'In February 2014 the House of Commons Public Accounts Committee published a devastating report on the way in which public services were contracted out to the private sector. It said that failure to manage performance across the board, not only showed that a far more professional and skilled approach to managing contracts and contractors was needed, but that contracts were not achieving the best for citizens. Alan White's well-researched book *Shadow State*, provides many examples that prove the Committee's case and will, I hope, act as an urgently needed call for action, particularly to improve the standard of contracting throughout Whitehall.'

Lord Ramsbotham, former HM Chief Inspector of Prisons for England and Wales

'This is a must-read for anyone who wants to know about the growing power and role of the private sector in delivering public services. It's comprehensive, written in a gripping style and chronicles many of the private sector's failures. It punctures the myth that the private sector is better at delivering public service.'

Dame Margaret Hodge MP

'The takeover of government activity by a cartel of unaccountable corporations is a major shift in the way Britain works. Alan White shines a light into this murky world. Everyone is affected by the shadow state. Everyone should read *Shadow State*.'

Andy Slaughter MP, Shadow Minister for Human Rights

About the Author

Alan White is UK Breaking News Reporter at Buzzfeed News. He has written for *The Times*, *Guardian*, *Private Eye* and the *TLS*, amongst other publications. His series of articles, 'The Shadow State', ran on the *New Statesman* website and were amongst its most read pieces. He lives in London.

SHADOW STATE

Inside the Secret Companies that Run Britain

Alan White

ONEWORLD

A Oneworld Book

First published in Great Britain, North America and
Australia by Oneworld Publications Ltd, 2016

ISBN 978-1-78074-574-9
eISBN 978-1-78074-575-6

Typeset by Hewer Text UK Ltd, Edinburgh
Printed and bound in Great Britain by Clays Ltd, St Ives plc

Oneworld Publications
10 Bloomsbury Street
London WC1B 3SR
England

To Fran and Zachary

Contents

Prologue
The 2012 Olympics
Security Fiasco

On 24 May 2012, BBC's *North-West Tonight* programme carried a little-noticed story about G4S, the company that had been brought in to provide security staff for the Olympic Games. The show reported that a whistleblower had been escorted from her place of work after claiming employees had taken shortcuts in their vetting procedures. She said the system was struggling because of the need to process thousands of applications ahead of the Games: staff had to get through a minimum of ten applications an hour and the documents had ended up piled in corners of the office in Stockton-on-Tees. The woman, Sarah Hubble, told the programme: 'It was an absolute shambles – you had people vetting potential employees who had not been vetted themselves.' She added that she had never received a criminal records check herself.

On 2 June 2012, the *Daily Mail* would report: 'After the report was screened on the television news, Miss Hubble, who was employed through employment agency Reed, said she was quizzed for two-and-a-half hours by several G4S directors. After initially denying she contacted the media, Miss Hubble said she admitted it was her when the company found evidence of her contact with a journalist on her phone, which bosses examined in detail.' Sarah Hubble was escorted from the building and told not to return.[1]

A couple of weeks later, *The Sun* ran another story about G4S's Olympics work. It claimed hundreds of sniffer dog searches for explosives at the Olympic Park in Stratford, east London, had not been carried out.[2] The operation was meant to stop terrorists smuggling a bomb into the site in a vehicle and setting it to detonate on a long-term timer. But the paper alleged that for three years, G4S 'ghosted' the searches of traffic entering the park. It said names of dog handlers on their days off were allegedly put down on shift rotas so it looked like they were working, but no searches took place. A source told the paper: 'The point about the searches was to stop someone smuggling a bomb inside. But the reality is a lot of the searches that were meant to happen didn't take place because the dogs and their handlers were only shown on paperwork and were never actually there. This has not just happened once or twice but regularly over the past three years. It is a farce.'

The paper reported that the alleged deception may have been carried out to avoid a £500 fine which LOCOG (the London Organising Committee of the Olympic and Paralympic Games, the Games' organizing body) would impose for every shift G4S could not cover. Two senior managers of the G4S dog section, Keith Francis and Ron Anderson, were suspended by the company while it carried out an internal probe.

It would be too much to suggest that these stories were warning signs for what was to come. But they do introduce two themes we'll encounter again and again when we look at the outsourcing business: lack of transparency in the first case, and incentives to game the system in the second.

In 2011, G4S was made the official 'security services provider' for London 2012. The intention was for it to provide training and management for the 10,000-strong security workforce, of whom 2,000 would be new staff recruited and trained by G4S and the remaining 8,000 would be from other sources. London 2012 chief executive Paul Deighton said the firm would help ensure security provisions were 'robust and of the highest professionalism'.[3]

But the announcement of the contract still caused concern. The group had been implicated in a number of scandals in recent years, perhaps most notably the death of Angolan immigrant Jimmy Mubenga on a plane two years earlier after three G4S security guards had pinned his head down while attempting to restrain him during his deportation.[4] There were concerns about the training and accountability of G4S employees. Was such widespread use of private security really a good idea? But these gripes came from the usual voices: campaign groups, predominantly on the political left.

In December that year, the government announced that the number of security guards for the Games would rise to 23,700 – more than double LOCOG's original estimate of 10,000. The number of security staff that G4S was contracted to provide had risen from the original 2,000 to 10,400. Its part of the contract was now worth £284 million, and the overall cost of security for the Olympics had risen from £282 million to £553 million.[5] This was widely reported in the media. What wasn't was the fact that LOCOG and the Home Office were concerned about the development of the security operation from an early stage. However, perhaps this was natural, given the scale of the operation – the concerns weren't focused on G4S specifically, but on the overall project including volunteers, the police and the armed forces.

In August 2011, Theresa May, the home secretary, commissioned Her Majesty's Inspectorate of Constabulary (HMIC) to conduct a review of the security arrangements. A month later, the report was produced, and it found some serious problems. LOCOG was eighteen months behind in producing its security policies and standard operating procedures, which was having a knock-on effect on its delivery of venue security plans. This, in turn, was causing delays in establishing an accurate picture of the number of staff that would be required.

Sir Denis O'Connor, HM chief inspector of constabulary, summed up the findings: 'This plan is not detailed enough at this point. [LOCOG] have had a lot of other things to do. It is now time to have a detailed plan so that the numbers make sense, the roles are clear, and you can recruit and train people with an end in mind.'[6] A second report was commissioned in February 2012.

But there was more we didn't know. In addition to the two HMIC reports asked for by the Home Office, we'd later find out that LOCOG had commissioned two reports of its own. In December 2011 it had asked the accountancy firm KPMG to produce an internal audit report, and, more significantly, it had commissioned a report by the accountants Deloitte in May 2012. This second report had been commissioned because LOCOG was concerned about the quality of the management information it was getting from G4S and about the way that company was communicating with its applicants. And as it turned out, Deloitte identified serious problems with G4S's management information and its overall operation: 'The current management information provided by G4S is fragmented, inconsistent and of variable levels of integrity in respect of sources, ownership and management . . . it is difficult to offer a high degree of confidence that end data figures provided in final reports to LOCOG provide an accurate picture of reality.'[7] The report also criticized G4S's communications with its applicants and recruits, indicating that its approach lacked detail, did not provide an understanding of the key messages which needed to be communicated at each stage, and was failing to address high attrition rates by engaging effectively with applicants.

It should be stressed that in the aftermath of what was to follow, Nick Buckles, the then CEO of G4S, would later tell the home affairs select committee that the recommendations were implemented within a week. However, the committee would conclude, several months later: 'Although Mr Buckles claims to have acted on all the relevant recommendations, the final outcome suggests that the changes to the data G4S were reporting to LOCOG were more presentational than substantial. The data were at best unreliable, if not downright misleading, and the most senior personnel in the company must take full responsibility for this.'[8]

What's most curious about the wealth of evidence that things might not have been going to plan is the fact that Assistant Commissioner Chris Allison, the senior Metropolitan Police officer who was in charge of Olympic security, didn't see all of it. He only ever saw the HMIC reports: he saw neither the KPMG nor the Deloitte one. He suggested that this might be because the consultants' reports were commissioned by LOCOG, a private company, and produced by other private companies.

On the other hand, David Taylor-Smith, chief operating officer of G4S, would later claim that for its part the company had never been given access to the internal audit report or the reports by HMIC, although it had been given the Deloitte report.[9] It might seem staggering in retrospect that the various parties weren't aware of the problems each was flagging up, but as we'll see, such miscommunication is a recurring theme in outsourcing.

At the same time, G4S's management fee was rising at a rapid rate. In March 2012, a report by the House of Commons public accounts committee (PAC) said it was 'staggering' that initial estimates about security costs were so wrong. The PAC's report stated that LOCOG had been forced to renegotiate its contract with G4S for venue security from a 'weak negotiating position'.[10] As the Games were due to start, the *Daily Telegraph* obtained confidential documents that revealed the component of G4S's fee dedicated to management had risen from £7.3 million to £60 million.[11] But by the time this revelation was uncovered, there was a far bigger problem at hand. Eighteen months into the contract – just a few weeks before the Games opened – things began to go very wrong indeed.

Throughout this entire period, G4S management was clearly confident that it was on track to meet its targets. It was obliged to produce management information, which it did, and it appeared to confirm that all was well. On 27 June, at a meeting of the Olympic Security Board, the company reported it was experiencing 'scheduling problems'. It said that this was primarily due to staff not being available to work during the opening ceremony, but that this was a 'small-scale, resolvable and temporary' problem, and the total shortfall would be fewer than 1,000 staff. G4S continued to assure LOCOG and the Home Office over the next few days that there wasn't anything other than a small problem.

How odd, then, that Charles Farr, director-general of the Office for Security and Counter-Terrorism at the Home Office, decided the next day to activate the contingency plan: on 28 June armed forces personnel from the Military Contingency Force were put on standby to help out at twenty-four hours' notice. Why?

At the home affairs select committee hearing later that year, he'd reveal that he'd been getting indications from 'other sources' that G4S's operation was not running as smoothly as the company appeared to think it was. He'd tell the committee that by 5 July it appeared to him that G4S was not getting to grips with the problem: 'I was basing this on data we were getting from the ground, rather than data I was getting from G4S ... I certainly wouldn't have relied on [information from G4S] by this stage as a single source of truth.'[12]

The company's view of how it was doing, however, hadn't changed. Theresa May spoke to Nick Buckles on 6 July and met him on 10 July, but he certainly didn't appear to think the problem had worsened and told her the contract would be fulfilled. Incredibly, on 6 July, Ian Horseman Sewell, one of the company's directors, told Reuters that G4S was capable of simultaneously delivering multiple Olympic security projects around the world: 'We are delivering a London Olympics now. If there was a similar event going on in Australia, I would be bullish that we could deliver this at the same time.'[13]

And the company's data suggested no problem: according to the home affairs select committee, on 1 July it provided statistics that showed 37,000 people had passed the G4S interview, 25,000 had been security screened, 21,000 had been accredited, 14,700 had been Security Industry Authority trained and 9,000 were ready to work. Then everything changed.

On 11 July, Nick Buckles and David Taylor-Smith visited the offices of LOCOG in Canary Wharf. They must have been feeling pretty apprehensive, because they were about to report for the first time that they weren't going to be able to deliver on the contract. There is no record of how the news went down. But they then travelled to the Home Office, where a meeting of the Olympic Security Board was due to take place. On the way, they telephoned Charles Farr, who notified Theresa May about the issue. He then went in to chair the board meeting.[14]

Off the record, insiders will tell you that there was a sense of absolute panic among both G4S's management and civil servants

– with tales of one manager sitting on the floor at the Home Office, surrounded by paperwork and close to tears. But when exactly did G4S first discover there'd been a shortfall of staff? According to the home affairs select committee inquiry, 'it seems the penny dropped on 3 July', when Taylor-Smith telephoned Buckles to tell him. Buckles was on holiday at the time, which as the committee deduced 'suggests that this was something more than a routine call'.[15]

Buckles didn't mention any problems when he met May three days later – the same day, remember, that Horseman Sewell was making his somewhat ill-advised statements on G4S's capacity to deliver projects around the world. And it wasn't discussed when Buckles met May on 10 July either. But the Home Office clearly felt there was a problem if the evidence of the contingency plans being put in place is anything to go by. The home affairs select committee would later describe the delay in reporting the problem as 'astonishing'.

Now the original contingency plans had to be revised. On 12 July, Defence Secretary Philip Hammond made the fateful announcement: up to 3,500 troops would be needed for security duties during the Olympics. May assured the House of Commons there was 'no question of Olympic security being compromised' as a result of the troops being brought in.

By that point, G4S had been paid £90 million. The police were called in at the football venues outside London, while the military were stationed at the venues in and around London. The government had no alternative course of action. Had the event been something like a football match, it could have been delayed. That simply wasn't the case when it came to the Olympics.

Indeed, the contingency plan saved London's Olympic Games. As the home affairs select committee would eventually conclude, it 'was only thanks to the far-sighted planning of officials at the

Home Office, LOCOG and other Olympic security partners that a catastrophe was averted. However, activating the contingency plan came at a price for many of those concerned.'

And as Lord Coe, chair of LOCOG, would tell the committee:

> I am acutely aware that I displaced family plans, the military came to the table, some of them had been on active duty until relatively recently, some were expecting to see more of their families during the summer months. I am very aware of that, and I would put immediately on record my gratitude to the contingency and the planning, and our ability to actually draw down. The military became one of the defining characteristics in the delivery of the Games.[16]

The day after Hammond's announcement, G4S announced it stood to lose up to £50 million as a result of the fiasco. The company added it 'deeply regretted' the problems. Shares closed down 1.5% at 278.7p, with more than £150 million wiped off the company's market value in two days. On 14 July, Nick Buckles said the firm would have to pay a penalty: he didn't disclose the exact amount but said it would be somewhere between £10 million and £20 million.

Buckles would appear before the home affairs select committee on 17 July the next year. He still wasn't able to explain what had gone wrong. He said he wished he'd never taken on the contract because it had become a 'humiliating shambles'. He added that G4S would pick up the bill for accommodating the army, and that it would pay bonuses if appropriate. However, he also felt it was right that because the firm expected 'to deliver a significant amount of staff', it would retain the fee. 'That's astonishing,' replied the committee chair, Labour MP Keith Vaz.[17]

Buckles also said he hadn't found out about the problems until 3 July, adding that as they 'dug into data day by day we realized the pipeline and people we thought we could deliver, we couldn't'. As a result, he'd returned from a holiday in America in a state of shock and on 11 July he realized the contract would not be delivered.

He added that the company wouldn't bid for contracts at the 2016 Olympics in Brazil because of the possible damage G4S would suffer if something like this ever happened again. In September 2012, the company said it had accepted the resignations of David Taylor-Smith and Ian Horseman Sewell over the failure. Buckles kept his job, but would step down eight months later in May 2013.

Also in September 2012 we found out exactly what had gone wrong at G4S's end. The company made its internal report public. It concluded: 'The monitoring and tracking of the security workforce, management information and the project management framework and practices were ineffective to address the scale, complexities and dependencies of the Olympic contract. Together this caused the failure of the Company to deliver the contract requirements in full and resulted in the identification of the key problems at a very late stage.'[18]

In February 2013, G4S announced it would take a bigger-than-expected hit. In total it would lose around £70 million on the London Olympics contract. There were costs of about £18 million relating to charitable donations, fees and marketing, an additional £2.5 million would be given to a military charity, and it would also spend £8.5 million on lawyers and accountants for negotiations with LOCOG. It was a £20 million higher loss than had been previously estimated, and it only came after months of negotiating with LOCOG.

As the home affairs select committee would conclude, in awarding the contract to G4S, LOCOG appeared to have been influenced by the company's size and reputation. The committee felt: 'This is not unreasonable – a bidder's previous performance on other contracts is something which any diligent procurement exercise should take into consideration – and it is a natural assumption that the world's largest security company would be a safe choice for such a large project.'

Paul Deighton, chief executive of LOCOG, told the committee: 'I think somebody else probably could have done it but [G4S] were the obvious and best candidates to do it. They are the biggest security company in the world. The government is their most important client. The eyes of the world are on this project. They were highly incentivized to succeed because of all those reasons and believed they could succeed.'[19]

And Deighton's right: the company clearly believed it could deliver – and indeed boasted it could be doing it simultaneously around the world, despite the fact (as Nick Buckles would point out) the contract was 'one of a kind … there wasn't a track record, there wasn't a blueprint'. It was also a hugely difficult task, involving the recruitment, training and accreditation of thousands of staff, all of whom – within a non-negotiable time frame – had to be placed in dozens of different roles across over a hundred venues.

And this raises an interesting question: if not G4S, then who? A government insider I spoke to during the research for this book made a very simple point: 'You know, if the government had wanted to get the army to do the job in the first place, they could have. So why did they ask G4S to do it? Because they thought it would save money.' What's more, the company's involvement in the biggest outsourcing scandal in history barely made it break stride in terms of its ability to land government contracts. Indeed, what's perhaps most telling about this scandal is that it was really the first time the issue of outsourcing had grabbed the general public's interest. Over the preceding thirty years, the industry had grown at a terrific pace, yet aside from a few reports, principally in *Private Eye*, it had generated remarkably few headlines in its wake.

While the implications of the scandal seemed severe for G4S at the time, they actually made little lasting impression on it or the industry. In fact, the coverage and media analysis barely shifted beyond what it meant for the Olympics. Once the army had stepped in, the story was swiftly forgotten. No one really seemed to ask if this was the only time a company had failed in the job the state had given it.

1

The Story of Britain's Outsourcing Revolution

The fundamental contradiction at the heart of most people's attitudes to outsourcing is this: we want to eradicate waste in our public services, yet we remain rightly suspicious of the consequences that come with introducing a profit motive. Furthermore, as the writer Sam Knight has put it:

> Outsourcers also threaten us because their growth entails the dismantling of something that was familiar. Public sector monopolies may not have always been effective, but at least they came with a story, an implied commitment to a common cause. They were, in some inescapable sense, *ours*. By contrast, the rise of the UK's public services industry – which now employs more than a million people and is the world's second largest, after America's – is an experiment that has been conducted largely without a narrative, and whose principal agents are large companies that belong to their shareholders.[1]

And this concern perhaps wouldn't matter, were it not for the scale of these companies and the depth of their involvement in the state. A study in 2011 suggested that the outsourcing sector employs 1.2 million people, and creates or supports a further 2.3 million jobs.[2] From that point on, it has grown rapidly – in just the first three months of 2014, the value of public sector outsourcing shot up by 168 percent, as monitored by the business service provider Arvato's outsourcing index.[3] Research suggests the market for public service outsourcing has an annual turnover of £72 billion: about twenty-four percent of the spend on public services in the UK.[4] As Stuart Weir, an academic at the University of Essex, has pointed out: 'The number of contracts in the UK has increased sharply by 47 per cent to 148 contracts a year since 2010 . . . And these figures date from before the major privatization drive in the NHS.'[5]

It's very difficult to get a full picture of the UK's outsourcing market. Indeed, the scale of government outsourcing is now so extensive that there have been times when even government departments have appeared confused about how many contracts have been handed out. In June 2014 the shadow justice secretary, Sadiq Khan, put a question to the Ministry of Justice about the sum total of its contracts – how much each contract was expected to cost over its lifetime, when they were due to end, whether financial penalties had been incurred and whether there was a break clause, among other details. He was told the MoJ didn't have data on this to hand, because it wasn't held centrally. In the end, it eventually sent him a list of forty-five contracts, although it turned out several private prisons and youth offender institutions had been left off the list, including Altcourse, Parc, Rye Hill and Thameside.[6]

What we do know is that four companies really dominate the landscape: G4S, Serco, Atos and Capita. One way of showing this is by looking at data on these firms and their relationship with government, which was put together by the National Audit

Office in 2013. We know, for example, that the money they brought in from government in 2012 ranged from around £500 million (Capita) to £1.2 billion (Serco). This is a lot, but worth seeing in context – Serco's worldwide revenue is around £5 billion, Capita's £3.4 billion. A small amount of this came from local government – that year Capita took in £506 million, G4S £71 million and Serco £382 million, but the overwhelming majority came from central government.

The two big spenders are the Ministry of Justice, which paid £500 million to Serco and G4S alone, and the Department of Work and Pensions, which paid G4S, Capita and Atos over £100 million each for its work, but pretty much every government department made payments of between £10 million and £50 million. Overall, these four companies' work cost around £4 billion – a small but, according to the National Audit Office, 'significant' part of central government's overall spend on goods and services.[7] So who are these firms? We'll look at Capita a little later, but a brief look at the three others shows that the market is being led by giant multinationals. The dizzying growth of outsourcing took place in line with the rapid growth of globalization in the late twentieth century.

Many people have heard of G4S, but few understand the company's scale. Its historical trajectory is hard to summarize, as so many takeovers and mergers have been involved in its evolution. It can be traced back to a Danish company called København Frederiksberg Nattevagt – the Copenhagen-Frederiksberg Night Watch – which began with twenty guards and was set up by drapery wholesaler Marius Hogrefe in 1901.[8] Its story really begins, however, many decades later, in 1985, when Nick Buckles took a job as a project accountant at Securicor (later the 'S' in G4S.) The *Financial Times* ran a profile of him in November 2013:

According to the head of one G4S subsidiary based outside the UK, when he first glimpsed Buckles at a regional management meeting about three years ago, the chief executive was wearing light-coloured trousers and loafers; with his long hair and open-neck shirt, he 'looked more like Elvis than a CEO'. In person he was – and remains – engaging. Another G4S executive, based in Asia, has said Buckles 'had this ability to know you – he would always make sure that he spent time with all of his senior managers at any opportunity he could get.[9]

In 2005, Buckles became CEO of G4S after Group 4 Falck – which grew out of that original Danish night watch – merged with Securicor. However, both companies had been rapidly expanding long before in the UK and Europe, in the core business of providing security for private businesses and individuals. It's now one of the biggest private security firms in what's become a burgeoning market: in 2011 there was one private security employee to every 170 citizens, compared to only one police officer to every 382 citizens.[10] In America, the ratio is twice as high, but the market has been growing across Europe for years.[11] However, the company had also been making gains in other, state-related areas. Securicor was managing detention at Manchester and Heathrow airports in 1970. By 1991 Group 4 was managing its first privatized prison, near Hull, and by 1993 Securicor had contracts for court and custodial escort services across London.[12]

It was only with the merger and the elevation of Buckles to CEO that the company really exploded into life. Under Buckles, the group spent about £1.5 million and acquired dozens of companies – according to the *Financial Times*, the group was active in the Middle East, around nuclear plants, and continued its drive into the British justice system, among other areas. As a result, its share price doubled in that time.[13]

But this aggressive growth wasn't met with universal praise. The subsidiary owner mentioned in the *Financial Times* piece also told the paper: 'We have always heard that the goal is to be the largest private-sector employer in the world. What kind of metric is that? It's size not quality. If you look at the environment they are operating in, in second-, third-tier countries, risks are very high; the opportunities for unethical behaviour are extremely high and, quite frankly, I think the business acumen of a lot of these folks is in question.'[14] But regardless of these fears, it's now the third-largest listed private sector employer in the world, behind Walmart and Foxconn.[15]

The other two companies follow a similar trajectory of dizzying growth. Atos, for its part, is a French multinational – the eighth-biggest IT provider in the world, formed in 1997 through the merger of two French IT companies (it subsequently acquired more, including KPMG Consulting and Siemens IT Solutions and Services). Serco, by contrast, is (sort of) British in origin: it began in 1929 as the UK subsidiary of the Radio Corporation of America (RCA).

RCA was a giant corporation that ran everything from car hire companies to publishing houses, but for most of the twentieth century its UK arm specialized in technical work in the defence and transport sectors: maintaining systems like traffic lights and missile defence.[16] When, in the 1980s, outsourcing began to stretch across Whitehall departments, the managers at RCA realized that, far from being scientists, their art was in managing the people with more mundane jobs at the bases they operated. So they reinvented their company as a management corporation. In 1984, RCA won the Ministry of Defence's first official outsourcing contract, to operate a big supply depot at RAF Quedgeley, in Gloucestershire, despite never having run a store or similar venture before.[17]

In 2012, Social Enterprise UK, an umbrella group for social enterprises, produced a report into outsourcing and attempted to list things that Serco operated. They included transport services (such as the Docklands Light Railway and Barclays cycle hire), hospital and pathology services management, security services for our borders, leisure services, prisons and young offenders' institutions, government websites, the National Nuclear Laboratory, maintenance for missile defence systems, air traffic control services, waste collection and more.[18] The disruption caused if the company went under would have a massive impact on Britain's public services. Suffice it to say, this company's business interests have moved far, far beyond those it had when it began.

The story of outsourcing in the UK

Where does the story of outsourcing begin? There's nothing new about the idea of the state engaging private entities to work for it. You could certainly argue that it started with the East India Company, which operated on behalf of the government in the eighteenth century, and could probably begin even earlier, going right back to a mediaeval king asking nobles to collect his taxes and run his courts. In the modern era, think, for example, of our much-loved general practitioners, who are essentially private contractors, and have been for decades. The Serco Institute, the outsourcing giant's now-defunct think tank, researched such projects as eighteenth-century contracts to transport convicts to Australia, and saw the line between public and private sector as 'a cultural artefact' according to Sam Knight: 'strongly held, but always shifting'.[19]

But to understand the development of modern outsourcing, we need to start in the 1970s, when the exchange rate system that had been set up with the Bretton Woods agreement collapsed. It meant that government-set exchange rates were suddenly unworkable – they had to be floated. Controlling inflation became the government's overriding priority.[20] Ideals like a comprehensive welfare system and full employment were shifted to the back-burner. Industries like gas and electricity were privatized, while the newly deregulated financial markets boomed. The aim was very simple: reduce the bill for public services.

Around this time, free-market theorists began to question the wisdom of large organizations – particularly governments – running their own affairs. Sam Knight has traced this school of thought to an academic at the London School of Economics called Ronald Coase, who wrote a paper entitled *The Theory of the Firm* in 1937, which asked why companies outsourced only some of their functions. Knight has described how a series of economic studies on waste disposal, which suggested cities using private firms made savings and had a higher quality of service, gave further weight to these beliefs.[21]

In 1980, compulsory competitive tendering (CCT) was brought in for construction, maintenance and highways work – industries which were rather easier to manage than some of those that would later be outsourced.[22] A couple of years later, regional health authorities began to use it for support services.

Around this time, the Conservative Nicholas Ridley MP began to argue that councils should concentrate on allowing services to be provided, rather than providing them themselves. Ridley was a fascinating character: older readers may remember his *Spitting Image* puppet, which was never without a cigarette dangling from its lower lip. He was, at heart, a passionate free-marketer. Margaret Thatcher once said of him: 'Free-market economics was always Nick's passion. And he had a longer, better pedigree in that respect than most Thatcherites ... His first vote against a Conservative government bailing out nationalized industries was in *1961*. To be so right, so early on, is not to have *seen* the light—it is to have *lit* it ... He would have been a superb Chancellor.'[23] The description is broadly accurate: Ridley actually opposed rail privatization, but he oversaw bus deregulation in Great Britain and came up with a famous plan to deal with trade union power.[24]

He may not have been the only one espousing these ideas, but perhaps his intellectual output best embodies them. In a pamphlet written in 1988, he claimed outsourcing would take politics out of the public service equation, making everything from education to refuse collection a simple transaction.[25] He described a utopian vision of a local council that existed in the American Midwest, which met just once a year to award service contracts to private firms. Education, building, refuse collection – these became merely financial exchanges in Ridley's eyes. And these ideas, to a small extent, were picked up by the Local Government Act of 1988, which extended CCT to things like refuse collection.[26]

In fact, some of today's outsourcing giants can trace their foundation to this initial drive to see local government working more closely with the private sector. Capita, for example, was founded by a man named Rod Aldridge, who was asked to investigate new ways for the Chartered Institute of Public Finance and Accountancy (CIPFA) to raise revenues.[27] CIPFA's tiny computer services division started up in 1984 – only a few years later, it had dozens of people working for it, and Aldridge launched a £330,000 management buyout, backed by the venture capital company 3i. By 1991, Capita – as it was now known – had increased its staff numbers by a factor of ten, and reached a turnover of £25 million.[28] The outsourcing industry had exploded. Serco, for its part, had 3,000 employees and revenues of £59 million in 1989. By 1999 it had 27,000 employees and revenues of more than £800 million.[29]

The 'white collar' services offered by companies like Capita were largely transactional and easy to define. Even at this early stage, however, reporters were expressing concerns about the marriage of state and private sectors. A 1996 piece in *Investors Chronicle*, for example, described how 'poorly managed computer systems, customers who don't pay debts and over-staffed personnel departments' were all 'meat' for a new type of UK company that had 'made minding other people's businesses a specialty'.[30]

This article was remarkably prescient in some ways, and remarkably wrong about how things would turn out in others. On the one hand, it correctly predicted that outsourcing's next growth area would be finance, 'including tax collection, payroll services and billings'. As it noted, Capita had recently won a deal to collect council tax in the London borough of Bexley – at ten years, one of the longest local authority contracts 'yet awarded'. It also pointed out other potentially 'fertile' markets – among them 'the privatized utilities and the increasingly commercial National Health Service'.

But where it got things very wrong was on the potential impact of a Labour government on the industry. Labour was considered a 'threat' to outsourcing. The article pointed out that Labour had pledged to abolish compulsory tendering, and it did do this when it got into government the following year – but only to replace it with BestValue, essentially a less prescribed and more wide-ranging version of the same, which aimed to make sure that outsourcing projects would preserve wages and standards.

The article also claimed that Labour was 'likely to put work tendered under the Tories' Private Finance Initiative [PFI] – another potential source of contracts – on the back-burner'. Prime Minister John Major had begun to use the PFI to finance and operate hospitals, schools and prisons – under this scheme, such projects were designed, built and managed by private consortia, but underwritten by the state, with the contracts typically lasting for thirty years. It was the best-known form of public–private partnership: legal contracts which allowed private companies to provide public services for the state. Before this, they had existed as one-off deals.[31] Contrary to the writer's suspicions, the use of PFI grew at a tremendous rate under New Labour.

And this fitted with the new governing party's ideology, which was supposed to represent a compromise between social democracy and the market orientation of Conservative neo-liberalism. In place of the 'free market', Tony Blair – and later Gordon Brown – often took the public position that Britain was at the mercy of the ebbs and flows of globalization. Their frankness about this would perhaps seem shocking now. In 2003, for example, Blair was asked to comment on the news that the UK insurance company Aviva, which traded as Norwich Union, would outsource jobs to India – as part of the process it would axe over 2,000 jobs. He said he was 'desperately sorry' for anyone whose job was at risk, but the outsourcing of jobs abroad was just 'the way the world is today'. 'We have not tried to pretend to people we can stop what is happening in the global economy,' he added.[32]

In this context, outsourcing was considered a natural development in a corporate-led world. New Labour picked up the

Conservatives' ball and ran with it. Public services were handed to the private sector on an ever-increasing scale ('What matters is what works,' Blair famously said in a 1997 speech). By 2001 the party's election manifesto even stated that private or voluntary sector providers should be brought in where public providers were failing to improve, or where they could add value to public services.[33]

Many of the early changes were seen in local government. In 2001 the *Local Government Chronicle* reported that the current outsourcing market within local government was worth £244 million a year but had a potential value of £1.7 billion. It said the reason for this 'was not the revolutionary effect of technology, but something far more basic – politics . . . The importance of politics in forcing through changes looks set to continue under a business-friendly Labour, should it win a second term.' It also mentioned the potential pitfalls of this brave new world, explaining how 'inequalities weighted in favour of the private sector, conflicts of interest and a lack of trust between the parties involved' were all problems that contracts faced.[34]

The tenor of the early coverage was often breathlessly optimistic about this brave new world. A 2002 report in the *Newcastle Journal* carried an interview with an Alan Gardner, business development manager at a company called HBS in Middlesbrough. HBS had won a contract from Middlesbrough Council outsourcing a 'whole range of administration, benefits and IT services, for 10 years at a cost of around £30m a year'. Gardner explained how his company had made these processes more 'efficient' through various processes of reorganization. Much of the article was given over to the excitement surrounding these 'radical' changes, but it did find time to note that the trade union Unison was already describing such changes as an 'attack on staff terms and conditions'.[35]

In spite of the speed of change, Tony Blair's autobiography doesn't make any explicit mention of outsourcing as an ideology. There's some mention of not ending up in hock to public sector unions, and some left-wing analysts have seen this as the fundamental goal for Blair's administration when it came to statutory services. John Grayson, a writer for OpenDemocracy and the Institute of Race Relations, has described New Labour's commitment to privatized justice and prison building under Jack Straw as requiring the unions representing workers to be defeated 'so as to enable the cutting of staffing levels and wage and pension costs'.[36]

But the lack of literature on outsourcing in these years is rather surprising, and perhaps indicates how slowly political thinkers grasped what was happening. Michael Barber, head of Blair's Delivery Unit, wrote a huge book called *Instruction to Deliver: Fighting to Transform Britain's Public Services* in 2008, which explains how New Labour attempted to reduce things like health waiting lists and crime, and improve school exam results. It, too, makes very little mention of the private sector. There is some mention of quasi-markets ('If they are to work, the government needs to regulate and intervene more'), but little beyond that.

But be under no doubt – central government's use of outsourcing was growing all this time. By 2009 – with Gordon Brown now in charge – even the normally sympathetic *Telegraph* was writing a story with the headline 'Meet Serco, the Company Running the Country'. The piece opened: 'Most of the general public has never come across the name Serco, but the company inspects Britain's schools, trains the armed forces, helps to protect our borders, maintains our nuclear weapons, runs our trains and operates our prisons.' The firm, which had just been 'propelled into the FTSE 100', would, the paper reported, expect to continue expanding, 'no matter which party wins the next general election'.[37]

How the outsourcing market affects us all

What's of concern is the way giants such as Serco have come to dominate the market. We will see how the growth of companies like this has forced smaller charities and social enterprises out of the market. There are a great many questions raised by the uncomfortable juxtaposition of profits and public service: indeed, said profits often don't even stay in the UK, let alone improve services. This matters because outsourced public services have an impact on the economy: they have an effect on our wages, and therefore they impact on what benefit demands we make. But more importantly, these services have an intrinsic effect on our social fabric and the knock-on effects can have huge impacts on the people they serve and their loved ones. What happens to a patient in a hospital, a child in a children's home or a prisoner in jail affects all of us.

People have been asking many of the questions we'll be looking at ever since New Labour's outsourcing drive picked up. One of the main ones, the question of efficiency, has never really been answered: New Labour rarely if ever carried out detailed comparisons of outsourced provision with that performed in-house, nor were assessments of savings made: that lack of assessment has carried on to this day. As Tim Banfield of the National Audit Office told Radio 4's *File on 4*: 'We've not seen sufficient evidence to back up the idea that it makes savings.'[38]

Under New Labour people also began to raise the issue of transparency. The government didn't keep a database of contracts, or price breakdowns for services, while commercial confidentiality laws stopped journalists and others scrutinizing the fine details of deals. This tied in with a third problem: competition. In this fragmented industry it was hard to work out. And this led to another question: were these big corporations specialists only in winning contracts, rather than delivering on them? The trouble was that even if long-term contracts (like the thirty-year PFI ones) were drawn up badly, it didn't really affect the politicians involved – they could cite savings made during their time in power and would be gone before any problems emerged.

The stance you take on these questions may come down to the simple question of how you perceive the relationship between government and contractor. Is outsourcing merely a case of simple pragmatism and a way of securing the best value for money? Or is it something rather more threatening – a way for the state to abdicate political accountability that furthermore introduces a profit incentive in place of the need to secure a public good? Is it right for giant corporations – paid by the state yet barely taxed, with shareholders drawn from among the country's elite, and lobbyists with access to the very top of government – to carry out mucky work in the crime, justice, welfare and immigration sectors among others?

Should such companies really be operating in sectors where many of the people with whom they deal are deeply vulnerable? Should there be secondary markets, so that the institutions these companies run – like care homes or asylum detention centres – can be traded around like any other product? Can a company like G4S or Serco really have fingers in so many pies, such as defence, welfare, health and justice, while maintaining the public's best interests?

If your immediate answer to such questions is 'no', you should consider the views of Mark Fox of the British Services Association, a policy and research organization for service and infrastructure projects. Fox is essentially the closest person I could find to a cheerleader for outsourcing: he regularly works with all the biggest firms to help them improve their performance – whether they're working for the state or otherwise. When I interviewed him on the subject he said:

[Outsourcing] is where people want to deliver a service. The question is how they do it . . . Do you buy ready-made meals? Then you've already outsourced food provision. [That's] a silly [example] but you get to a bigger scale. What you're talking about is not outsourcing. You're talking about a decision politicians make about what they want to provide, then they go to the electorate and say 'We will do this, will you vote for me on that basis?'

So I would say to you, you're talking about politics, not outsourcing: if you want to provide certain services in certain ways, that's a political decision. You then get into the business of saying 'How do I provide those services in the context of promises I've made about taxation and spending?' So already we're not talking about outsourcing, we're talking about party politics. People have legitimate, sensible views about what should be provided where. It's up to individuals to make those decisions.

So what do we mean by 'outsourcing'? As we've seen, the definition of the word is nebulous – and the range of services these companies provide is extremely wide. For now, suffice to say our subject is the delivery of services that have, in recent British history, been provided by the state but which are now delivered by private companies.

In the Prologue we saw what happened when one of the companies involved made a mistake. The state simply stepped in and bailed the firm out. But more often than not, the question of whose mistake it was – and what to do next – is far from simple.

2

The Asylum Industry

In October 2010 Jimmy Mubenga died 'a very public death', in the words of Jerome Phelps, CEO of the charity Asylum Aid, 'on the last row of seats on a full British Airways flight that was sitting on the runway at Heathrow airport'. The flight was waiting to go to Luanda, in Angola. As Phelps would write on a website a few days after it happened:

> The interior of a passenger flight is a non-place, familiar to the point of banality. Most of us have sat many times in seats indistinguishable from Jimmy's. We can all imagine ourselves there. But few of us can imagine Jimmy's one-way flight. An unbridgeable gulf separated him from the passengers sitting in front of him and across the aisle. Some were going on holiday or to visit family; many were travelling to work in the profitable Angolan oil industry.[1]

One witness, Kevin Wallis, would say he heard Mubenga heaving as though being sick, and saying 'I don't want to go' and 'I can't breathe, I can't breathe', for at least ten minutes before he fell unconscious.[2] Wallis was one of the people sitting across the aisle from Mubenga when he saw three guards restrain him: two were sitting either side and held him down, pressing his head between his legs, while a third leaned over the passenger seat from the row in front and occasionally did the same when he managed to push back up. His leather jacket had been taken off, and some passengers had been moved away. The three guards worked for G4S, which at the time had been contracted to oversee Home Office deportations.

Wallis also said: 'I think they were scared of him ... they put so much pressure on him because he looked a big lad. The three security guards were big blokes as well.' A second witness told the *Guardian* he thought the men were on top of Mubenga for forty-five minutes. He said: 'There were three guys trying to hold him. This led to them pushing everyone further up the plane, so we were all pushed into first class ... You could hear the guy screaming at the back of the plane. He was saying: "They are going to kill me." That's what he repeatedly said.'[3]

Mubenga was laid down in the aisle after it was clear that he'd lost consciousness, whereupon the captain, police and paramedics were alerted. Wallis said that the security guards must have notified the crew: 'He just went quiet for a good while, then they checked his pulse and they must have thought it was very, very low. They [the guards] brought him up then, and I saw his head and everything. They checked his neck pulse and his wrist pulse. That is when they looked a bit worried.'

He added: 'The paramedics tried to resuscitate him on the floor beside me. They chased the security guards and said: "Get out of the way, we don't want to know you." The security guards were trying to have a look to see what was going on, but the paramedic – a young lady, she was – said: "Will you get out of the way?"'[4]

Detectives interviewed a number of passengers – Wallis among them – and then allowed them to board another flight twenty-four hours later. Around that time, Wallis discovered the man he'd heard screaming for help had died. As the story began to break, G4S put out a statement in which it said a man 'became unwell' on a flight while being deported. The Home Office said much the same thing. The *Guardian*, which broke the story of his death, only realized there was something up because its reporters tracked posts from passengers on the plane who were using Twitter.

What happened was written about for years to follow. And yet most of the coverage never really got to the bottom of what this case really said about the outsourcing industry. The first question is: who was Jimmy Mubenga? I met with Jerome Phelps after reading his piece about the case. A quietly spoken, thin middle-aged man, Phelps has been running Asylum Aid since 1993. He told me: 'I met him in Harmondsworth [detention centre] – our organization knew his case well. What struck me about him, because it was quite unusual, was that he was a very east London guy. He seemed very aloof from his environment.'

Mubenga was a 46-year-old man who had fled from Angola with his wife and son in 1994. His lawyer said he was a student leader who had fallen out with the government of the time. His wife claimed that the government had killed her father and threatened Mubenga, so they'd had to leave.[5] It had taken a long legal battle, but eventually the family had been granted exceptional leave to remain.

They had another four children over the next sixteen years, and eventually settled in Ilford. Mubenga worked as a forklift truck driver. His wife told the *Guardian*: 'Jimmy was a good man, a family man. He would do anything for the children. He would take them to school and pick them up, if I ever went to school they would all ask: "Where is Jimmy?" Everyone knew him and he was a kind man. People liked him.'

But in 2006, it all went wrong. Mubenga got into a fight in a nightclub, and was convicted of actual bodily harm. He would have to serve two years in prison. And this meant that he had to be deported: any foreign criminal jailed for more than twelve months is subject to automatic deportation. He was transferred to an immigration centre. Phelps would describe his life after serving his sentence as being a 'nightmare of indefinite immigration detention and increasingly desperate struggles in a legal system that refused to allow him to stay with his family'.[6] He had, Phelps said, applied to court to be released on bail seven times when he knew him, only to be refused seven times, a situation he 'couldn't bear' his family to see.[7]

I asked Phelps if this might not have been the first time Jimmy had got in trouble. He replied: 'All I know is that he seemed like a very dignified, mature man, one who regretted the decision he'd made and the impact it would have on his family. He was so distressed because his entire life was here. I honestly think the reality of his situation was that he'd made one mistake.'

Phelps would eventually write:

So I wonder, and I imagine Jimmy wondering, how it can be proportionate to take away his family and the whole life that he had built here, for that one mistake. How, had he been British, he would have been given a chance to rebuild his life after he finished his sentence. How instead, a public authority could think it a good idea to spend so much money and resources on depriving a young family of its father, to send him to a country he had not seen for fourteen years, where he expected persecution for his political activism and for having claimed asylum.[8]

A year after Mubenga died, staff working for the chief inspector of prisons saw G4S personnel using 'offensive and sometimes racist language' on a flight to Nigeria. In a report on the incident, the chief inspector stated: 'Quite apart from the offence this language may have caused to those who overheard it, it suggested a shamefully unprofessional and derogatory attitude.'[9] It was only the start of the controversies surrounding the asylum industry that would be brought into sharp relief by Mubenga's death.

In July 2013, an inquest jury at Isleworth Crown Court recorded a majority verdict of unlawful killing in relation to Mubenga's death. The case brought all sorts of uncomfortable truths to light. It transpired that two of the guards had racist jokes as text messages on their phones, some of which they'd forwarded (sample: 'I walked past a blind black guy begging in the street. He said, "Any change mate?" I said, "No, you're still a nigger."').[10]

G4S, for its part, has always stated that disciplinary action would always be taken against any staff when racism is discovered. However, Emma Norton, the legal officer for the campaign group Liberty, responded: 'It is clear that neither UKBA [the UK Border Agency] nor the private security companies have taken steps to ensure that racists are not employed to perform this terribly sensitive and difficult job.'

This was part of her furious public statement, in which she mentioned

a ludicrous account that Jimmy Mubenga somehow forced his own head between his knees, causing his own asphyxia. Unforgivable indifference to the dying cries of a man who, according to one witness, called for help around 50 times as he slowly suffocated. These are the actions of the private security guards entrusted by the Home Office to ensure the safe removal of Mr Mubenga from the UK. What utter contempt for human dignity and life ... The Home Office is also culpable. The department has long used a restraint policy designed for inmates in prisons against people being removed [in] aircraft. The Home Office has known for years that the policy is unsafe.[11]

As she pointed out, Liberty had tried to look at the policy, but had been refused permission by the Home Office. She said that the department had assured them that detainees might 'learn' the techniques if they were made public and would be able to counter them. That meant the organization hadn't been able to show the policy to its restraint expert. She added: 'Don't worry, says the Home Office – our own experts have taken a look: they assure us that, while the techniques aren't designed for aircraft, "their use [is] not fundamentally dangerous and could be safe so long as staff had adequate awareness of potential issues such as positional asphyxia".'[12]

The Medical Foundation for the Care of Victims of Torture catalogued the following injuries sustained by failed asylum seekers upon their removal from the UK:

Loss of consciousness; tooth coming loose, bleeding from the mouth; testicular pain; difficulty passing urine; nose bleed, sprained neck from having neck forcibly flexed (head pushed down); bony tenderness over the cheekbone from a punch to the face; abrasion over the cheekbone from being dragged along the ground; lip laceration (splitting) from having head pushed down against the ground; bruising under the jaw and tenderness over the larynx from fingers being pressed to the throat; laceration over the temple from having head banged against hard object ...[13]

This was corroborated by a 2008 report from the charity Medical Justice, which described 300 allegations of such assaults. Clare Sambrook, an award-winning investigative journalist who has covered the industry for years, told me that she felt the Labour government of the time didn't take the report seriously, and that it instead 'attacked the doctors and lawyers who brought the abuses to light'. And there was a further statement in the wake of the case from Amnesty International UK's arms, security and policing director, Oliver Sprague. He released a statement in which he said: 'Several former G4S staff told us about how they'd raised concerns about the use of dangerous restraints and the life-threatening risks they posed, but across a 20-year period nothing changed.'

Sprague went on to claim the charity had heard that contractors had been banned from using restraint holds that impaired breathing to a dangerous degree, and that 'so-called "Carpet Karaoke" was being used – where security staff would force the person's face into a carpet with such force that they were only able to scream "like a bad karaoke singer".'[14]

When you take all of these statements and evidence together, the only conclusion you can reach is that the death of someone during removal was only a matter of time. And of course all this led to a simple question: were the guards at fault, or were they just carrying out their orders? One place to start is with the statement that G4S put out in the wake of the verdict:

Our employees were also trained, screened and vetted to the standards defined by strict Home Office guidelines. We believe that at all times we acted appropriately and in full compliance with the terms of our contract with UKBA and it should be noted that the Crown Prosecution Service found no basis on which to bring criminal charges against G4S in this case. It would not be appropriate for us to comment on behalf of our former employees who were separately represented throughout these proceedings.[15]

It was a difficult sentiment for the layman to interpret. Was the company blaming rogue staff members for the death, or the rules that it'd been given by the Home Office? If it was the latter, was the company in any way culpable? There certainly seemed to be some evidence: testimony submitted to the home affairs select committee revealed that G4S managers had been alerted to the dangers. As the *Guardian* reported: 'According to their testimony, G4S received repeated warnings from staff, whose complaints included that training had to change "before there was a serious positional asphyxiation incident resulting in a detainee's death".' The paper claimed that one letter to managers said the problem had to be met 'head on' before 'the worst happens', even going so far as to tell G4S bosses that the company was 'playing Russian roulette with detainees' lives'. This rather contradicted earlier evidence from the company's managers to the committee, who said they were 'not aware' staff had raised concerns.[16]

The system through which failed asylum seekers are removed from the country is, at the best of times, shrouded in secrecy. Cases like the Mubenga death would be extremely complex even if there weren't an intersection between the state and the private firms it employs, but the relationship is prone to making things seem a great deal more suspicious.

For example: no doubt, government officials and G4S managers would tell you that the initial statement put out at the time of Mubenga's death, about how he'd been 'taken ill', was an innocent error – a result of how difficult it is to share accurate information in a breaking news situation. As a journalist, you'd be inclined to have some sympathy with that line. But at the same time, it's impossible to ignore the fact that the complicity between state and contractor can shield both parties from accountability in a job that demands transparency.

One experience I had while covering the story encapsulates this. In the wake of the Isleworth judgment, a number of problems with the process at the time of Mubenga's death had been highlighted. I approached G4S for a comment about what was being done. They told me I should approach either the Home Office or another outsourcing firm, Tascor (now part of Capita), which had taken over the overseas escorting contract. I contacted the Home Office and was given a generic statement: 'We have received the report and will respond to its findings in due course.' This was disappointing, so I followed up with a list of further questions. I was advised that, because they concerned operating procedure, I should take them to . . . G4S, who weren't even contracted to provide the service any more.

After the Isleworth verdict, Gaon Hart, the senior Crown advocate within the Crown Prosecution Service's (CPS) Special Crime Division, gave a statement about why he was unable to prosecute G4S – because he couldn't prove exactly why Mubenga died. He also provided a clear explanation as to how the relationship between the state and its contractors creates a buffer against, for example, corporate manslaughter under common law: 'The law would require me to prove that a sufficiently senior person within G4S, who could be said to "speak for" the company, failed to act as a reasonable person should do in their position and that the failure was so bad that it should be considered criminal.'

The experts suggested there were shortcomings in the training given to the security guards. They said that the training on how positional asphyxia might occur and the warning signs for identifying positional asphyxia were both flawed. In addition, the experts criticized the lack of specific training by G4S for use in restraint on board an aircraft. But here's another factor that would make prosecuting the company for these training failures difficult: G4S followed training recommended by the UKBA and the National Offenders Management Service, which had been found to be '"safe and fit for purpose" after official review', as Hart pointed out. He concluded: 'I appreciate the outcome is not what the family of Mr Mubenga would have hoped for.'[17]

Hart's wasn't the only official statement that showed exactly how the interaction between government and contractor clouded the question of culpability. The coroner's report highlighted the fact that G4S's guards were operating to a system of 'zero hours' payment that meant they'd be rewarded if they could keep detainees quiet until their plane had left the runway. It also pointed out that while the guards had been trained to restrain people, they hadn't been trained to do so in the unique environment of an aircraft.

On the subject of payment, the coroner had this to say: 'It seems to me that incentivizing the completion of removals by monetary award necessarily carries with it the risk that removals will go ahead in circumstances where otherwise they might be aborted. Having a financial interest in getting the job done does give rise to real concerns that inappropriate methods might be used to that end.' And on the issue of accreditation: 'The evidence points not to a mere lack of robustness either in the procedures of G4S or the Home Office but to an agreement to dispense with the need for accreditation, apparently to address delays within the UK Border Agency in processing applications for accreditation.'[18]

All these statements did little to placate Mubenga's wife, who wanted justice for her husband. She had previously told the *Guardian*: 'He was crying for help before he was killed. We can't understand why the officers and G4S are not answerable to the law as we or any other member of the public would be.'[19] It was hard to disagree.

As we'll see, Jimmy Mubenga is not the only person to have been restrained to death by guards from outsourcing companies. There's a clear need for our legal and political systems to improve the standards for accountability and it extends far beyond this case, or indeed the assaults mentioned earlier. Indeed, as Clare Sambrook pointed out to me in 2013: 'G4S [and other outsourcing companies] operate[s] in many countries where such matters don't come to light.'

The year after the unlawful killing verdict, there was a new development. In March 2014 the CPS confirmed that the three guards who restrained Mubenga would be charged with manslaughter (back in 2012, it had declined to bring charges over the death).[20] Something had changed: the CPS said 'new information' had come out of the inquest verdict that was delivered in July 2013. It had also considered whether G4S could be prosecuted for gross negligence, which would have required evidence of a 'controlling mind' being guilty. It decided this wasn't the case.

However, in December 2014, the three guards were found innocent. During the trial, the jury was not told about the racist jokes on their mobile phones (indeed the CPS asked that online reports about them be taken down), nor about the unlawful killing verdict the previous year.[21] Deborah Coles, the co-director of Inquest, a charity offering advice to people bereaved by a death in custody and detention, said: 'It is difficult to reconcile the verdict with the evidence heard at the trial that over twenty people heard Jimmy Mubenga say "I can't breathe."'[22]

Jimmy Mubenga was killed unlawfully, this much we know for sure – but no one has ever been held accountable.

Yarl's Wood

Of Britain's thirteen immigration removal detention centres, the one which has attracted the most headlines over the years is Yarl's Wood in Bedfordshire, a squat building tucked away on an industrial estate near a Formula One car testing wind tunnel and an indoor skydiving centre. That's because it's full of women (with just a few men who live in family units). Today, it's operated by the outsourcing firm Serco, which took over in 2007. It boasts a fancy website, the sort that might suit a primary school or the like. It describes itself as 'a fully contained residential centre housing adult women and adult family groups awaiting immigration clearance. We focus on decency and respect in all aspects of care for our residents and use continuous innovation to further improve and develop our service.'[23]

In 2013, as a result of covering a case we'll get to later in this chapter, I wanted to find out about the centre's history. I made contact with a researcher at the charity Medical Justice, who'd been going through old newspaper cuttings from since the place was built in November 2001, during the boom years of asylum detention services (it was huge by the standards of what had gone before: it cost £100 million, and was designed to hold 900 asylum seekers). And what struck me was that every year, there seemed to be a different problem. From her report:

2002: In February, a huge fire destroyed half the building, reportedly triggered after a 51-year-old woman was physically restrained by staff. When the fire started the head of Group 4 security ordered all staff to exit the timber-framed building, locking the detainees and some staff inside. Five people were injured.

2003: An undercover *Daily Mirror* reporter took a job as a security guard. The front page of the newspaper told how he 'discover[ed] a culture of abuse, racism and violence that SHOULD appal us all'.

2004: The prisons and probation ombudsman published a report on the investigation into the *Daily Mirror*'s allegations. Thirty recommendations were made. The report concluded: 'Most of the things [the reporter] said happened did happen. However, I have also concluded that these do not indicate a culture of racism and improper use of force.'[24]

And so on, every year through to 2013, including (among other cases), a suicide, a guard getting a woman pregnant, a report by Her Majesty's Inspectorate of Prisons (HMIP) described by one MP as 'appalling', and two hunger strikes involving around 100 women. If any prison had seen this many stories about it, surely it would have been shut down?

A few months after I'd read the Medical Justice report, in October 2013, a detainee alleged the women held there had been subjected to unwanted sexual advances and abuse by security guards and other officials. The *Observer* was given evidence – which it handed over to the police – from *Tanja* (throughout the book, names in italics have been changed to protect anonymity), a 23-year-old Roma woman, who'd been released from Yarl's Wood in March 2012. She described sexual contact with three male guards. She claimed attempts were made to deport her within days of her informing Yarl's Wood's management, and that one security guard had inappropriate relations with at least four women.

Tanja told the newspaper: 'A lot of officers were taking advantage of the girls that were detained. They would promise favours or offer to make life easier, saying they would have more chance of winning their case or staying in the country.' It reported: 'In a formal witness statement she has sent to Bedfordshire police, she states that one Serco official, with whom she was sexually involved, told her: "Don't worry, there is no way they can deport you."'

Most troubling of all were her claims that the sexual contact wasn't all consensual: 'I said I was scared and I did not want to ... There were two occasions when I was made to do "blow jobs" when I did not want to. [The guard] was well aware that I did not want to.'[25]

Her lawyer said there was evidence of 'systemic supervisory defects' in the centre's management. At the heart of this was the question of power within a relationship. The paper noted Tanja's lawyer had written to the UKBA, claiming: 'Our client has indicated that she was a reluctant participant in some of the sexual contact and, given the huge power imbalance, at least some of the conduct by the officers she complains about may amount to assault. Furthermore, she has suggested that there have been attempts by officers to destroy and suppress evidence of their misconduct.'[26] Serco would eventually pay damages and dismiss three staff members.

The lawyer's claims were supported by Nick Hardwick, the chief inspector of prisons, who had visited Yarl's Wood that month. He found no evidence that a 'wider culture of victimization or systematic abuse' had developed following the new allegations of abuse at the 400-bed centre. But he said: 'We were concerned to find that two staff had engaged in sexual activity with a female detainee, something that can never be less than abusive given the vulnerability of the detained population, and these staff had rightly been dismissed.'[27]

Hardwick raised other concerns: it was felt there weren't enough female staff, for an establishment overwhelmingly full of women, and that a number of women had been detained for too long – one had been held for four years, which, when one considers the fact that none of these people have been charged with an offence, seems needlessly cruel. And as mentioned earlier, the inspection said pregnant women were being held without the 'exceptional justification' required.

If Yarl's Wood's managers thought that would be the end of negative media coverage, they were very wrong. In March 2014, Christine Chase, a forty-year-old Jamaican woman, died at the centre after suffering what was thought to be a heart attack. A few days later, there was an urgent question in the House of Commons by the shadow home secretary, Yvette Cooper, who said there were claims that staff at the centre also refused the NHS's offers to help other inmates who were distressed. Home Office minister James Brokenshire confirmed there would be an investigation.

Then, in April that year, UN special rapporteur Rashida Manjoo said she was barred at the gates of the centre, on instructions 'from the highest levels of the Home Office'. She said: 'If there was nothing to hide, I should have been given access.'[28] The Home Office claimed her visit had never been agreed. And the very next month there were damaging revelations that seemed to point more clearly to a culture of secrecy surrounding the centre.

The *Observer* obtained an internal Serco report into an alleged sexual assault by one of its staff, a male nurse, against a female detainee. The police also investigated, but the allegations couldn't be substantiated. Serco's report said the woman had made it up, and a female guard who believed her was given 'objectivity' guidance. However, the Commons home affairs select committee was rather less satisfied. Keith Vaz MP told the BBC he was concerned that the report was never brought to parliamentary attention: 'That review contains very serious concerns about the way in which alleged abuse has been dealt with by a company that is in receipt of millions and millions of pounds of taxpayers' money.'[29] He added that his committee had received a number of anonymous emails from detainees in which they described poor treatment.

Despite the fact that the HMIP report had found no evidence of a wider culture of 'victimization or systematic abuse', the MPs on the committee decided in June to visit the centre after they spoke to Serco's managers, who admitted that over the past seven years ten staff had been dismissed over allegations of improper sexual contact with female detainees, as a result of thirty-one investigations of sexual offences. One of them was the nurse who'd been the subject of Serco's internal investigation.

At the time the internal report was revealed, a former senior Serco official went to the *Observer*. He claimed an anti-immigration culture was 'endemic' among staff, and that vulnerable women had been deported without their mental health being properly assessed. He told the paper: 'Officers would say openly: "They need to go back, they need to leave the country, they're only coming here to use NHS resources." A common phrase was: "They're only putting it on to block their removal." I've actually heard [senior staff] say: "These people are putting it on." It was endemic ... even the senior management structures were saying this, it was a mindset.' The *Observer* added: 'The whistle-blower, who resigned from Serco last year after raising concerns, corroborated allegations from former detainees that some women felt they had to flirt with staff to obtain everyday essentials such as toiletries.'[30]

Another whistleblower stated his concerns over the issue of mental health a month later, in June 2014. Noel Finn told the BBC he'd repeatedly raised concerns about the assessment and treatment of women with psychological problems, but no action had been taken. He said: 'The system wasn't driven for mental health. It was more driven about "Are they fit to fly, physically?"' He described an occasion when a woman he'd assessed as being at risk had later burned herself with boiling water, but she'd been left untreated for sixteen hours: he was 'basically told to shut up' when he asked how it happened. He also described 'a toxic culture, where guards would flirt and be inappropriate'.[31]

And what was the end result of all this coverage? In November 2014 Serco's contract to run Yarl's Wood was renewed for eight more years, and it was paid £70 million for the job.[32]

Only two months later, the charity Women for Refugee Women interviewed thirty-eight detainees. The charity's report claimed that – in clear contravention of Serco's guidelines – 'almost all [of the women interviewed] said men watched them in intimate situations, such as while naked, partly dressed in the shower or on the toilet'. Among the women interviewed, thirteen said they'd been seen naked, twenty-nine said they'd been seen partially dressed, twenty-nine said they'd been seen in bed, sixteen said they'd been seen in the shower and fourteen said they'd been seen on the toilet. Serco responded that the claims were 'uncorroborated'.[33]

Then, in March 2015, *Channel 4 News* went undercover in the centre and discovered detainees self-harming and staff referring to the inmates as animals, 'beasties' and bitches. One guard was recorded saying 'Headbutt the bitch.' Another said: 'They are all slashing their wrists, apparently. Let them slash their wrists ... It's attention seeking.'[34] Those of us who'd covered the centre for years were rather more depressed than surprised by the footage, and nor were we surprised by the collective political shrugging of shoulders from most politicians that followed. Labour hardly has a guilt-free history concerning mistreatment of asylum seekers, but Yvette Cooper spoke for many when she told the House of Commons: 'There is no point in ministers pretending to be shocked at news of abuse. This is not news ... This is state-sanctioned abuse of women on the home secretary's watch and it needs to end now.'[35]

Channel 4 also uncovered anxiety about medical care – a concern about the centre which receives rather less coverage. Back in 2013, Medical Justice offered to put me in touch with pregnant women who were being held in the centre. Every woman I spoke to asked if I would change their name. They were scared of the UKBA, and scared of going back to the centre. The first was a woman I called *Samantha*. She'd fled to England from Africa a few years before (she didn't want me to name the country), and told me that, because of her role in strike actions and civil disobedience, she'd been raped by two policemen, while her husband had been murdered. Her appeal to remain in the country had dragged on for years (as we'll see soon, this isn't unusual). During this period, she'd given birth to one child and was now expecting another. I would later write up her description of Yarl's Wood in a piece for the *New Statesman*:

My daughter, by that time fourteen months old, had measles so I'd had to leave her with a relative while I went to the reporting office. They told me I was being taken to Yarl's

Wood. Then they brought her to me. She had wet Pampers, and no other clothes. They just dumped her in front of me.

There is no standard of care there. The food was so bad my daughter lost weight. The male staff would just burst into the room at four in the morning. She was terrified. The staff don't care. They stick all the kids in a nursery: another child tried to strangle her. In the end my lawyer had to write to them about that.

It's a dirty, filthy place. You never go outside. There are some bad people in there. My daughter and I were in our bedroom when a huge fight broke out. There was screaming, mothers being pulled apart from their children, people with bleeding noses. It spilled into our room and there were four or five men and women trying to restrain another woman: one of the men accidentally had his leg on top of my daughter in the scuffle. I was screaming: 'You'll kill her!' They lied afterwards – they told the TV news crews it didn't happen. I know what I saw.

I started to go mad in there. I honestly wanted to kill myself. If it hadn't been for friends I'd made before going in I think I would have. It made me ill.[36]

Samantha was released after three months. Shortly afterwards, she suffered a miscarriage. She attributed it to the stress she suffered in detention. Medical Justice had also interviewed *Samantha* for a report about the treatment of pregnant women in detention. There were many more voices quoted there:

I don't want to remember those horrible moments of my life which I spent in detention, when I cried for food and cried due to pain. I was in a detention centre for seven months. I had severe morning sickness which lasted five months. I couldn't eat the food which was provided for detainees. I remained there living just on fruit, juices, biscuits, crisps and popcorn for five months. I got weaker day by day.

I lost 6kg of my actual weight – it should increase in pregnancy. The doctors and nurses there shouted at me many times. They mentally tortured me by saying that I was on hunger strike. I was never on hunger strike: I love my baby so why would I go on hunger strike? I requested and begged the officers many times to allow me to go to eat something in the cultural kitchen because I always felt hungry – but they refused.[37]

I mentioned some of the others in my report, among them *Maria,* who was restrained and forcibly removed to her home country by four escorts, only to suffer a stillbirth a few months after her return. Another, *Aliya,* developed acute psychosis after she was prescribed anti-malarial medication in anticipation of her forced removal. Perhaps the most horrifying story of all was that of *Anna,* who had complained for weeks about abdominal pains, attended A&E with two guards in company, miscarried, attempted suicide, and was admitted into a psychiatric ward.

It's a hugely sensitive and difficult issue. Many of the women in detention will have been victims of rape, trafficking and torture: in Yarl's Wood, eighty percent of women claim to have been raped or tortured.[38] A third will have been put on suicide watch while there.[39] While the Home Office claims to have a policy of not detaining pregnant women, it does detain them: this was corroborated by an HMIC inspection of the centre in 2013, and it has no idea of how many pregnant women are kept in detention.[40] What we do know is that there were nearly 100 in Yarl's Wood in 2011, yet according to Medical Justice's research, only five percent of them were successfully removed. For that matter, there are also a number of children under the age of eighteen being kept in adult detention centres, in clear breach of legal guidelines – the Refugee Council has found that at least 127 children have been classified as adults since 2010, and the Bureau of Investigative Journalism uncovered more cases in 2015.[41]

Medical Justice said the medical treatment the women at Yarl's Wood received was not up to NHS standard. Both the Royal College of Midwives and the Royal College of Obstetricians and Gynaecologists responded to the report. The former said: 'We believe that the treatment of pregnant asylum seekers in detention is governed by outmoded and outdated practices that shame us all. Midwives must care for and serve all mothers and babies regardless of their immigration status. We, therefore, encourage and urge the Home Office to act on the report's recommendations without delay.'[42]

During his tenure as prime minister, David Cameron has had little to say on Yarl's Wood besides a brief line about how 'detention is an important part of a firm but fair immigration system'. However, in April 2015 he announced that a review of immigration detention would be undertaken by a former prisons and probation ombudsman for England and Wales, Stephen Shaw. The report was published in January 2016. It concluded that not only did the government drastically need to reduce the number of immigration centres it used, but, shockingly, that there was no correlation between the number of people being detained and the number of people who ended up being lawfully deported. He called for one centre where children along with their families are detained – Cedars, near Gatwick – to be closed.[43]

The problem with immigration

Why have there been so many problems in the system? To return to the case of Jimmy Mubenga briefly: the legal implications for the government, had G4S been charged as an entity by the CPS over Mubenga's death, would have been intriguing. To what extent would the company have blamed the incident on the lack of clarity in the instructions it had received from the government? One suspects it might have had a strong case, if the state of the body giving the orders is anything to go by.

The immigration detention industry began to boom in the early 2000s. Jerome Phelps from Asylum Aid told me: 'Ministers' diaries of the time are full of entries about asylum panic. The numbers in asylum grew under the Tories, but when they're in power there's no one to the right [outside UKIP] to complain about it. So Labour inherited a dysfunctional system, and then the numbers began to grow even more, primarily due to the Balkan conflict.' There was a new political agenda: one, stop people claiming asylum, and two, try to deter them from doing so.

And what evolved from this was fast-track detention, launched under Tony Blair's government in 2000. Under the system, claimants are locked in high-security detention centres and interviewed, and within three days a decision is supposed to be made. As the *New Statesman* writer Daniel Trilling put it:

> Difficult cases – survivors of torture, families, pregnant women, people with physical or mental conditions, potential victims of trafficking – aren't supposed to be processed in this way: the fast track was designed for single people, largely those coming from 'white-list' countries (asylum claims originating from such countries are more likely to be false) ... Target-driven deportation and removal statistics dictate who leaves and when, rather than the needs and desires of the individual human being at stake.[44]

As it happens, since Trilling wrote these words, a High Court action brought in 2014 by Jerome Phelps's organization was successful, and the detained fast track asylum system has now been deemed unlawful for vulnerable groups like asylum seekers. That system increased the rate at which people were detained, but it was perhaps less of a problem than the sheer length of time that they were kept captive without trial. It's still not unusual to spend a year or more in a detention centre while attempting to be granted asylum. In 2015 a Freedom of Information (FoI) request revealed that ninety people in detention had been held without trial for a year, twenty people for more than two years, and one had even been held for five years. Two thirds would be released, costing the government nearly £5 million in compensation claims.[45] The cost of detaining migrants subsequently granted permission to stay was £242,515.52 in the first quarter of 2014 alone.[46]

In the background, the governance surrounding this rapidly growing industry has lurched this way and that. It began when home secretary Charles Clarke resigned because his department had lost track of released foreign-national prisoners. His successor, John Reid, now Lord Reid of Cardowan, promptly remarked that the then Immigration and Nationality Directorate was not fit for purpose. Phelps described this to me as a long-forgotten event which still has knock-on effects today: 'It's a very politicized realm and it affects contractors and civil servants: people back then were scared of losing their jobs, they seemed traumatized, battered, always looking for the next punch.'

The mess over prisoners resulted in the creation of the Border and Immigration Agency, which dealt with immigration control, and then in 2008 the UKBA, following a merger with UK Visas, which dealt with applications for entry clearance into the UK, and customs staff from Her Majesty's Revenue and Customs. All the while the policy of not granting too many people asylum was at odds with an increasingly dysfunctional system. The fact the new agency was not equipped to deal with the task it faced was made clear by the fact it shut down five years later, and as the *Guardian* pointed out: 'The stunning thing is that some people still stuck in the backlog of 310,000 cases that sealed UKBA's death warrant are actually a direct legacy from [a late 1990s] breakdown in the system.'[47] The backlog of cases had soared into the hundreds of thousands due to a failed IT project.

As anyone who's ever worked in government knows, rejigging rarely if ever solves fundamental systemic problems. The UKBA's history was largely an absolute shambles. In 2013 an FoI request showed that almost half of the enforced removals the government attempted were cancelled: 14,435 effected versus 11,085 cancelled. Given each cancellation cost £186, this was a huge waste of money above all (£10 million over five years) – never mind the human cost, as outlined by Emma Mlotshwa, chief executive of Medical Justice: 'This is a system in chaos. We deal with countless cases of enforced removals which are cancelled. The whole thing causes needless trauma to detainees. Taking someone to the plane and then back to a detention centre, keeping them under imminent threat of deportation, is inhuman and treats detainees no better than cargo.'[48]

The fact it took an FoI request to reveal the extent of the chaos faced by the organization lends credence to the conclusion Theresa May would reach in 2013 as she abolished it: that it was 'secretive and defensive'. We can't say for sure if the body's reliance on outsourcing firms – which grew and grew over the years – was motivated by a desire to shift responsibility or by a lack of confidence in its own capacity to do what was now a job it simply couldn't handle. However, we can say for sure that the saving of money – as it always is – was a motivation, and that the expertise of those to whom it gave the jobs wasn't always a primary consideration.

The work we ask outsourcing firms to do is often concerned with the dignity of vulnerable people. In a civilized country, there shouldn't be any muddiness over the question of accountability when this work is carried out. One immigration lawyer (who wished to remain anonymous) gave me a particularly unsympathetic view of the asylum industry several years ago, when I was researching a piece on the matter: 'You sort of feel like it's "out of sight, out of mind". These centres are out in the middle of nowhere: no one really knows what's going on in them, what the quality of staffing is like – you ... think the government's decided: "This is ugly work but someone has to do it, so let's keep it as far away from scrutiny as possible."'

And behind this mismanagement are thousands of human stories. While the most dramatic, like the case of Jimmy Mubenga, are relatively well known, most are not. Here's a story that brings together most of the themes we've seen over the course of this chapter and shows how they interrelate: the way the asylum industry deals with human beings, the thorny and complex background behind the people making asylum claims, and the secrecy with which the whole process operates.

Rose Akhalu used to live in a little flat in Benin City, Nigeria, with her husband, a nurse. They had no children (in fact, Rose had suffered a miscarriage), but they were happy. Then, in 1999, he was diagnosed with a brain tumour. She worked in local government and earned 22,000 naira – at the time about £80 – a year. If he was to be treated, they needed to raise £8,000 (₦2,000,000) and go to South Africa or India for treatment. And they couldn't, so Rose stood by as he lost his sight, and then his speech, and finally she watched him die.

Rose's husband's family took all of his possessions – including his money. She wanted to challenge them, but was dissuaded by her mother, a traditionalist who told her she should be thankful to God that she was still young and had her life ahead of her. Rose was alone in the world. She set about putting her life back together.

And a few years later, in 2004, she'd managed it. She won a Ford Foundation scholarship to study in England, along with only twenty-two other people. Her choice of course was international development at Leeds University. The plan was to establish an NGO so young girls would be educated and not make the mistakes she had in the aftermath of her bereavement. She'd already started educating young girls in her community, under a tree near her house, telling them they had the right to go back to school even if they'd got pregnant.

One thing that had kept her sane during these difficult years was her faith in God. So she joined a Catholic church in Leeds, St Augustine's, a little parish on the outskirts of town. The area is poor, but the church itself is a warm and welcoming community. The first time I spoke to Rose, over the phone (I didn't know where she was at the time; she was afraid to tell me), she told me about how the church was the most important thing in her life: 'I'm a member of the choir and I lead the Bible study group. On Mondays I serve the older people tea, coffee and cake. After food we clean up and play dominos and bingo for biscuits. It's like a day centre for women. They love it and the volunteers love it too. I've made so many friends in the church: I spent Christmas and Boxing Day with Paul and Dot . . .'

I spoke to one of her fellow parishioners, Claire McLaughlin, who backed up exactly what she was saying: 'She's quite a private person. But she's really interested in other people.' The two women began working on community initiatives for young girls. Claire told me: 'She works with asylum seekers, and goes out doing street pastoring work in Harehills – she's never evangelical with the people on the street: she just wants to help them.'[49]

But it all went wrong. One day, Rose went to have a vaccination, only to be told her blood pressure was too high. She was sent to Leeds General Infirmary, where a nephrologist ran tests and diagnosed renal failure. What this meant for Rose was dialysis, three times a week. That meant her original plan, to return to Nigeria once her course was completed, had to be abandoned. In 2009 she had a kidney transplant, which requires a special cocktail of drugs to stop your body rejecting the foreign organ that's been put in it.

The next year, her consultant wrote to her former MP, Fabian Hamilton, explaining how the treatment had complicated her residential situation. The transplant had been successful but she would need regular hospital check-ups and immunosuppressant drugs for the rest of her life. And that was a problem, because it meant returning to Nigeria was all but impossible. As I wrote when I was covering the case:

> Rose was no 'health tourist'. But it was her misfortune that the medication to protect from rejection of the kidney would cost £10,000 per year in Nigeria – a sum Rose would never be able to earn given the wage differential (85 percent of the population live on less than $1 a day), high unemployment and the fact she is of retirement age in that country. She had no support network there, besides three siblings, all of whom lived in poverty. Moreover, as medical experts – Nigerian and British – have testified, the sanitary and medical facilities she required could not be provided. If deported, she would die within two to four weeks.

So Rose began the long and arduous legal process of fighting for the right to stay in Britain. She checked into UKBA reporting offices without quibble. And one day, in March 2012, she was told that she was going to be detained. Staff from Reliance – the firm contracted by the UKBA – told her she was being transported from Leeds to Yarl's Wood.

She was put in a van which would take her to the centre in Bedfordshire. Early in the journey she asked to use the toilet (her kidney problems made the request a matter of some urgency). She was told she'd have to wait until they got to a police station, whereupon it'd be 'safe' for her to go. After asking for the toilet again and again for half an hour, she was taken to one of Reliance's offices, where there was a changeover of guards. Through the van's window, she could see the entrance to the toilet, and she frantically stood up, begging to use it. The officers told her she'd have to stay in the back, and tried to find a plastic bag into which she could urinate – they eventually handed her the one used by male detainees. It didn't work: she urinated all over her hands and inside the van, in full view of the CCTV cameras.

I remember speaking to her a few months after the incident, and hearing the trembling anger in this mild woman's voice: 'I felt humiliated and degraded. I was treated like a common criminal. As if I had no dignity, no rights and no voice.' She told me that she and the van were left covered in urine, and that as a result she suffered a urinary tract infection because she was stuck in her urine-sodden clothes until she arrived at Yarl's Wood that evening.

And that was when I first began to take an interest in Yarl's Wood, and what happens there. Because if Rose had to be locked up there, who else was? As it happened, she didn't talk much about it in general – she said more about the Colnbrook centre in west London, where she'd been locked up in a male cell because there wasn't enough space in the female ones. She talked about the couple of weeks she spent there, describing a room 'stuffed with cigarette smoke and rubbish. The officer left another woman and I there, so we started banging on the door, asking for him to let the cigarette smoke out of the room. The officer's boss came and threatened us, telling us we'd be moved somewhere worse. Eventually a cleaner was sent.'[50]

In case it's not obvious, the Home Office had decided that Rose was a health tourist, even though she'd applied for her scholarship in 2002 and only suffered an unforeseen renal problem five years later. The legal battle began: her solicitors won an injunction which prevented the Home Office from deporting her until a renewed application for permission to proceed with judicial review was heard on 24 July 2012. She also had the support of her MP, Greg Mulholland.

Indeed, in an age of political equivocating, his public statements were endearingly blunt: 'I will be writing to the Home Secretary to ask why, despite being granted an appeal hearing, the judge thought it acceptable to allow UKBA to continue harassing Roseline and continue to seek her deportation from the UK. As well as the distress caused, this has been a farce and has wasted considerable amounts of taxpayers' money. The system clearly needs to be looked at so this cannot happen.'[51]

Yet in September that year the Home Office refused her appeal. This generated the publicity that caught my attention. The Bishop of Ripon and Leeds spoke out on the campaigning website OpenDemocracy:

Roseline has made a life in this country (gaining qualifications here) and is loved and respected in her community in Leeds. It saddens me to think that, having been accepted and cared for in the UK to the extent of being given a kidney transplant which has transformed her life, she should now find herself being forced to return to Nigeria where she would not be able to receive the medical treatment she needs to survive.[52]

He was far from being the only one to speak out: Rose's consultant and the National Kidney Foundation – which pointed out that its donors would think it a waste of time if they believed recipients were going to be allowed to die – had made representations to the Home Office. Even the actor Colin Firth, who famously played a human rights lawyer in *Love Actually*, joined in: 'Our Home Secretary has effectively condemned an innocent woman to death – a decision surely repugnant to every person in this country. It should be reversed immediately and Rose should be allowed to live.'[53]

Rose's lawyers appealed to the First-tier Tribunal (Immigration and Asylum Chamber), and in November, Judge Saffer overturned the Home Office's decision. At the hearing the Home Office finally accepted that she would definitely die if returned to Nigeria. As I wrote at the time: 'Astoundingly, it continued to maintain that her removal was proportionate and not in breach of her human rights. However, the judge found she had come here legally, was diagnosed while here legally, that the cost of treatment was not excessive, and that she had established a private life of value to her.'[54]

Her MP felt that any appeal on the part of the Home Office would be 'a serious misuse of the public purse', but that didn't deter it from lodging one in December. The judge refused its appeal, and the department took it to the Upper Tribunal (Immigration and Asylum Chamber). Rose's solicitor put out a statement: 'I cannot comprehend why the Home Secretary is continuing to pursue Rose through the courts after conceding at the last hearing that if Rose is deported to Nigeria she will not be able to access medical care and will die a painful death within four weeks of her return. Not only is such conduct deeply inhumane, it is also a complete waste of scarce public funds on unnecessary and time consuming litigation.'

All the while, I couldn't understand why a government department seemed to be – to put it bluntly – condemning an innocent woman to death. Rose emailed me a few lines when I was researching my piece, and touched a nerve, perhaps because of the simplicity of what she said, and the fact that death wasn't even her uppermost consideration:'I'm very happy here in Leeds as I've made so many friends. Leeds is now my home. To think that I might be removed made me feel very bad and empty – the thought of losing my wonderful friends is very painful. And they don't want to lose me either.'

It took quite a few phone calls before I finally began to get a grip on why this was happening: it was about case law that would make life easier for genuine health tourists. In fact, Rose's lawyers had been arguing her case under Article 8 of the European Convention of Human Rights: a right to a private and family life, because it's currently legal to deport someone even if they will become terminally ill on arrival in a new country. Eight months after I'd first covered Rose's case, judges in the Upper Tribunal rejected the Home Office's appeal. Her friends were jubilant. Her solicitor pointed out that the judges had found her case to be exceptional. Rose's friends thanked me for helping me bring her case to the public's attention.

I was left with a lot of questions about the outsourcing industry – many of which we've touched on in this chapter – but the biggest was a simple one: why does the government *really* want private firms to do this kind of work? As we've seen, it's certainly unpleasant work, but is it all about keeping unsavoury incidents at arm's length? No doubt, there is that element to this decision.

As recently as August 2015 the MP for Hornsey and Wood Green, Catherine West, was barred by the Home Office from visiting Yarl's Wood, ostensibly to protect the inmates' 'privacy'.[55] But for the most part the perpetual negative media and parliamentary reports have had very little impact on policy, whichever party is in government. Nor has it ever forced any improvements in standards – that month the chief inspector of prisons reported that conditions at the centre had deteriorated to such an extent that it was 'a place of national concern'.[56] In fact, the most obvious answer is a simple one: it's a good way to save money.

3

Disabilities and Employment

For several years now, there's been an outcry on social media about the way outsourcing companies have treated disabled people. The most regularly presented narrative is that the human suffering arising from the nature of this treatment is simply a by-product of a right-wing government's cuts to services for the most vulnerable.

The tale of how we got here is rather more complex than that. However, it begins with an outsourcing firm whose name is now notorious in the context of disability services. Atos, a French multinational that specializes in IT services, was asked by Labour in 2008 to assess 2.5 million people on the newly introduced employment and support allowance (ESA), which had replaced incapacity benefit for people too ill or disabled to work. Incapacity benefit had been assessed using a test known as a personal capacity assessment (PCA), which actually had a lot of similarities to the new test that Atos would carry out for the ESA – the now-infamous work capability assessment (WCA).

The WCA was supposed to be more modern and fair than the PCA, and for carrying it out Atos was to be paid £110 million a year. What barely anyone noticed was that the notion of saving money was built into the scheme from day one. A 2010 explanatory memorandum from the Department for

Work and Pensions (DWP) explained that 'net savings' would be increased because the assumption was that twenty-three percent of people given this new test would be found fit for work.[1]

Critics soon claimed the WCA made it very difficult for health professionals to exercise their professional judgement. It was a 'logic integrated medical assessment' – a computer-based system – and fairly early on it became clear it simply wasn't able to take in how complex the needs of severely disabled or sick people are. In 2010, two years after it had been brought in, a DWP review identified 'procedural problems'. As Iain McKenzie, Labour MP for Inverclyde, put it: 'It is ridiculous to have people making an assessment based on a tick-list that looks like it should be used for an MOT on a car.'[2]

Nevertheless, that year the scope of the tests was expanded under the coalition, so that long-term incapacity benefit claimants would also be assessed by it. In 2012, the British Medical Association condemned the WCA as unfit for purpose. And the next year Professor Malcolm Harrington, a government welfare adviser (who had carried out the 2010 review), suggested the expansion happened after ministers ignored his advice not to push ahead immediately with the plans. The DWP said there was no record that Harrington had formally issued a warning to ministers.[3]

These were the bare facts as of 2014: there were 1.6 million claimants on incapacity benefit, assessed at a rate of 11,000 every week. On average around thirty-five percent of challenged decisions were overturned at tribunal; this number had dropped a little, but it still amounted to one in ten of the total assessed. It cost £70 million in 2013/14 to assess the appeals.[4]

The human cost behind the figures

Some of the stories we've seen so far have hinted at the way that large-scale state projects end up reducing complex human problems to balance sheets. Nowhere is that clearer than in the case of the WCA. From about 2011 – when campaigners really began to express their dismay – it took years of concern being expressed on both mainstream and social media before the issue was discussed at length in the House of Commons. There had been hundreds of such stories shared on Facebook and Twitter, along with documentaries on Channel 4 and BBC One, but the criticism of the WCA was still dismissed by many MPs as politically motivated. However, after a Commons debate in January 2013, such characterizations were rather thinner on the ground – MPs from across the political spectrum shared the experiences of their constituents, and it seemed a tipping point had been reached.[7]

Stephen Gilbert, Liberal Democrat MP for St Austell and Newquay, was one of the first to speak, saying the problem was not the 'principle but the practice'. And in this case he felt the latter was 'dehumanizing and degrading'. He went on to add: 'If we in this House cannot give voice to these people, who are some of the most vulnerable in our society, I really do not know what we are for.'

One story in particular was widely shared around Twitter and other social networks. Iain Wright, Labour MP for Hartlepool, described the distress of a female constituent in her early fifties who suffered from Crohn's disease. She had a large section of her bowel removed and suffered two bouts of diarrhoea a day, but was classed as having 'limited capacity for work'. Wright went on to say:

Her assessment and appeal were degrading, insensitive and unprofessional. She was described throughout her appeal notes as a man. Incorrect dates and fictitious telephone calls were placed on her files – in other words, lies. Mrs M. was told that she could wear a nappy for work. What sort of country have we become? What sort of ethical values do the government have, if that is the degrading and crass way in which decent, law-abiding constituents of mine are being dealt with?

Steve Rotheram, Labour MP for Liverpool Walton, described a case he had heard about from a constituent, Janine, in Liverpool: 'Her dad was thrown off sickness benefit in November after an Atos work capability assessment and was declared fit for work despite suffering from chronic obstructive pulmonary disease. Six weeks later, on Christmas Day, Janine's father died.'

John McDonnell, Labour MP for Hayes and Harlington, drew attention to Callum's List, a now-defunct website that aimed to bring attention to cases where people had died as a direct result of the WCA. He pointed out in Parliament: 'The first [now second] example on the list was that of Paul Reekie. Some members may have known Paul, an award-winning writer and poet in Leith, Scotland. He did not leave a suicide note, just two letters on the table beside him. One was about his loss of housing benefit and the other was about his loss of incapacity benefit.' Campaigners and journalists have drawn attention to many such cases since.[8]

Pamela Nash, Labour MP for Airdrie and Shotts, gave us this:

I have had a frail lady sitting in my office who had only recently finished chemotherapy but had been told she was fit for work. I have had a lady who suffered ninety percent burns to her body – she spends every day in severe pain – and was told that she was now ready to join the work programme. I could list hundreds of others – sadly, these are very familiar stories. These people are having their lives ruined by a system that was designed to support them.

There were plenty more stories – scores, in fact. Madeleine Moon, Labour MP for Bridgend, said her constituency phones were often 'clogged with crying people'. Eilidh Whiteford, SNP MP for Banff and Buchan, said she had 'encountered incontinent patients being asked to make four-hour round trips on public transport. I have also encountered constituents who have had to make very long journeys by public transport only to find that their appointment is not double booked, but triple booked.' She was one of many MPs who made similar complaints.

Michael Meacher, Labour MP for Oldham West and Royton, said he could not 'easily contain my own feelings at the slowness, rigidity and insensitivity with which Atos and the DWP have responded — or very often not responded — to the cries of pain that they have heard repeatedly'. He presented four demands: an independent assessment of the suitability of the work capability assessment; acceptance that current criteria and descriptors don't take into account fluctuating conditions; full and transparent details of the Atos contract (adding that they should not be hidden by claims of commercial confidentiality); and assurance that the medical expertise of disabled persons' doctors and related professionals was fully taken into account.

But there were still many serious questions, one of which was asked by Heather Wheeler, Conservative MP for South Derbyshire: 'One of my early letters to a previous minister asked about the point when we say that the system is not working;

frankly, I have not had an adequate reply. When someone drops down dead within three months of being assessed as being perfectly capable of going back to work, what is the review process for Atos?'

As already seen in the case of *Alice*, perhaps the most egregious examples of bureaucratic cruelty concerned the issue of mental health. At the debate Pamela Nash said she had been 'seeing people who have claimed employment and support allowance as a result of a physical disability or illness ending up with mental health problems owing to the stress of going through the system'. And Madeleine Moon had described a female constituent who'd been left with post-traumatic stress disorder after a sexual assault. The number of tribunals she'd been forced to attend after she'd been found fit to work had caused her to attempt suicide. Moon concluded: 'This lady is being hounded by the state: there is no other way of describing it. There is no excuse for this behaviour. This is a company that is not playing fair by this country's most vulnerable people.'[9]

What was being done? The answer was detailed in a response to a question from the journalist Kate Belgrave: 'We have put in place a network of Mental Function Champions to spread best practice across the business and offer advice and coaching to other professionals carrying out WCAs. We invited leading external experts in mental health to help us shape the role for the Mental Function Champions, and we now have 60 Champions.'[10] But there were a number of problems with them.

Belgrave and I looked into the issue. After a number of frustrating attempts at getting clarification (at one point she began to wonder if they existed at all), she discovered that the 'mental function champions' were merely providing guidance over the phone – not sitting in on the interviews. Given that there was widespread agreement that the WCA didn't deal with the issue of mental health very well, it barely seemed enough.

So 2013 was the year when it was finally accepted that the WCA had been a failure. For the government's part, Conservative DWP minister Mark Hoban would point out at the January debate that three in ten people who were assessed now got ESA. He also claimed it was unhelpful to 'demonize' the system with 'adverse media coverage'. John McDonnell MP, however, said: 'The concern expressed by members about an issue of public administration in all [these stories] is unprecedented in recent decades. There is example after example of human suffering on a scale unacceptable in a civilized society.'[11]

The demise of Atos and the rise of Maximus

Arguably the most telling exchange in the debate didn't involve MPs' constituents at all. It involved the Conservative MP Robert Halfon and the Labour MP Kevan Jones, and it was about the outsourcing process. Here's the Hansard entry:

> **Mr Kevan Jones (North Durham) (Lab):** The hon. Gentleman is correct in saying that the first contract with Atos was introduced by the previous government, but why did the present government renew and extend that contract even though they knew about all the problems that he and others have raised in the House?
>
> **Robert Halfon (Harlow) (Con):** This is where I agree with the hon. Gentleman. I was very disturbed when Atos got the contract for the personal independence payments.
>
> **Mr Jones:** That happened under this government.
>
> **Mr Halfon:** Yes, that is what I am saying. The reasons that were given included the fact that the infrastructure was already in place, and the cost of changing the contractor.[12]

What they were saying was that one party made a mistake when it drew up the contract; the other was left in a situation whereby it had no real way to remedy it.

Atos might have hoped that all of the rage regarding the contract would eventually be displaced onto the government. But a steady trickle of worrying stories put paid to that. Insiders will tell you that of all the mistakes the company made, the biggest was accepting a contract like this without predicting the degree of media scrutiny that would come with it. In 2011, two employees were investigated over allegations that they made inappropriate remarks on Facebook about the people they assessed, referring to them as 'parasites' and 'down and outs'.[13]

Two years later, two nurses who resigned from the company because it was 'cut-throat' and 'ruthless' described how they were criticized by their managers for being 'too nice', and a doctor working at the company also blew the whistle: the BBC reported on the case of Greg Wood, a former military doctor who 'decided that he could no longer tolerate working for the fitness-for-work assessment firm Atos earlier this year when he was asked, for perhaps the 10th time, to change a report he had made on a claimant, in this case making it unlikely that the individual would be eligible for sickness benefit.'[14] Indeed, some felt that it was his evidence that in part led to the DWP announcing in July 2013 that it would bring in additional providers alongside Atos, although the official reason cited was one of its own audits, which identified an unacceptable reduction in the quality of written reports produced following assessments.

It would be easy to point the finger at the various revelations that emerged during Atos's tenure and conclude that the contract failed purely because a private company was given a job for which it was entirely unsuited. But it's worth noting that the assessment with which it's most closely associated – no doubt much to the frustration of the company – was drawn up not by Atos, but the DWP. Its descriptors were written by the department, which gave the company strict rules that it had to stick to.

And the contract meant fundamental reform just wasn't affordable – or, indeed, practicable. At the January 2013 debate, Ian Lavery, Labour MP for Wansbeck, asked if Michael Meacher's suggestions were just putting 'a sticking plaster on a gaping wound'. He asked if both the contractor and the test itself should be scrapped. But as Dan Rogerson, Lib Dem MP for North Cornwall, pointed out: 'The problem with that suggestion is that all the people who have been through the process and have won appeals will have to go back to square one.'

After a damning report by the public accounts committee (PAC), which criticized both the DWP and Atos, the latter told the *Financial Times* in February 2014 that it was seeking to end its involvement in the contract. It said staff carrying out work capability assessments for Atos had received death threats online and in person. It pledged to carry on undertaking the tests until a new company was in a position to take over.

The signs had been there that the DWP wanted Atos out of the contract too. A month earlier, it had quietly stopped making 'repeat referrals' to the company – that is, referrals where a claimant had been found to have limited capability for work but would need to return for repeat assessments.[15] However, by all accounts, staff at the DWP were furious that the company had gone public. A spokesman said: 'Atos were appointed the sole provider for delivering work capability assessments by the previous government. In July we announced Atos had been instructed to enact a quality improvement plan to remedy the unacceptable reduction in quality identified.'[16]

It's perhaps worth noting that the death threats, which, according to media reports, were the primary motivation for Atos's exit, were subsequently called into question. Shortly after the news came out that Atos wanted to leave the contract, the Disability News Service (DNS) website asked the company for evidence of these threats, whereupon Atos was unable to provide a single example. It was also, according to DNS, 'unable to explain why there had apparently not been any prosecutions for such "death threats" or assaults when its assessment centres were usually littered with CCTV cameras'.

This sparked a furious reaction among campaigners. John McArdle, a prominent campaigner from an organization called Black Triangle, told DNS the Atos claims were 'an outrageous libel against sick and disabled people', and added: 'If we could sue them, we would.'[17] Atos had claimed it was recording 163 incidents a month in which members of the public were assaulting or abusing its staff. But a response from the DWP to a DNS Freedom of Information request showed that of 1,678 'security incidents' recorded by Atos in 2013, only five could be 'easily identified as assaults on staff'.[18] The company, for its part, said: 'It's not true to say we are unable to share data, we have declined to do so for reasons of staff anonymity,' though it gave no explanation as to why the evidence couldn't be presented in a redacted form.

However, Atos continued to claim that it was being inundated with threats: indeed, Lisa Coleman (vice president), Helen Hall (director of communications) and Dr Angela Graham (clinical director for the WCA) made more claims to the House of Commons work and pensions committee in June 2014, talking about a rise in 'issues' and claimants coming 'into assessment centres with knives' and '[threatening] to throw acid in the face of the receptionists'. When asked by journalists for more details, they refused to provide any, instead referring them to a pre-prepared statement. And the DWP directed journalists trying to get more information about the issue back to Atos (you may remember a similar never-ending circle of non-information in Chapter 2, with G4S and the Home Office).

In March 2014 disabilities minister Mike Penning said a new company would be appointed in early 2015: 'I am pleased to confirm that Atos will not receive a single penny of compensation from the taxpayer for the early termination of their contract. Quite the contrary, Atos has made a substantial financial settlement to the department.'[19] The DWP said 'one national provider' would be appointed to take over the contract.

A couple of months later Judge Robert Martin, the outgoing head of the tribunal that hears appeals related to social security benefits, wrote in the *Judicial Information Bulletin* that the WCA had undergone 'virtual collapse' because of problems with the delivery of reforms and the removal of legal aid funding for challenging benefits decisions. He described how the number of cases being adjudged had dropped from more than 50,000 in July 2013 to 8,775 in March 2014.[20]

Who would take on this broken system? The answer was revealed in October 2014: an American company called Maximus, which took over in March 2015. It's a large multinational that offers a range of human services, but has not done so without controversy – most notably in 2007, when it settled a lawsuit with the American government at a cost of $30.5 million after it was accused of being involved in the falsification of Medicaid claims.[21]

Shortly before taking over the WCA, Maximus signed Sue Marsh, a disabled Labour activist who ran a popular blog called Diary of a Benefits Scrounger, to be its 'head of customer experience', on a salary of £75,000 a year. Prior to this, Marsh had been extremely vocal in her criticisms of both the WCA and the DWP, especially on Twitter, where she had thousands of followers. Her fellow campaigners were outraged.

A few weeks later, there were media claims that a subsidiary of the firm in Australia had been manipulating the government's welfare-to-work contracts, by putting clients through pointless training courses to trigger payments.[22] We'll soon hear about much the same sort of scandal in Britain. In January 2016, there were further negative headlines surrounding Maximus: a whistle-blower who worked at a subsidiary of the firm in the UK filed a complaint to the US Securities and Exchange Commission alleging that directors of the company sold over £7.9 million of shares late in 2015, ahead of news that the company was perform-ing badly on the contract.[23]

However Maximus performs, in the end, the history of the test isn't a story about the profit incentive – it's about misman-agement, political impotence in the face of badly drawn contracts, and market failure. The WCA has been changed again and again, but because of all this its fundamental problems in the years I've covered it have never been addressed.

The Work Programme

One of the Department for Work and Pensions' other main roles, besides the payment of benefits, is to try to improve participation in the job market. To this end, the Work Programme was introduced in June 2011, the biggest-ever single scheme to get the long-term unemployed back into work (it replaced a selection of Labour schemes including the New Deal and Future Jobs Fund). Unlike many outsourcing projects, it boasted a lofty aim: those given the task of getting people back into employment were not only to be drawn from the public and private sectors – they would be from charitable organizations too.

The first thing to note is the huge controversy over how well it's actually working for people. The DWP has claimed there has been a significant improvement in performance, year on year, and that the structure of the system – by which everyone contracted to get people into work is paid on the basis of the results they achieve – gives taxpayers the best deal possible. In 2012 just 18,270 people out of 785,000 had found work, which as many commentators pointed out, was actually worse than doing nothing.[24]

By the end of June 2013, this figure had risen to 168,000 out of 1.14 million.[25] Some sort of rise was only to be expected, because it could hardly perform any worse. The general consensus among analysts is that if the Work Programme is improving, it's doing so at a glacial pace. A report by the Centre for Economic and Social Inclusion in March 2014 found: 'There are no significant signs of increasing performance by the Work Programme. It could have been expected that with the increase in economic growth that performance would pick up, however this might not yet have fed through in the figures. In addition, more employable claimants may have got jobs before they reach the Work Programme.' It did, however, add that 'there are positive signs with much higher sustained employment than expected and a more even spread of performance across the country'.[26]

A National Audit Office (NAO) report in July 2014 essentially concluded that while the Work Programme had improved, it was no more effective than any of its predecessors in the welfare-to-work sector. Robert Devereux, the DWP's permanent secretary, said he disagreed with this conclusion and had debated it for 'hours' with Amyas Morse, head of the NAO.[27] Margaret Hodge MP, chair of the PAC, gave a statement:

The Department for Work and Pensions has not delivered the much needed improved performance on the Work Programme since my committee last examined it in late 2012 and it is very clear to me that it still has a mountain to climb if it is to help those most in need.

I am angry that the Department has failed the vast majority of those referred to the Work Programme from Employment Support Allowance, one of the 'hard to help groups' – with 89% completing the programme without finding and staying in work. It is completely unacceptable that contractors are on average now spending only £630 per person supporting this group, compared to an original £1360.[28]

There have also been big questions over the way statistics have been deployed by the government to defend the Work Programme. In April 2013, *Private Eye* magazine (which has consistently provided the best coverage of the scheme) exposed some rather selective use of the figures by the government. It reported that the first results of the Work Programme in November 2012 showed that the contractors were not meeting performance levels – the magazine claimed that the DWP knew performance was 'worse than useless', and so employment minister Mark Hoban responded by meeting with Kirsty McHugh, the head of the Employment Related Services Association (ERSA), the organization which lobbies for employment companies. According to the magazine: 'She told Hoban: "On performance overall, I think it is really important that both the industry and department are robust in terms of defending the WP as much as we can." In a later email Hoban thanked her for "discussion around the November publication and the simplicity of messages required for public consumption."'

What this meant, *Private Eye* claimed, was that Hoban told McHugh he was keen to use the ERSA's figure of 200,000 'job entries', which was simply the number of people who had begun jobs – it didn't specify the number of people who either didn't begin jobs or failed to hold on to one. McHugh told him: 'Our view is that the existence of Minimum Performance Levels [the data which includes outcomes as opposed to referrals] is in the public arena and we need to prepare for questions around them.'[29]

The DWP press release didn't contain mention of minimum performance levels. In June 2013 much the same thing happened when the scheme's second-year results showed that most contractors hadn't met these targets – the DWP released ERSA figures rather than its own, and as *Private Eye* would later note, Hoban's claim that these figures 'demonstrated the growing success of the scheme' were, he claimed, 'a big improvement from year one when no provider reached their contracted level'.

It might be going too far to claim Hoban's preferred way to present the data was entirely motivated by the desire to put a positive spin on it. After all, that month, he commissioned a review of minimum performance levels that stated the first statistical analysis had been 'confusing to the public'. But his preference for the companies' unofficial data, like so many outsourcing issues, looked less than transparent.

Private Eye would also go on to debunk his claims that 'providers are only paid when they deliver results', which neglected to mention that contractors received several hundred pounds for each person who had been attached to the scheme, whether they remained on it or not. G4S, the magazine noted, had said it was 'delighted to be the second best performing prime contractor nationally', but had actually missed seven of its nine minimum performance levels, based on how many people find work without G4S: so in the majority of cases its performance was 'worse than doing nothing'.[30]

There's a more fundamental criticism, as Alistair Grimes of the think tank Rocket Science put it on *File on 4* in 2013: 'The long-term unemployed are where they normally are – moving further back in the queue because more people are coming into the queue who are better qualified.'[31] And indeed, in March 2014 *Channel 4 News* reported that the DWP's own assessment of how the Work Programme was performing suggested it was continuing to fail. The show claimed the '"Work Programme evaluation: interim meta-report" was signed off ready for publication in September 2013, but has been sat on ever since'. An unnamed Whitehall insider had told Channel 4 that ministers had taken the decision not to publish it because it would have been an embarrassment. As Channel 4 went on to say, while the report wasn't written in 'strident language', it confirmed the Work Programme was failing in one of its central tasks.

In June 2014 the government's Major Projects Authority, which oversees such schemes, downgraded it from 'green' to 'amber', which meant there were significant problems with how it was being run. The announcement was buried away in an obscure link on the DWP website. By that point, burying bad news had become something of a priority, because far more worrying issues had emerged than those detailed so far.

Fraud

One of the main issues that Channel 4 picked up on was the fact that, according to the report, '"creaming and parking" are still significant problems, and [the] whole payment-by-results contract structure didn't seem to be doing what it was meant to do. The authors report "participants with health conditions and disabilities . . . being seen less often and being offered less support than other groups".'[32]

What is 'creaming and parking'? It wasn't the first time we'd heard the phrase: in May 2013, after six months of inquiries, the Work and Pensions select committee's second report into the Work Programme found much the same. It essentially boils down to helping the jobseekers for whom it was easier to find work. Here we see another recurrence of the theme we'd touched on when discussing the contracts under which the guards in the Mubenga case were working. When you introduce a private company, you introduce a profit incentive, and there is a question here: will it encourage your contractor to do a good job, or will it simply encourage them to game the system?

Those who take a pessimistic view of the answer to this question are quick to point out that 'creaming and parking' are the least of the Work Programme's problems, and the implications of this spread far beyond the scheme itself. Allegations of fraud have dogged the Work Programme ever since its inception. The alarm bells rang in September 2012, when the PAC said the DWP had missed 'vital evidence' of possible fraud, particularly at the firm A4e.

Margaret Hodge said the DWP had 'not been proactive in setting in place systems which root out fraud'.[33] A4e responded that a recent audit of the firm had found no evidence of fraud. But in December the next year, four people were charged with fraud and forgery at A4e, after nine arrests had been made in September. In a statement on the company's website, A4e chief executive Andrew Dutton said the company had 'fully cooperated with police'. In February 2014, the four accused pleaded guilty to a total of thirty-two offences.

That year, I got wind of a story that gave some indication as to how such behaviour manifests itself. A former Work Programme participant got in touch with me because he'd written to David Blunkett, his local MP, to raise concerns about how A4e worked and above all that it had fraudulently attempted to take credit for a job he had found himself – by coincidence, a temporary position in A4e's Sheffield head office in late 2012 and early 2013.

He told me:

> I was asked to sign [forms by A4e]. One form is the Customer Consent Form, the second is the Work Programme Agreement and the third is the Employment Start Declaration. These are the forms that are used by the Work Programme Providers to validate participants' information to the DWP in order to receive their payment for 'succeeding in finding sustainable employment' ... According to the statement in the DWP Guidance, I am fully within my rights to refuse the use of these forms, as I did. The main reason for my refusal was that A4e did absolutely nothing to help me find any job, let alone my current one at the time in their own offices! Apart from being underhanded, it is also unethical for them to claim any taxpayer's money for something they didn't do.

The claimant told me the company regularly took credit for jobs they didn't find. An A4e spokesperson insisted to me that they deserved credit because they were there to help if the job didn't work out: 'Contractually, once an individual has been referred to us by the Jobcentre Plus, they are obliged to remain on the programme for 104 weeks. For those who might find employment during this period, the benefit of being on the programme is that at any time their circumstances change, for example, when they might fall out of work, they are able to seek further support and training to help them find another job.'[34]

A4e wasn't the only company implicated in such behaviour.

Back in 2012, the Work and Pensions select committee had heard from Eddie Hutchinson, an accountant who was appointed head of internal audit at the firm in the autumn of 2010. The *Daily Telegraph* would report that 'within weeks of starting, his attention was drawn to what he described as an "ever-increasing volume of frauds", sometimes more than one potential case a day, Mr Hutchinson said in evidence to Parliament ... He claimed his work running the audit department was "regularly disrupted" by having to investigate "recurring incidents" of fraud and irregularities.'

Prior to working at the company, he'd investigated suspected fraud at another Work Programme contractor, a company called Working Links. He described a 'common theme in relation to DWP contracts', with falsified signatures and incentives in the bonus system that encouraged staff to make false claims 'without fear of reprisal' – staff would resign whenever dubious behaviour was uncovered. Hutchinson said he'd faced a 'stonewall' from the managers at Working Links over the issue. According to the *Telegraph*: 'He has produced a note from the chief operating officer which objects to Mr Hutchinson's description of a "prevailing culture" of fraud. The note says its PR team prepared "defensive briefs" to deal with the fallout if newspapers got wind of any fraud.'[35]

And there have been many more concerns raised about the issue of fraud on the Work Programme, not all of them by journalists or whistleblowers. Consider the words of Stephen Lloyd MP, interviewed in 2013 for Radio 4's *File on 4*:

Some of the primes [the large corporations like A4e that subcontract out work to smaller charities and other bodies] took the attachment fee [the money paid by the government for attaching job seekers to the programme, irrespective of what happens next] and banked it. I've met forty to fifty two-year returners in the last few months and I'm hearing from too many they were either seen occasionally and a lot of them don't feel they had the support.[36]

A pretty staggering accusation to make of your own government's flagship policy.

As *Private Eye* would point out in January 2014: 'According to the DWP's Report on Contracted Employment Provision – slipped out a year late – in 2012/13 the government received more allegations of fraud by workfare contractors than in previous years.'[37] Indeed, the details only came out after a Freedom of Information request was answered that month that had been submitted in July 2013.

The report didn't name any of the companies involved, instead citing 'substantial media and parliamentary scrutiny', which referred to the case above. Three cases had apparently been referred to police but there weren't any prosecutions because 'proceedings were considered by the police to be unlikely to result in a conviction or were not considered to be in the public interest.' It appeared, the magazine said, that the companies involved had simply paid back taxpayers' money to the DWP.

The problem with payment by results

One of the most important and under-reported flashpoints in the Work Programme's short history happened on Friday, 13 July 2012. Eco-Actif Services, a non-profit company that helped find work for the hardest to employ, including ex-prisoners and ex-substance abusers, went bust. It shouldn't have. At the time, it had £1 million worth of advance orders on its books and a turnover of £700,000.

So what happened? What we're beginning to turn to is the

issue of market failure. Not only is there the question of who else we could get in to, say, police the Olympics or run an immigration detention centre, but there's the question of who does the job when the company we've chosen fails. If fraud is a relatively easy problem to resolve, the issue of risk is far tougher. As we've seen on several occasions, mistakes by outsourcing companies carry the potential for gigantic financial losses and huge levels of media criticism. It's a problem the current government is extremely aware of, and as we'll see, the collapse of Eco-Actif resulted from its attempts to do something about it.

When the coalition came to power, it was concerned by the issue of transparency in the outsourcing industry. Without any central database of contracts, how could it tell which companies were dominating the scene? It had the sense that a few giants like Capita, G4S and Serco held most of them, but what was the true extent of their dominance? And without the answer to this question, it lacked the answer to another: were these big corporations specialists only in winning contracts, rather than delivering on them? A badly drawn-up contract to which companies had no real obligation to adhere potentially worked for both parties – a local or national politician could sign off on a long-term deal promising value, and the saving could be cited throughout his or her tenure. By the time any problems emerged, he or she would likely be long gone.[38]

And the coalition thought it saw an answer to all this in a long-forgotten New Labour policy. It was called payment by results (PbR). The term first appeared in a 2002 Labour paper on NHS financial reforms. It was subsequently picked up in 2008 by the Department for Work and Pensions, which asked for a greater focus on the area in its commissioning strategy.

There's considerable Whitehall buzz around the idea. Quietly, it seems to have become one of the most important aspects of the government's plan for delivering services for vulnerable people. In 2013 I attempted to produce a rundown of exactly how many projects had been associated with it, and was surprised to find how far it had spread. It's been mentioned in conjunction with:

- The Work Programme and Troubled Families Fund, run by the DWP
- The Troubled Families Financial Framework, run by the Department for Communities and Local Government
- Schemes run by the Ministry of Justice aiming to reduce reoffending among inmates
- The Youth Contract, run by the Office of the Deputy Prime Minister, aiming to get young people into jobs
- Acute healthcare services, run by the Department of Health in hospitals
- Children's charities like Barnardo's, and Sure Start children's centres, run by the Department for Education

And there are more, with pilot schemes also taking place. These policies, many centring on early intervention, are aimed squarely at helping the most disadvantaged of society who have been left furthest behind by the economic changes described above – the families with generational unemployment, the criminal, and the drug-addicted, for example. There is, of course, a question about the fundamental philosophy of PbR. As its title suggests, it seems like there's an implicit assumption that people won't do a good job unless some coin is flashed in their general direction. But this is perhaps offset by the idea that the localism inherent in the idea will give you a greater diversity of providers, more fairness and more accountability.

The Cabinet Office minister Oliver Letwin spelled his vision out in a 2013 column for the *Guardian*: 'In effect, central government is saying to local governments: "You have the power and the knowledge to bring the right people together in the right way in your locality to crack these problems which affect the whole country; and we will make it worthwhile for you to invest time and effort in doing so; but we'll do that by rewarding success, rather than by forcing you to tick boxes and follow processes we prescribe."'[39]

Which brings us to Eco-Actif. The Work Programme's PbR model sees 'primes' – A4e, G4S and the like – subcontract out work to smaller businesses and charities. The model is supposed to diversify providers and offset some of the risk entailed in signing such contracts, because the larger companies are able to put up the investment required – so Eco-Actif was actually a subcontractor to 3SC (which is a social enterprise, a business that seeks to invest any profits it makes back into dealing with the problem it's attempting to solve, rather than giving it to shareholders), and 3SC was a subcontractor to the prime, which in this case was A4e. It seems in this case Eco-Actif's risk was hardly reduced – its founder, Anna Burke, had actually put up £20,000 of her own money into winning the contract.

Eco-Actif had insufficient working capital to keep going while it was waiting for cash under the PbR scheme. It couldn't raise bridging funds, because, according to Colleen Baldwin on the Indus Delta website for employment professionals:

When it approached banks and other established and social finance providers, potential investors turned them down giving three grounds: the government's Work Programme was too high risk; the prime contractors were not passing sufficient funds to the ultimate delivery organizations to make sufficient surplus to finance any loan; and their association with A4e (which had attracted hugely negative headlines around that time) was a matter of great concern.[40]

So it's more than a little ironic that a charity designed to get people back to work should, due to signing up to a government programme, find itself contributing to the unemployment statistics. Only a year earlier, Dave Yip, director of Xantus Consulting, an IT advisory firm, had posted a little-noticed blog on the *Guardian*'s Public Leaders Network website, in which he noted:

> PbR is a big company game played by cash rich suppliers. The client, whether public or private sector, is ostensibly playing poker; offering a high risk bet, often because they are unable to clearly enumerate the size of the prize at the outset or cannot define the end goals clearly enough ... For smaller companies, a loss on this scale from just one contract – whether through the fault of the company itself or circumstances beyond its control – could wipe out an unacceptable amount of annual profit.[41]

Many more commentators would raise concerns that charities were being used as 'bid candy' by larger firms in order to win DWP contracts. Anna Burke would later say: 'The whole of the Work Programme is cherry-picking. We were a small charity signing a contract with a giant A4e and their lawyers. Chris Grayling just says it's "More fool you" to charities who signed bad contracts.' This was echoed by 3SC, which told the *Guardian*: '[Eco-Actif's] trouble was they cared more about the hard cases than the easy ones. But you can only get income from the low-hanging fruit.'[42] Burke never said that the PbR system was a bad idea in principle, even when journalists asked her about the £8.6

million dividend A4e's director, Emma Harrison, had received in 2012, the year Eco-Actif went under.[43]

These sorts of concerns were repeated by a friend of mine who talked to me for this book (she wished to remain anonymous). She works in the welfare-to-work sector for charities and has done work both on and off the Work Programme. She told me that the Work Programme job generally entailed a huge client list, which meant her day was typically spent making short phone calls to check in on her clients and give some general tips, hoping that the least troubled individuals would sort themselves out so that a fee could be banked. There'd then be more time for the more difficult cases, but that day 'never seemed to come'.

Fundamentally, this is about whether the system is fair or not. In 2015 the National Audit Office issued a report that stated PbR was not only a challenging form of contracting, but clearly couldn't work for every service – undermining quality and value for money if badly implemented.[44] Ministers' optimistic rhetoric on PbR simply doesn't match the evidence. Clearly they need to make it easier for charities to bid for contracts by guaranteeing upfront payments. The potential gains for big companies and losses for small ones just haven't seemed fair. At the time of Eco-Actif's closure *Channel 4 News* obtained leaked A4e figures that showed that more than 93,000 unemployed people on the company's books had earned the company more than £41 million of attachment fees, but just 3,400 of them had found sustained work.[45] There was also a huge regional variation in the figures – possible evidence of a growing temptation to concentrate on those for whom jobs were easiest to find.

A4e is now known as People Plus, the name change due to the fact that its owners – Staffline Group – felt its brand was too tarnished to continue trading under its original name.[46] Whether this is due to its underperformance over the years, or the afore-mentioned fraud case, we do not know. Staffline had bought A4e from Emma Harrison, the Sheffield-based entrepreneur who originally set up the company. She made £20 million from the deal.[47] The Work Programme certainly worked for someone.

In the midst of such eye-watering figures and such hugely complex government initiatives, it's very easy to lose sight of the fact that human figures lurk behind these tales. For what it's worth, the running theme throughout all of these stories is not so much conspiracy and duplicity as mismanagement. The problem with administering these projects badly is that standards can fall by the wayside in the drive for profit. Hardly a suitable model upon which to base more government outsourcing projects, you may think. You'd be wrong.

4

Selling Off Lady Justice

Gareth Myatt was a small fifteen-year-old: he was four foot ten and weighed just six and a half stone. He'd had a difficult childhood and, in 2004, he ended up where many troubled children do: G4S's Rainsbrook secure training centre in Northamptonshire. He'd been sent there after he stole a bottle of beer and assaulted a social worker.

Three days into his six-month sentence, he refused to clean a toasted-sandwich maker. He was acting up. So two members of staff followed him to his room and began to remove things from it. One of them was a piece of paper on which his mother's mobile phone number was written. He lunged at the staff member who took it. The two men – joined by a third – restrained him, using the technique we encountered when we learned about the Mubenga case: a seated double embrace. Two of them forced the boy into a sitting position, while the third held his head.

What happened next was subsequently described by a member of staff at the inquest into his death: '[Another staff member] looked back and said [Myatt] had . . . shat himself. The struggling seemed to go on for a while and then he seemed to settle down. After a few minutes we realised something was wrong. I looked at his face and he had something coming down his nose and he looked as if his eyes were bulging. I can't remember much more. I've tried to get it out of my mind.'[1]

Myatt had choked to death on his own vomit. The inquest revealed that at least four other children had complained about not being able to breathe while in the position. There were also questions asked about the culture of the place: the court heard that on two occasions, officers described children who had been restrained the highest number of times as 'winners'. Officers undergoing training were given nicknames – including 'Crusher', 'Mucker', 'Mauler', 'Rowdy' and 'Breaker', though the duty operations manager said this was just a 'tasteless joke', and that there wasn't a macho culture.[2] At the inquest into Myatt's death, the prison's director, John Parker, admitted that he'd never read the Home Office manual governing the use of restraint in his prison.[3]

Four months later at Serco-run Hassockfield secure training centre in County Durham, fourteen-year-old Adam Rickwood got into an altercation with staff. He had a history of mental health problems and had been put on remand for an alleged wounding charge. On this occasion he'd been ordered to leave the social area but sat on the floor, refusing to go. Back-up was called. This time four officers restrained him: one on each arm, one holding his head and another his legs.

The staff who held Rickwood face down in the cell were using a technique called 'physical control in care' (PCC), described as 'non-pain compliant' in official literature, but which authorizes 'distraction' techniques that do cause pain if the staff feel they're needed. Five years ago the Children's Rights Alliance for England managed to obtain the PCC manual, and found that staff were authorized to cause pain to the thumb, ribs and nose if required – in Rickwood's case the staff member, fearful his fingers would be bitten, had pushed the outside of his hand in an upward motion against Rickwood's septum, bruising his nose.[4]

Hours later, his body was found hanging in his cell. There was a note there, asking what gave the staff the right to hurt his nose. Rickwood was the youngest child to die in penal custody in twenty-five years. There were two inquests following his death: the second of them, in 2011, found that there was a serious system failure in relation to the use of restraint at Hassockfield, which was a contributing factor in his death.

Why dredge up these two stories, now over ten years old? Firstly, because they again raise many of the questions over accountability and policy that we encountered when we looked at the Mubenga case. After the Rickwood case, a coroner emphasized that the use of force was unlawful, because it should not simply be used to enforce 'good order and discipline'. It seems the government's contractors weren't following these rules between 1998 and 2004; but did they ignore them or misunderstand them? It's a tricky question to answer – not least because the Youth Justice Board (YJB), the organization that has overall responsibility for children in care, never properly reviewed the rules.

The Labour government tried to change the rules so that force could be used for good order and discipline, but in July 2008 the Court of Appeal rejected its case. What that meant was that thousands of children in detention centres over a period of ten years would have a case that they had been assaulted. In 2012 a private case was brought to the High Court by the Children's Rights Alliance in England (CRAE). It aimed to make the Ministry of Justice contact children who had been assaulted so they could seek redress. The judge concluded these children 'were sent [to secure training centres] because they had acted unlawfully and to learn to obey the law, yet many of them were subject to unlawful actions during their detention. I need, I think, say no more.' He decided the MoJ had no legal obligation to contact them, but said: 'It probably requires just one former detainee, looking back at his or her experience in ... secure training centres and having conducted the necessary preliminary inquiries, to pursue a well-publicized claim and others will be alerted to the potential of pursuing matters.'[5] During the hearing it was estimated that force was used an average of 350 times in four secure training centres, and that there might have been as many as eighty-five incidents of unlawful force every month, for ten years. But what was the result of this potentially hugely costly judgment? At the time I researched the issue, nothing.

I approached Carolynn Gallwey at Bhatt Murphy, the solicitors who represent CRAE. She told me very few children had come forward: 'It's sad that children haven't come forward. I think the biggest factor is that the children to whom I've spoken all come from the most dysfunctional backgrounds you can imagine. Bluntly, they're used to abuse. I suspect the main reason we've not heard from them is purely because they don't suspect the treatment they've received is in any way illegal.'[6]

However, unknown to me, the *Guardian* had actually been investigating the issue – and had tracked down some former inmates who had been assaulted in secure training centres. As a result, in October 2014, fourteen people received thousands of pounds in compensation from G4S, Serco and the YJB, and the latter gave them an apology. One claimant told the paper: 'I was there to help me obey the law, but instead the STC [secure training centre] staff themselves acted unlawfully by physically abusing me again and again.'[7]

We continue to use force on the estimated 2,000 children

in custody in England and Wales. A 2011 report by the Howard League for Penal Reform found there were 6,904 incidents of reported restraint in 2009/10, of which 257 resulted in injury. In one child jail, the Howard League reported that 13 of the 229 restraints had led to complaints from children that they couldn't breathe. The charity also reported that its lawyers had represented children who had suffered from broken bones including wrists and elbows, teeth knocked out and bruises all over their bodies. Hundreds of injuries are reported every year.[8]

The Howard League's report on the subject is full of testimonies from young children who have left secure training centres and youth offending institutions. It makes for horrifying reading. There are threats of violence ('One of the officers spoke to me through my door and said that they were "going to make me scream later"'), and outright physical and mental assault: 'Several times while I was being restrained, they deliberately hurt me by bending my thumb down so that it touched my forearm. This was really painful. I often had bruises under my upper arms and scratches down my arms after PCC. I sometimes had panic attacks when I was in my room after a PCC.'[9]

In 2013 a new system of restraint called minimizing and managing physical restraint (MMPR) was brought in at four child prisons – including Rainsbrook – and it was rolled out across all the others in 2015. The techniques described in the manual are unclear, because the version available to the general public has nearly 200 redactions, and Freedom of Information requests from campaigners to reveal more detail have been unsuccessful: only the government and those it contracts know in full what's allowed. As one campaigner wrote in the *Guardian* in 2014: 'Various bodies oppose the UK's idiosyncratic reliance on pain as a form of restraint, including the UN torture committee, the European torture committee, the UK's four children's commissioners, the prisons inspectorate, and the Association of Directors of Children's Services.'[10]

The Gareth Myatt case has obvious similarities to the Jimmy Mubenga incident we looked at in Chapter 2. The same company – G4S – was involved, as was the same technique. Indeed, in the wake of the announcement that Mubenga's guards would stand trial for manslaughter, Lord Ramsbotham, the former chief inspector of prisons, wrote an article illustrating how often the same mistakes had been made, and cited the Myatt case.

Back in 2012, Ramsbotham had described as 'perverse' the initial CPS decision not to bring charges against the officers in the Mubenga case, because he was chairing an independent inquiry into enforced removals, and had learned that 'the Home Office continued to require plainly inappropriate, pain-compliant, Prison Service restraint techniques to be used by detainee custody officers, not having bothered to find out that these had been rejected both by NHS special mental hospitals [except in extreme circumstances where they needed to remove weapons] and [organizations] such as the Liverpool police on Mersey ferries'.

As for Rainsbrook, in 2008, a guard was convicted of actual bodily harm after dragging a 13-year-old child across a tarmac floor and up a flight of stairs before putting him in his cell.[11] Worse was to come in May 2015, when Ofsted inspectors looked at the centre and found that children had been caused 'distress and humiliation' after being subjected to 'degrading treatment' and 'racist comments' from G4S staff who were high on illegal drugs. Six members of staff were sacked as a result. Frances Crook, the campaigning prison reformer, said it was 'the worst report on a prison I have ever seen'.[12] There were a number of troubling echoes of the Myatt case. According to the 2015 inspection, there had been delays in reporting MMPR incidents to the government team monitoring its use: one incident had taken six months to report.[13] G4S said the prison would be given new leadership, and it got it in the controversial form of John Parker, the director who had been in charge when Myatt died. However, in September that year, it was announced that G4S had lost the contract.

It was replaced by an outsourcer called MTCNovo.[14] In January 2016, I reported that this new contractor had no less of a troubled history. It described itself as 'a new venture between the third, public and private sector, which has been established to provide rehabilitation and offender management services across London and Thames Valley'; this was true, but the 'private' element was largely composed of MTC (Management and Training Corporation), a Utah-based firm that grossed more than $500 million in yearly revenue and had been embroiled in a series of scandals in America that included violence and poor healthcare at its prisons. It had even been linked to a corruption case after a police commissioner had received kickbacks for private contracts (though it denied any knowledge of the affair).[15]

Only a few months before the Ofsted report, G4S had written to the House of Commons justice committee to complain that heads of prisons were being 'undermined' by government policy, and that they should be given control of healthcare, education and training wardens in order to be more 'responsible and accountable'.[16]

However perverse it might seem, one has to ask if the company had a point. The negative issues regarding outsourcing in immigration services largely revolve around this issue of training. The cases may seem tragic, inhumane and cruel – but however cold it sounds, one of the most practical solutions is better oversight and management. In the case of our prisons, however, the ethical issues around outsourcing run rather deeper: here we really have to question what impact the introduction of a profit incentive has on the people who are compelled to 'use' this particular state service: is it possible to bring it in and maintain a justice system that's fit for purpose in a developed, civilized country?

The issue stayed out of the headlines for several years – but in 2016 it returned with a vengeance. At the time G4S lost the Rainsbrook contract, the justice board announced it had won a new contract for Medway secure training centre in Kent. Only a few months later, in December 2015, seven staff members were suspended after the BBC's *Panorama* filmed evidence of unnecessary force, foul language, and failing to report their actions. Among the allegations, *Panorama*'s footage appeared to show that a teenager was slapped several times in the head, that young people's necks were unnecessarily pressed on, and that restraint techniques were inappropriately used – including pressing on a teenager's windpipe so he had problems breathing. The programme also alleged the guards boasted about using a fork to stab an inmate in the leg and tried to conceal their behaviour from the centre's CCTV cameras. G4S wrote to the BBC in an attempt to stop broadcast of the footage, arguing it was 'unauthorised and illegal'.[17]

However, shortly after the programme was broadcast, it apologized for its staff, and went on to sack four of them. That week, five men were arrested: four on suspicion of child neglect and one on suspicion of assault. I reported that the behaviour shown on the programme might be rather more historical than many assumed: a contact at the Howard League for Penal Reform told me that its lawyers had dealt with numerous concerns raised by or on behalf of young people at the prison 'dating from at least 2008', but that 'invariably complaints are not upheld, often because of a lack of CCTV evidence corroborating the child's version of events'. It was my understanding that there had been at least half a dozen cases where this had happened since 2008.[18]

In February 2016 I interviewed Paul Cook, the company's director of children's services, about this scandal.[19] Prior to doing that, I'd reported on my discovery that guards at Medway had previously been sacked in 2013 after children were called 'fucking cunts' by them on Facebook.[20] The Guardian would later claim there had also been complaints about staff 12 years before that.[21] Cook informed me that he'd found the Panorama footage appalling, and that G4S guards at all three of the company's centres would now all wear body cameras.

There had been rumours that the company was to sell off its youth prisons, but I couldn't get confirmation from it at the time I spoke to Cook. However, days after I spoke to him, it confirmed that not only was it to sell off its youth prisons, but all of its children's homes. It didn't explain the decision, though it seems reasonable to assume this latest round of negative coverage had proved one storm too many.

HMP Oakwood and private prisons

In April 2012, HMP Oakwood, in Wolverhampton, opened at a cost of £180 million. The G4S-run prison would house more than 1,600 inmates. Its website claimed it would be known as 'the leading prison in the world' within five years.[22] It was part of a general governmental policy – one that had been operating for many years – whereby smaller centres up and down the country were replaced by 'super-prisons'.

In its first two years, Oakwood featured in scores of unfavourable headlines. In October 2013 the Wolverhampton *Express and*

Star printed a picture of a prisoner on the roof of Oakwood and reported that officers had told parish councillors that prison gangs were 'running the institution' and that it had been just a matter of time before any of them escaped on to the roof. The paper reported that the 'rooftop protest by three prisoners lasted more than five hours and came just days after the jail was branded "Jokewood" in a damning official report,' that 'prison officers have been voicing their concerns since the £150 million prison opened in April 2012' and that 'councillors say they feel "hood-winked" because bosses have repeatedly insisted the prison is well run and secure.'[23]

The paper's report followed a surprise inspection by Her Majesty's Inspectorate of Prisons (HMIP), which concluded: 'The inexperience of staff was everywhere evident and systems to support routine services were creaky, if they existed at all. The quality of the environment and accommodation mitigated against some of the frustrations and without this risks could have been much greater. Against all four healthy prison tests, safety, respect, activity and resettlement, the outcomes we observed were either insufficient or poor.'[24]

The *Guardian* ran another damning report into the prison the next year. One prisoner told the paper: 'I've been in jails all over the country. But this was the worst. It's a shit-hole staffed by kids who should be stacking shelves.' He added that it was easy to get drugs and alcohol: 'It's easy to get hooch, even easier to get Black Mamba [synthetic cannabis]. The parcels are chucked over the fence'.[25] He also claimed urine or excrement was regularly thrown at the guards. 'There's no respect,' he said. An anonymous G4S employee said there was a problem with the inexperience of staff at the prison.

Then, in June 2014, the prison journal *Inside Time* published an anonymous letter from someone whose relative was serving a life sentence and had been relocated to Oakwood. They said there were 'serious problems with the lack of regime and staff morale', and that they had been told drugs were being brought in and 'smoked on the wings in full view of the staff'. They also alleged that tension was beginning to build among the inmates 'because of the lack of a regime, [and] very poorly trained staff who have no idea what to do . . . The staff are ill equipped to deal with the situation and would appear to be giving in to demands of prisoners instead of setting down a regime and sticking to it.' The writer concluded by describing the prison as a 'ticking time bomb'.[26] It was only in 2015 that some good headlines emerged about the place, after a report by the chief inspector of prisons said it had 'turned a corner'.[27]

One could certainly be forgiven for asking what G4S and the government had been doing for the previous two years. But then, the thing about HMP Oakwood – and its ilk – is that it saves money. In 2013/14 the cost of keeping a prisoner there was expected to be £12,000 a year. The cost is £22,420 for the average equivalent jail.[28] The contract is valued at £349 million. According to an FoI request by *Private Eye* magazine, it would cost £498 million to run it in the public sector. The MoJ has decided it's not in the public interest to show exactly how these savings will be generated. So perhaps the question is this – how representative is Oakwood of the private sector as a whole?

Only 13 of England and Wales's 134 prisons have been privatized. In the MoJ's 2012/13 ratings, Oakwood and Thameside in London received the lowest rating of one out of four ('overall performance is of serious concern'), while two others had a two rating ('overall performance is of concern'), eight had a rating of three and one had a rating of four. This doesn't sound so bad, but of the 121 publicly run prisons, only one received a ranking of one, and only ten achieved a rating of two. And as the BBC reported: 'The HM Chief Inspector of Prisons' annual report for 2011/12 suggests there has been an improvement in prison performance, with 82% of jails receiving a positive score for safety, compared with 75% in 2005/6.'[29] Violence is four times higher at Serco-run HMP Doncaster than at a comparable-sized state-run prison.[30]

Arguments have been made in favour of the private sector on the basis of quality, but frankly it's rather hard to take them seriously, given that they have come from institutions that receive funding from the companies they champion. For example, the think tank Reform produced a report in 2013 entitled *The Case for Private Prisons*, which suggested private prisons offer better value for money and lower reoffending rates. Three of Reform's 'corporate partners' are G4S, Serco and Sodexo, which run all the private prisons in Britain.[31] The argument wasn't supported by the Prison Reform Trust, nor by prisons minister Jeremy Wright.[32]

The suspicion persists among campaigners that private prisons are more prone to cutting corners than those run by the state. Only a few days after the October 2013 stories emerged about Oakwood, a surprise inspection at HMP Holloway found Serco-Wincanton (a joint venture between Serco and European 'supply-chain solutions provider' Wincanton) was transferring female inmates to the jail in vehicles shared with men for long periods without a privacy screen. HMIP said the male prisoners got out first, leaving the female inmates in the 'grubby' vehicle, because reception areas in men's prisons have a fixed cut-off time. The director of the Prison Reform Trust, Juliet Lyon, told ITV News that Serco-Wincanton had risked the safety and wellbeing of women who had suffered sexual violence.[33]

When you allow companies to run public services for profit, any accusations of bad practice will always look more serious. The suspicion will linger that problems aren't born of incompetence or rogue members of staff, but that the profit incentive has something to do with it. Fortunately prisoners – rather like asylum seekers and illegal immigrants – are not a group of people for which the British electorate has a lot of sympathy. If they were, perhaps the Howard League for Penal Reform's dossier outlining years of failures in the sector, handed in to police on 13 May 2014, would have attracted more headlines.

In the section on Sodexo, it includes 'allegations made that a woman who had miscarried at HMP Peterborough was left to clean up after herself while the foetus remained in her cell' (an internal inquiry would deem no disciplinary action was necessary, though Jenny Chapman, shadow justice minister, said she doubted the inquiry's conclusions). It also states: 'An investigation into the death of 35 year old Michael Watson, who died of a heart attack at HMP Forest Bank, found a plethora of failings, including a delay of getting him to hospital for 11 hours after he complained of chest pains and cancelling previous hospital appointments for him which could have afforded him life-saving treatment.'[34]

There's more on the treatment of the terminally ill. In the section on G4S, the dossier says: 'An investigation into the death of a prisoner from terminal cancer at HMP Birmingham found that on a trip to hospital, prison staff kept him waiting for 40 minutes in handcuffs on the street, in full view of the public, whilst they went to a Greggs bakery for their lunch. Further, they kept him restrained, either by double-cuffs or on a chain, while he was dying in hospital.'

The dossier raises a number of difficult questions about the outsourcing of justice services. It's fundamentally concerned about 'the effects of privatisation on the expansion of the prison system for the primary benefit of lining shareholders' pockets'. And it concludes: 'To make profit, the private sector needs business – there are questions to be asked about whether the aims of such companies are fundamentally at odds with the aims of reducing the prison population and reoffending.'[35] To judge from the litany of problems highlighted by the dossier, private-sector-run prisons offer little for those who'd like to see the prison system as an effective, constructive way to integrate offenders into society. And our failure to prevent reoffending, of course, comes at a massive social cost that affects us all. At the same time, it seems like money has been saved. But that's not always the case: when outsourcing goes wrong in other areas of the justice system, the cost is likely to be financial too.

The court translation scandal

When you talk to supporters of outsourcing, they often put forward a very simple argument in its favour: it saves money. They believe they have the evidence to prove it, and successive governments have believed them. What they're also very open about is the fact that they can't prove the companies that'll be brought in will do the job any better: even if there was a strong imperative to prove this case, they couldn't, because the data simply does not exist.

Early in the 2010–15 coalition's history, the MoJ was handed an unprecedented savings target of twenty-three percent. Kenneth Clarke, justice secretary at the time, said he'd 'worked out the maximum I could possibly save, offered it to them [the Treasury] on the last day and they agreed. With the help of a former Treasury official as permanent secretary we did our own hatchet job on our department.'[36]

Part of the plan was to decrease the number of prisoners in

UK jails, but it was scrapped: in fact capacity fell while prisoner numbers rose. At the time of writing, there are around 85,000 people in jail – over ninety-nine percent of maximum capacity.[37] So the MoJ began to look at other ways in which money could be saved, and it found an area in the court system – specifically, court interpreting. In August 2011, the department signed a five-year, estimated £90 million contract with a small private language service provider called Applied Language Services (ALS). It meant that at the start of January 2012, a new framework came into place for the system by which interpreters in court were selected. Previously, most of the 2,200 qualified interpreters – largely self-employed – were selected from the National Register of Public Service Interpreters, an independent voluntary regulator for the profession.

The first thing that should be said about this move is that there were, in theory, good reasons for it to happen. The existing approach was time consuming: each court had to devote separate resources to booking interpreters and they often made many unsuccessful contacts before they found an interpreter. Each court had its own arrangements, which meant that there was a huge variance in quality and in the amount they were spending. As a report by the Office for Criminal Justice Reform stated: 'HM Courts Service had almost no central management information about language services, for example on the demand for specific languages or the performance of interpreters under the various arrangements.'[38] There wasn't a market benchmark for how much they were paid, and some of the pay deals seemed, in the MoJ's view, far too generous – many had a minimum three-hour charge despite the fact few jobs lasted that long (some interpreters said they needed this just to make ends meet). Of the interpreters they did find, some of them didn't have the right security and quality guarantees. The MoJ felt it was hard to remove interpreters from the central database when they'd done a bad job, although the nature of local bookings meant courts and tribunals would generally just choose not to use them again.[39]

There were more serious problems. The report found: 'In a small number of cases there was evidence that people had even impersonated interpreters in court, and security arrangements had failed to pick this up. Finally, the existing approach meant that some court cases did not go ahead because of shortages and other problems. In 2010/11, 18 Crown Court and 373 magistrates' court cases were ineffective because of problems with interpreters.'[40]

Something clearly had to be done, and it seemed like the department had found a cheap and effective answer. However, it hadn't foreseen that before the contract went live, ALS would be acquired by Capita. Both ALS and the MoJ denied that they knew about this acquisition at the time the contract was signed. A year later, Ian Swales MP would mention this sale in a Westminster Hall debate on what would become a scandal. He claimed that it was a good example of how outsourcing companies 'really make money' by winning and then selling on public sector or PFI contracts.[41]

Capita was expected to provide interpreters for all but a handful of cases. However, interpreters didn't like this new arrangement, which cut their pay and allowed people with fewer qualifications to do their jobs. So they boycotted it, causing absolute carnage, with around a third of assignments not completed in the first month, causing huge delays across the legal system. Though the number of completed assignments rose by the end of the year to eighty-six per cent, it still left thousands of hearings where interpreters were not being provided.[42]

By December 2012, the Commons public accounts

committee had produced a report that heavily criticized the decision to contract out the service. Its chair, Margaret Hodge, said the project was an 'object-lesson in how not to contract out a public service' as 'almost everything that could go wrong did go wrong.'[43] It pointed out that despite being warned in a credit rating report that ALS was too small to take on any contract worth more than £1 million, the ministry handed it a deal worth up to £42 million a year. The MoJ had failed to carry out 'due diligence' before signing the deal and had so little understanding of what was needed that bidders were able to lead the process – when the system went live only 280 specialist staff were available from ALS, even though 1,200 were needed, and it wasn't even confirmed if they were qualified and security cleared.

The department had also failed to conduct a proper pilot or to phase the roll-out of the system, and began the process, according to the *Telegraph* website, 'without knowing the cost of interpreters or the languages which were required in which locations and at what notice, and still cannot provide details of the costs caused by delays to trials. It also started the process without knowing how many interpreters were needed, or where.' The figures showed that in one three-month period (February to April 2012), an interpreter failed to attend court on 682 occasions – indeed, when the system launched, Capita could only meet two in five of its bookings.[44]

'The result was total chaos,' Hodge said, adding that it should have been evident that the company was 'clearly incapable of delivering'. She described a 'sharp rise in delayed, postponed and abandoned trials; individuals have been kept on remand solely because no interpreter was available and the quality of interpreters has at times been appalling.'[45]

It got worse. It turned out that Capita had counted as an interpreter anyone who had registered an interest on the firm's website, without checking their qualifications, experience and suitability: 'We heard that some names were fictitious and one person had even successfully registered their pet dog,' Hodge said.[46] Indeed, there were a number of amusing stories to come out of the fiasco. One man, charged with perverting the course of justice, was accused – via the interpreter – of being a 'pervert'.[47]

And what sanctions had been imposed on the company as a result? It had been fined £2,200, a move that, in the report authors' view, made clear the MoJ was happy for contractors 'to get away with over promising and under delivering'. Richard Bacon, a Conservative member of the committee, added: 'The MoJ must learn from this debacle and pay far more attention to the basics of contract management in future.'[48] In truth it wasn't a laughing matter. As Aisha Maniar, a freelance translator, wrote in a blog for the Institute of Race Relations:

> Interpreting services are used mainly in criminal and immigration proceedings. Interpreters have played a crucial role in a number of major cases over the past year, including child cruelty, trafficking and murder. Without an interpreter, none of these cases would have seen justice. The interpreter's task in interpreting accurately and without prejudice, taking into consideration the social, cultural and behavioural codes of two languages and cultures is no small feat; it takes an exceptional amount of skill and ability. The interpreter's role in the final verdict is by no means incidental or marginal.

And Maniar went on to describe how foreign language speakers could ask for interpreters to 'mitigate the difficulties often faced by giving evidence in court or standing trial, particularly if they are asked to relate traumatic incidents'.[49]

Whatever improvements were being made certainly took

their time: there were plenty more stories the next year. A furious crown court judge had to adjourn a murder hearing because a Mandarin interpreter refused to turn up, claiming he would 'not be making enough money'. Anxiang Du, from Coventry, was accused of killing four members of a family in 2011, but the clerk at Nottingham Crown Court said the interpreter told him it wouldn't be worthwhile for him to attend. The judge, Mr Justice Flaux, said: 'It would be completely unfair on Mr Du to go ahead without an interpreter. To say I am annoyed is an understatement. I will be asking for a written explanation. It is a complete disgrace.'[50] The hearing was postponed until July, and Du wasn't found guilty until November 2013.[51]

In February that year, the House of Commons justice select committee weighed in too, asking whether the deal was 'financially sustainable'. Its report also condemned the MoJ's actions in seeking to prevent court staff from taking part in the committee's inquiry, which it said 'may have constituted a contempt of the house'. The report showed the committee apparently 'gave serious consideration' to asking the house to pursue the matter, and echoed the public accounts committee's concerns about the ministry's due diligence and risk mitigation procedures. The committee chair, Liberal Democrat Sir Alan Beith, said: 'The department did not have an adequate understanding of the needs of courts, it failed to heed warnings from the professionals concerned, and it did not put sufficient safeguards in place to prevent interruptions in the provision of quality interpreting services to courts. The MoJ's handling of the outsourcing of court interpreting services has been nothing short of shambolic.'[52] In a parliamentary debate he went on to say: 'The standard of court interpretation needs to be restored, preferably by bringing back those whose experience can return the service to the standards that the courts used to expect.'[53]

So again we see quality of service being sacrificed at the altar of financial savings: in fact, the MoJ's response, published in April 2013, barely addressed the committee's points regarding the widespread disorder now taking place in the system, instead stressing that 'better value for money for taxpayers' had been achieved. It conceded that performance 'under the contract has not been of a satisfactory level', but it did say that it was trying to entice more qualified interpreters – increasing their pay by just over a fifth.

As Maniar argued in her blog, quality had taken a hit: 'The current agreement makes use of a three-tier system, with Tier 3 interpreters being insufficiently qualified to interpret in court [therefore they should only be used as a last resort]. But according to the progress report by the NAO, there has been a sharp increase in the use of Tier 3 interpreters; by November 2013, they were dealing with 10 percent of the month's bookings.'[54]

But this time there's another question to ask: was money actually being saved? As Maniar noticed, 'the "savings" boasted by the MoJ took no account of costs of delay and additional work in court cases.'[55] A 2013 statistical bulletin from the MoJ showed that courts weren't being provided with interpreters nearly once every ten times.[56] On each occasion this led to days being lost at crown court, it cost around £10,000 – by December 2013 it had cost the Crown Prosecution Service around £17 million in total.[57] The pressure group Professional Interpreters for Justice gathered data over one week in November 2013 which showed a pre-trial hearing for an attempted murder in Ipswich delayed, a defendant in a speeding case having a friend interpret for him, magistrates in Spalding adjourning a drunk-driving case due to lack of an interpreter, and a sentencing hearing in Bradford being adjourned.[58]

Things hadn't improved much by 2014. The MoJ and Courts

Service were hauled before the public accounts committee in January, when the committee noted that Capita had failed to fulfil more than 23,000 requests, which, given that an extra £2.8 million had been put into the contract the year before, didn't exactly suggest value for money.[59] Would the MoJ be terminating the contract? The committee was told it would not. That month a telling little detail was revealed by the National Audit Office (NAO): Capita had actually been fined the maximum amount possible under the terms of the contract – and that amounted to £46,319. Shadow justice minister Andy Slaughter gave a statement in which he said:'It's a disgrace that ministers have still failed to get a grip [on this] after two years.'[60]

A year later, there were still stories coming through about the service. In January 2015 we learned about a Romanian man who'd had to rely on an English-speaking friend at Grantham magistrates' court and the failure of Capita to send a Spanish interpreter for the sentencing of a man who'd tried to smuggle drugs into the country.[61] The government had brought in consultants Optimity Matrix to review the service, and it recommended a simplified system with two tiers depending on qualification and experience. The government decided to put this off until the next time the contract was tendered, while Optimity Matrix's suggestion that a professional development programme would be a good idea was also thrown out.[62]

Back in February 2013, when the justice select committee reported on the fiasco, it was particularly exercised by the fact that while the previous translation system had its faults, it didn't need fundamental, root-and-branch reform: 'This is a cause for concern at a time when the same department is likely to be responsible for a large complex centralized commissioning programme for implementing the rehabilitation revolution,' it said.[63] And it's therefore no surprise that when we turn to this aspect of outsourcing in the justice system, we find a very similar story.

The probation 'revolution'

In December 2012 the *Daily Mail* carried an excoriating attack on the probation service with the headline 'Nearly 50,000 Criminals Spared Jail Offend Again within a Year: MPs Claim "Shocking" Figures Show Failure by Probation Officers'. Priti Patel MP was quoted and said: 'There is clearly a problem with the probation service which is not working well to deal with this issue.'[64] The story was based on the MoJ's quarterly reoffending statistics. The only problem was that this short-term picture didn't show that reoffending had in fact slightly decreased, every year, since 2000. The figures also included criminals who had received sentences under twelve months, for whom the probation service has no statutory responsibility.

Had the briefing for this story come from the opposition? That seemed unlikely: Patel was a Conservative MP. One couldn't help but notice these lines: 'Justice Secretary Chris Grayling is set to announce within weeks that charities and businesses will be brought in to tackle entrenched reoffending as part of the "rehabilitation revolution". Yesterday he said the majority of probation work would be outsourced.' It was, in fact, the most obvious indication thus far that the government was laying the ground for another outsourcing 'revolution' – to be known as 'Transforming Rehabilitation'. Grayling was, of course, the man who initiated the Department for Work and Pensions' Work Programme, which, as we've seen, operates on payment by results (PbR) lines. We've looked at some of the Work Programme's failings, but perhaps the most relevant criticism was the fact that it was simply wheeled out too quickly in comparison with Labour's New Deal.

In January 2013, I spoke to Mark Ormerod, chief executive of the Probation Association. I asked him what the next step in the process would be and it turned out he and the other probation chiefs were somewhat bemused by the whole thing:

> A government announcement would be helpful. We've been waiting for a response to the consultation since June. It's not even clear who's supposed to implement what, but we know it's supposed to happen in 2014/15. We're not opposed to the idea of PbR, but it doesn't seem very far away and the only way we can see it happening is some kind of central contracting process but that cuts across a tremendous amount of work that's being done at a local level.[65]

PbR requires contractors to put money on the table themselves at the outset, and we've seen the downside to this idea when looking at the case of Eco-Actif. Sebert Cox, chairman of both the Probation Association and Durham Tees Valley Probation Trust, was concerned about how the involvement of charities would work. He told me that there simply weren't enough of them, and the ones that could potentially do the work were squeezed financially. 'One has to be sceptical about who'll be coming forward to do this,' he said: it appeared he was concerned the likes of G4S and Serco would come in because they could promise to cut costs.[66]

At this point, various sources had given a vague idea of how the changes would be implemented – it appeared the outsourced work would be targeted on those serving twelve months or fewer; they would apparently be supervised so they had places to live and were signed up to drug treatment programmes. It seemed a positive move, but I was concerned at how little the probation bosses actually knew about how the scheme would work. Ormerod had already raised concerns about accountability and transparency with the MoJ: 'You have that potential situation where various organizations look at each other and say "I thought you were responsible for that" or "That's not in our contract."'[67]

Savas Hadjipavlou, business director of the Probation Chiefs Association, expanded on this: 'If you compare probation work with other areas that have been outsourced, it tends to work where the business is transactional and clearly defined – things like civil service pensions.' Probation, by contrast, involves humans, who fluctuate in terms of how they behave and have to be constantly monitored. And moreover, it also requires plenty of different authorities to do this: mental health and drug addiction services, the police, the local courts and more.

As Hadjipavlou said: 'The idea it can be easily mapped into a simple PbR model is rather difficult to understand.' For him, the probation officer's role is to bring these agencies together: 'You have to preserve that, as against the purity of the PbR model which says you're not interested in the contents of what's done, you're only going to pay for the result.' This idea that behaviour can fluctuate was a huge concern for him:

High-risk people can be low risk if they're taking their medication, if they've got mental health problems that are managed and so forth – that takes us back to measuring success. All those who go into prison with a Class A drug problem, for example, have a reoffending rate of 90 percent. Government aggregates large groups and looks at the average but no sensible way of looking at success would do it by that measure.[68]

And there was the rub: outsourcing and complex human behaviour don't always mix. How do you tell if someone is high, low or medium risk? Are people really that simple? Aren't these definitions changing all the time? When making the same point, the politics.co.uk editor Ian Dunt has cited the issue of domestic abuse: 'Perhaps an offender has a minor conviction of some sort and authorities are aware they have problems at home. They are low risk. Then something changes. Neighbours hear fighting in the house and inform the police. The risk level has changed and it has to be managed accordingly. Supervision needs to increase.'[69]

For Ormerod it led to a central question – how can you pay by results, when the results are so hard to measure?

> With the Work Programme, getting someone in a job stops benefits being paid so you get an immediate cash reward. The immediate aim with this is to close prisons because you've got reoffending down, but that's a very protracted cycle. We're talking about making a long-term behavioural change – there's no point saying 'We'll pay you after a week'. It's a far more inchoate environment in terms of working out whether success has been achieved and then saying we can pay you something.

This is central to many of the initiatives we've looked at already. Outsourcers will tell you how they can save money. But few can promise to make things better. Qualitative improvements are impossible to claim because they're dealing with people, who are hugely complex, so it's often near impossible to measure outcomes in a meaningful way. There also isn't robust data on how the state is doing to begin with, so even if the companies had a better system of tracking performance, they'd have nothing to compare it to.

Like many public service leaders, none of the people to whom I spoke had an issue with the fundamental idea of PbR. But when it was being introduced in such a chaotic and rushed fashion, they could be forgiven for wondering if ideology was trumping pragmatism. In May 2013, Grayling expanded on the plans in Parliament. We learned what we'd expected to hear: that the probation service, which currently deals with 250,000 cases a year, would remain responsible for the 30,000 high-risk cases, while control of the roughly 220,000 low- to medium-risk offenders would pass to private firms and voluntary groups.

When I spoke to him again, Savas Hadjipavlou was still concerned that the issue of risk hadn't been satisfactorily resolved. He said: 'There's a difference in relation to accountability. Originally the public sector was simply accountable for everything that might go wrong. There was a suggestion it would have people in outsourced offices – that's gone away and now a series of triggers are proposed. If the offender is of a certain risk level to go to contracted services there are triggers that mean they come back.'[70]

It was one of those solutions that made less sense the more you thought about it. There was barely any detail on what these 'triggers' meant. MoJ documents about the scheme shown to probation managers referenced a 'change in circumstances', but what this really meant was barely defined. It wasn't clear what would actually happen when a client was deemed a serious enough case to move back to the public sector. Nor was it clear if the private sector's work would simply be forgotten.

This meant there was a very simple question: who was to be blamed when things went wrong? In the worst possible scenario, what happened when one of the private sector's offenders ended up killing someone?

Ormerod told me:

We understand the provider would be accountable if they hadn't pulled the triggers. It would come to a review of the case in the way that happens now. The issue we drew attention to is that it's more likely to go wrong because you've introduced an interface. Things go wrong when communication breaks down. And it gets more complicated when some of the triggers have been pulled ... When the person goes forward and backwards between providers it becomes more difficult to assign responsibility. Whose fault is it? Risk levels change in about twenty-five percent of cases. In some of the cases we've looked at, the risk levels change substantially. Low- or high-risk cases are easier to manage. They're the minority though. It's the bit in the middle where change is dynamic and contextual.[71]

In the context of the things we've read about during the implementation of the Work Programme, it seemed entirely possible that providers could be incentivized to pull triggers for dubious reasons. Ormerod's answer was diplomatic, but he clearly recognized where I was coming from: he told me that while the public sector could carry out renewed risk assessments, 'it's difficult to regulate it by contract.' And Hadjipavlou was no less uneasy: he told me this was an attempt to say the public sector 'wasn't responsible for the whole thing', but that risk assessment simply wasn't a 'precise science'. He expressed his doubts that the new process was capable of the 'fine granularity' needed to look at people 'intelligently'.[72] And this reminded me of the problems around the work capability assessment: we barely needed reminding of the problems engendered by a tickbox approach to a complex, human problem.

Indeed, it seemed at this point that there hadn't been any real attempt to address directly any of the problems unearthed during the Work Programme's existence. Grayling's plans were announced in the month the work and pensions select committee published its second report into the Work Programme – the very report that concluded that 'creaming and parking' – picking off the easiest cases to work with while ignoring the more taxing ones – was endemic.

To my mind, a diversity of providers was a good thing. After researching my first book about street gangs I became convinced of the power of the voluntary sector to tackle crime successfully: I saw how such charities regularly employed people from the local community who had understood the issues and got more respect from clients than people from bodies like local councils. But how were charities to avoid being outflanked by huge outsourcing companies? There didn't seem to be an answer. And just because these new workers might empathize with their clients better, it didn't mean they had the professionalism of the people they were replacing. No doubt many of the former state workers would simply shift across to the private sector, but the only mention made of this issue was the creation of a new 'probation institute'.

There were also concerns over how probation staff would be moved to their new employers, perhaps not without good reason. In June 2014 Labour alleged that names were 'drawn from a hat', but Grayling denied this was the case. Only a month later, in a parliamentary answer to shadow justice secretary Sadiq Khan, justice minister Andrew Selous described the allocations as an 'automatic assignment process' with 'local evidence-based assignment criteria'.[73] Which, bluntly, sounded rather like drawing names from a hat.

Quite apart from the lack of data to support the idea of

probation privatization, there was one more big problem – the time frame. Ormerod told me: 'The speed at which we're expected to ready ourselves is just breathless. There is more detail now but that only makes you realize more clearly how much has to be done in a very short timescale.'[74] It felt rather incredible that the government was rushing the scheme through (I would describe the plans in 2013 as 'a frantic attempt to put ideology into action before an electoral deadline, rather than any kind of considered response to the problems of reoffending'), when the risk to public safety was so very clear.

In October 2013 hundreds of experts descended on London for the first ever World Congress on Probation. No doubt they'd have been bemused to find the service was being sold off and even more puzzled over the numerous articles that had been written highlighting how risky the sell-off actually was. That month *Private Eye* obtained a scoop: a leaked letter from the local probation trust boards, which hold the local staff accountable, said the 1 April 2014 deadline for handing over seventy percent of probation work to companies or charities was both 'unrealistic and unreasonable in that it undermines employer/employee relations, has serious implications for service delivery and therefore increases the risk to public safety'.

The magazine went on to point out there were still no detailed plans for an integrated IT system, that the boards were being forced to consult staff over moves to the new companies or to what was left of the National Probation Service, and that staff would be struggling to keep on top of their workload while ensuring the safe and robust transfer of all cases. As it concluded: 'No doubt these thorny issues will be dealt with by the new army of "transformation managers" about to be recruited (Official MoJ guidance was that any objection to a transfer [from a member of staff] "brings that person's employment to an end").'[75]

By April 2014 any of the silenced workers who were hoping to have their fears allayed would have been somewhat disheartened by the performance that month of MoJ officials in front of the public accounts committee. That thorny issue of risk, about which I'd first heard concerns a year earlier, reared its head again. Margaret Hodge wanted to know the cost of transferring cases between the probation service and the new private companies. It seemed a reasonable question when, according to her figures, one in four offenders changes risk category while being supervised. *Private Eye* once again had a field day with the responses. It mocked Michael Spurr, chief executive of the National Offender Management Service, who 'didn't recognize' the one in four number, but said he didn't have the exact figure: 'I don't think it's fair for me to pluck a figure out of my head at this minute.'[76]

And as it went on to report, it was no better when MPs tried to find out how the contracts were to be paid and what percentage would be set fees as against PbR if a private company could prove it had helped reduce reoffending. Hodge asked if there was any evidence on the efficacy of PbR. Antonia Romeo, director general of the MoJ's Transforming Rehabilitation programme, said there was very little. And, of course, this fits in with a narrative surrounding most new outsourcing projects: evidence is always going to be thin on the ground when you're a global trendsetter.

But as the magazine pointed out, Romeo's answer wasn't quite accurate, because according to the charity Human Rights Watch (HRW), every year US courts sentence thousands of misdemeanour offenders to probation overseen by private companies that charge their fees directly to the probationers. Often, the poorest people wind up paying the most in fees over time – the charity has found that in many cases they will only have been put on probation because they need time to pay off fines and court costs linked to small crimes. The companies are, in HRW's words, more like 'abusive debt collectors' than probation officers.[77] And when these people can't pay, the companies 'can and do secure their arrest'.[78]

I'd also been worrying about the issue of service ownership since the story had broken that the service was to be outsourced: what if we had a similar situation to the one we've already encountered with Capita taking over from ALS in the court translation contract? According to Romeo, there'd be a 'discussion' with the MoJ. But there was no assurance that companies couldn't sell: 'I am deliberately trying not to find myself in a position where I reveal too much during the process of a live competition.'

Private Eye would conclude:

> Top marks for obfuscation during the two hour grilling went to Dame Ursula Brennan, permanent secretary at the MoJ. Hodge wanted to know how splitting the service between the privately owned CRCs and the Probation Service, while at the same time expanding it to cover a predicted extra 50,000 inmates who currently receive no supervision after prison, could be delivered within £850 million. [Brennan answered:] 'We are not saying, "Here is how we do it now. We are going to do something that adds cost to it." We are saying, "Here are all the costs now. They are going to lie in different places, and the procedures are going to look different."'[79]

By this point, around £9 million had been spent on consultants: if they were there to provide clarity over the process, it didn't seem to be happening. It took the best part of a year for Sadiq Khan, the shadow justice minister, to pass significant comment

on Grayling's plans. When he did, however, it seemed the gloves
were well and truly off. He wrote:

> I've heard some truly alarming reports on the chaos privatiza-
> tion is causing: staff shortages caused by rocketing sickness
> levels and dozens of unfilled vacancies are crippling the
> service.
>
> As a result, a backlog of cases is building up, including
> offenders who have committed serious, violent crimes like
> domestic violence. Oversight of sex offenders has been handed
> to staff without the right expertise. High-risk cases aren't
> receiving sufficient supervision. Court reports are going
> unwritten. Senior management time has been sucked into
> restructuring, neglecting day-to-day duties rehabilitating
> offenders. New software designed to assess the risk that
> offenders pose to the public was rushed into service without
> adequate staff training. It is a shocking state of affairs, which
> could have catastrophic consequences for public safety.[80]

Khan went on to raise many of the same concerns and points
that I and many other reporters had: we had heard, time and
again from probation professionals, that the service only really
works when it pools its resources with other bodies like local
authorities, the health service and the police, so that the specific
needs of offenders could be tackled. But instead, the new scheme
replicated the Work Programme, in Khan's words, 'outsourcing
service delivery to a handful of large private providers while
local probation trusts are abolished and long-established working relationships ripped apart'. And as he pointed out, this was
happening without any meaningful piloting or testing.

One sensed the ideological fervour behind the reforms was so
great that it simply had to be rushed, which was why Khan went

on to say that it was unacceptable, in an election year, for Grayling to sign away a whole swathe of the justice system on ten-year contracts: 'It's undemocratic, binding the next secretary of state, whoever they may be, to this policy and reducing their ability to choose an alternative route to reform.' He demanded the contracts weren't signed this late in the parliament, and that they include get-out clauses to allow a new government to walk away free of financial penalty – of course, it's worth noting this was a luxury the coalition wasn't afforded with the Atos work capability assessment, for example.

However, in September 2014, the *Guardian* reported that if contracts were cancelled the penalty incurred could be between £300 million and £400 million, under an unprecedented clause that guaranteed bidders their expected profits over the ten-year life of the contract. According to the MoJ, the clause was included only because of Treasury guidance.[81] It rather negated Khan's original claim: 'If contracts remain unsigned at the next election – and Labour wins – I will bin them. If anything is in place by May 2015, I will get the best legal minds to find all possible ways to get out of them.' He offered a Labour vision built on local, publicly run probation trusts, close to those they were supervising: 'Trusts have told me they'd take on supervising short-sentence prisoners within existing budgets. This makes a mockery of government claims that privatization is necessary to free up resources to cope with prisoners serving less than 12 months.'[82]

In the end, it never happened: Labour lost the general election. Still, it was a remarkably stringent intervention. Until then, there had been little evidence that the Labour Party had hardened its attitude to privatization. It seemed the relentless pace at which Grayling had pushed his reforms had finally turned the tide, on one policy at least. Ironically, though Khan never had a

chance to put his plan into action, the contracts did stop someone else from changing Grayling's plans. His successor at the
MoJ, Michael Gove, who became justice secretary in 2015,
immediately set about ripping up a number of his predecessor's
high-profile schemes. It was widely suspected he'd have binned
the outsourcing of probation too – but whether or not that was
the case, the contracts would have made it impossible.

In early 2015 journalists spotted that the firms involved were
offering jobs at lower rates than qualified probation staff
received.[83] Soon, the expected jobs cuts would follow. Shortly
before the general election, Sodexo Justice Services, which had
been given contracts to run six of the twenty-one community
rehabilitation companies in England and Wales, announced jobs
cuts of more than thirty percent, totalling around 700 posts,
within the next year.[84] At the same time, we learned that ten
senior probation trust executives received six-figure severance
packages: Sally Lewis, the outgoing chief executive of Avon and
Somerset Probation Trust, for example, received £293,000.
Napo, the probation officers' union, seized on the figures as
evidence that the plan had never been 'fully costed' by the
government.[85]

It had even more to say on the news, which broke around the
same time, that Sodexo was planning to allow offenders to report
in at electronic kiosks that used fingerprint recognition software
to reward good compliance from prisoners: 'The use of call
centres and machines instead of highly skilled staff is downright
dangerous and will put the public at risk,' said Ian Lawrence, the
general secretary.[86] There was more on the costs of redundancies
a month later, when justice minister Andrew Selous revealed that
the cost of payouts for those taking voluntary redundancy had
totalled £16.4 million.[87]

By April 2015 the *Guardian* managed to interview some

current and former probation officers about the changes. One complained about the physical screens put up between the National Probation Trust and the Community Rehabilitation Company, despite both sharing an office: 'There is this idea that because we're separate organizations now we can't allow the other organization to see our work because it's confidential, which is absolute nonsense because six months ago we were all working together . . . There's no flow of information, no knowledge sharing. It's this huge demarcation that's being created.'

Su McConnell, a manager in what had been the Devon and Cornwall Probation Trust, had recently quit the service over the changes. She told the paper: 'I was trying to manage a team and that team was just being split up, and I could see it; careers were being wrecked. Some staff who had invested a decade of training to do the thing they wanted to do were suddenly staring into the abyss.'[88]

Whether it's in the courts, prisons or probation, the Ministry of Justice has outsourced at a breakneck speed in recent years. In part, it's been done to save money – but in all three cases there's an earnest belief that private companies can bring imagination and creativity to the sectors within which they operate. However, the problem is that the decisions to outsource appear not to have yielded any particularly impressive results yet, while the rush to impose this brave new vision has upset established workers within the justice sector. The truth is that in both court translation and probation it's too soon to say exactly how effective the results will be. But private prisons have been around for years, and the results have been mediocre at best. The comprehensive 2015 general election win for the Tories does, however, mean that the pace of reform can be a little less breathless. What's more, the new justice secretary, Michael Gove, has shown little of his predecessor's zeal for contracting out his department's functions. In justice, many services are still to be outsourced, yet those that have been have generated a slew of scandals. In other sectors the outsourcing vision is even more nascent, but many of the same concerns are beginning to prevail.

5

NHS for Sale?

The Health and Social Care Act 2012 is a huge, complex Act of Parliament. It will be years – perhaps decades – before we know for sure which elements of it have merit and which don't. It's the most wide-ranging reorganization of the National Health Service in England to date. According to its entry on the House of Commons website, among other things, the Act:

- establishes an independent NHS Board to allocate resources and provide commissioning guidance;
- increases GPs' powers to commission services on behalf of their patients;
- strengthens the role of the Care Quality Commission (CQC);
- develops Monitor, the body that currently regulates NHS foundation trusts, into an economic regulator to oversee aspects of access and competition in the NHS;
- cuts the number of health bodies to help meet the government's commitment to cut NHS administration costs by a third, including abolishing primary care trusts (PCTs) and strategic health authorities (SHAs).[1]

What's particularly interesting is the fact that around £70 billion of commissioning (i.e. procurement of services) was transferred from the abolished PCTs to several hundred 'clinical commissioning groups' (CCGs), partly run by general practitioners in England. It was hugely controversial. Some supported it – one 2011 letter to the *Daily Telegraph* from a GPs' consortium called it 'a natural conclusion of the GP commissioning role that began with fundholding in the 1990s and, more recently, of the previous government's agenda of GP polysystems and practice-based commissioning'[2] – but a 2012 *Guardian* data investigation found overwhelming lack of support among the royal colleges and organizations representing the medical profession. Among the bodies that didn't support the bill were the Royal College of Physicians and Royal College of Surgeons, along with the British Medical Association (BMA).

Why? The worst-case scenario was that private sector operations and pricing would be introduced into the NHS, and that local NHS providers could end up outcompeted, and thereby bankrupt. There were concerns about management expertise, with widespread fears that a larger number of GPs' consortiums (as opposed to fewer, larger health authorities) would mean that commissioning skills were (in the words of the BMA) 'spread more thinly'.

There were worries too about fragmentation of the service, and a lack of accountability – such as we've encountered through earlier chapters of this book. Indeed, there would be more tiers to the NHS, with five national bodies – the Department of Health, the National Institute for Health and Clinical Excellence, the CQC, the NHS Commissioning Board and the economic regulator Monitor – raising questions about whether accountability could be muddied. If the fears over accountability were to be allayed, it was important that transparency was maintained in this brave new world.

How Sudbury fought privatization

The Suffolk town of Sudbury is not what you'd call a hotbed of political activism. It's a small market town with a population of around 13,000, sitting by the river Stour, surrounded by rolling, verdant countryside. But in 2012 it became the setting for a battle that would tell us so much about how communities all over the UK might respond to the new-look health service.

In mid-2012, Serco was awarded a contract to deliver community health services to the county of Suffolk – a £140 million three-year deal.[3] According to campaigners, it bid £10 million less than rivals. The PCT for Suffolk had, however, told Serco that quality had to be maintained as part of the contract. Soon after winning the contract, it began to consult staff. The consultation wasn't sent to the county council's health scrutiny committee, nor to the local involvement network (now Healthwatch) – which it should have been, because it proposed to cut staff numbers from 790 to 653.

Campaigners began to fear for higher-band nurses and therapists. They wrote to the chief executive of NHS Suffolk in November, and said:

> [It is not] any consolation that job losses will take place through 'mutually agreed resignation' or MARS – just another clever way of getting rid of people at minimal cost ... we are told that staff who refuse to agree to MARS are likely to be given jobs which will require them to drive all over the county as and when required, as well as work to new shift patterns into the evening – an impossibility for staff with young families. This is nothing short of blackmail.[4]

As I went on to report in the *New Statesman*: 'The campaign group [Sudbury WATCH] received an anonymous letter suggesting that after the contract was awarded to Serco in March 2012, it was subsequently renegotiated over the next few months, in a manner favourable to Serco in breach of procurement rules, and that a substantial sum of money had been paid in September 2012, before the contract started to run in October.'

The letter contained more worrying details: it claimed that the company registered with the CQC to run Suffolk health services (not Serco but a sub-company called Integrated Clinical Services) was set up a month before the contract was awarded. It also went on to claim that the SHA had driven the decision; Serco had no track record in running community health services, so NHS Suffolk should have scrutinized the bid more carefully, it alleged.

However, when I put these claims to NHS Suffolk, they rebutted them:

The procurement process was run in an entirely proper, appropriate and normal fashion. This process adhered to the guidelines set out by the Cooperation and Competition Panel, which include a formal complaints and appeals procedure. No formal complaints or appeals have been received.

After being named as the preferred bidder, Serco and NHS Suffolk went through the standard procedure of due diligence and contract finalization with a schedule of contract payments being agreed. Integrated Clinical Services is a company that was established by Serco with the agreement of NHS Suffolk, NHS Pensions and Suffolk Community Healthcare staff as the appropriate vehicle for employing staff and ensuring they retained their proper NHS pension rights.[5]

In December that year, Peter Clifford, the head of the campaign group, told the *Suffolk Free Press* that he was 'not prepared to see

Sudbury's health services wrecked again'. He added: 'Combined with the cuts to occupational therapist numbers, community nurses, specialist and district nurses, general health workers and physiotherapists, the end result will inevitably be a serious reduction in the quality of rehabilitation and general care of the elderly.'[6] His group took legal action, instructing solicitors that, as the consultation was about patient care, it should involve the public. If the consultation wasn't stopped, proceedings could begin.

Serco claimed that the number of sackings had been overstated by the campaigners, and that the figure of 137 positions lost had been reduced to 95. However, a spokesman for Sudbury WATCH told me: 'The number is a red herring. This is about getting rid of experienced professionals. One thing that is for sure is that staff are demoralized. In fact, we understand that at present the company has received too many applications for voluntary redundancy.'[7]

The acting CEO for NHS Suffolk tried to dissuade the campaigners with a post on his website, which said:

> The Clinical Commissioning Groups will have the same priority for ensuring good patient care and value for money. Local scrutiny and public input will continue through the usual channels, through the emerging Healthwatch, the Health Scrutiny Committee and the Health and Wellbeing Board. In addition, Serco, like all providers, will be required to carry out regular patient experience surveys to help improve and shape services.[8]

The campaigners were advised their legal action was unlikely to work. They told me: 'The legal action against NHS Suffolk and Serco has run into the sand at present because we are up against so much secrecy, fudge and obfuscation. Plus a lack of account-ability: NHS Suffolk telling us to ask Serco, Serco telling us to ask NHS Suffolk.'[9]

As we've seen so far in this book, it's extremely difficult to see how things like quality – or in this case 'efficiency' – are meas-ured. Serco claimed efficiency savings would be generated through hand-held computers. Sudbury WATCH said that while there would be increased assessments of patients, they'd be carried out by less experienced staff, and so the quality of inter-action would diminish. The group claimed the company was ultimately relying on crude activity analysis of dubious and unreliable statistics gathered in Suffolk in the past couple of years.

Once again, the issue of transparency came to the fore. Sudbury WATCH's spokesman told me:

> Our biggest problem has been securing information. Before the work was outsourced, the PCT's job was to consult publicly. They could be challenged, but now commercial confidentiality laws mean it's been very hard for our lawyers to pin them down over their decision making. There's a real sense you're dealing with a private company, not the NHS. Freedom of Information requests are met with commercial confidentiality defence, and Serco isn't even subject to the Act. The tail's wagging the dog.[10]

Serco would go on to win the contract, but in the end no one really won. In 2015 Serco announced it would be withdrawing from the contract after making losses of £13.7 million. West Suffolk NHS Foundation Trust and Ipswich Hospital NHS were named preferred bidders for the new contract. It was to be brought back in-house.[11]

We're seeing more and more stories like this. In February 2014 we learned that NHS chiefs were promising a limited public consultation over an £800 million contract for older people's health services in Cambridgeshire, but a quick look at some of the tender documents released by Cambridgeshire and Peterborough CCG revealed that censors had got to them: there were just four pages, out of sixty-nine, that hadn't been blacked out.[12]

The reason that the situation in Suffolk had interested me was that I wondered how the government's stated aim of increasing integration would actually work. A patient in Suffolk could potentially be welcomed to one of the county's acute hospitals, but then be sent to a non-acute bed commissioned by the CCG. That bed would be in a care home run by the Partnership in Care (a private business), but would be visited by nurses now working for Serco. The future of public health looked fragmented, to my eyes.

The out-of-hours GP scandal

Two months before Serco was awarded the contract by NHS Suffolk, it emerged that it was under investigation by the Care Quality Commission for providing an 'unsafe' out-of-hours GP service in Cornwall.

Whistleblowers had contacted the NHS to claim that Serco was manipulating results when it wasn't meeting targets, which led to an unannounced NHS inspection. The sources had said that it had allowed queues of up to ninety patients at a time to build up on the telephone helpline, and had blamed delays on patients so that it could meet its targets. It also, according to the *Guardian*, rang at least one patient who had waited too long to see a doctor to give them a new waiting target instead, and repeatedly took visiting doctors off roving duties in order to operate clinics and hotlines because it had too few staff on duty to cover the county. On one occasion the *Guardian*'s sources said only a single GP had been on duty.

The CQC was contacted by Dr Gareth Emrys-Jones, a retired former chair of the GP cooperative that used to run the out-of-hours service for Cornwall as a not-for-profit company. 'I have been approached by a significant number of people representing all classes of employees at Serco who felt unable to whistleblow directly but who perceived the service to be unsafe because of a lack of clinicians and inadequate cover for the needs of the patients of Cornwall,' he told the *Guardian*. 'They have cited incidents where it appears that data has been altered in order to achieve compliance with quality standards that they knew had been missed. These related to an extended time period and were not one-off incidents. I was concerned for the staff and for the service because if the allegations are true it would have serious implications,' he went on to say.[13]

As a result, the Commons public accounts committee asked the National Audit Office to investigate. According to its summary, a clinical review of the service in June 2012 found no evidence that the service was or had been clinically unsafe. But a forensic audit found that two members of staff made 252 unauthorized changes to performance data. It should be stressed that this represented only 0.2% of all interactions with patients during the six-month period. As a result of the data changes, the performance Serco reported to the primary care trust was overstated in seven instances.[14]

The NAO also found that during 2012 Serco regularly had insufficient staff to fill all clinical shifts and redeployed some GPs to cover them, taking them out of the cars available for home visits. In July, the CQC reported that the out-of-hours service did not have enough qualified, skilled and experienced staff to meet people's needs. When it inspected the service again in December 2012 the commission found that, although the number of clinical staff had increased, Serco needed to take further action because there were not enough health advisers to handle incoming calls.

The NAO concluded:

Serco has not consistently met the national quality require-ments for out-of-hours services set by the Department of Health. Performance against the requirements declined signif-icantly following the introduction in May 2012 of NHS Pathways, as required by the primary care trust, a new system for assessing patients' needs when they call the service. Serco has since taken steps in response to the problems, including using more clinical staff to support the health advisers handling calls, and performance is now recovering.

Perhaps more worryingly, the CQC had highlighted a bullying culture. The NAO said: 'Whistleblowers' concerns had not been identified by routine management controls or by the primary care trust itself. Serco had a whistleblowing policy but evidence suggests that whistleblowers were still fearful of raising concerns. Serco and the primary care trust have since reminded all staff of the importance of raising concerns and the protection available to whistleblowers.'[15]

However, such systemic problems become old news in the privatized world. In late December 2013, Serco agreed to the early termination of its contract for out-of-hours GP services. It said cancelling the Cornwall contract (along with a similar one in Braintree and a loss-making agreement for community healthcare in Suffolk) would cost it £17 million in one-off charges: 'Serco has agreed with NHS Kernow to bring forward the end of its contract for GP out-of-hours services in Cornwall. Serco's operation of the contract to date has experienced some operational challenges.'[16] And what was perhaps most telling about this saga – although hardly anyone seemed to pick up on it – was the fact that Serco had won the contract with a bid that undercut the local GP cooperative by £1.5 million. As with other such bids, we can't see exactly how the savings were made – commercial confidentiality law prevents us.

The suspicion that arises due to the lack of transparency means there are already questions about the unhealthy influence of the profit incentive on the NHS. It's certainly not the case, however, that profits from non-clinical support services are high: companies like Serco are actually carrying losses or struggling to break even on more generous NHS contracts. In June 2014 the Bureau for Investigative Journalism (BIJ) discovered that thousands of NHS patients – some seriously ill – hadn't received vital medicines on time because Healthcare at Home, a company which had been contracted to deliver them to their homes, had failed to do so. It had been investigated in April by the General Pharmaceutical Council (GPhC), along with the CQC, which found that 'a proportion of patients did not receive their medicines at the scheduled time. The consequent telephone enquiries from these patients overwhelmed Healthcare at Home's customer service team. This led to complaints being unresolved and patients being left confused and uncertain about when and whether their medication would arrive.'

As the BIJ reported, the GPhC put the problems down to two key issues: outsourcing distribution arrangements to another company, and a growth in the number of patients of about three thousand after another provider withdrew from the market. But the really interesting aspect to this story is that Dave Roberts, chief executive of the National Clinical Homecare Association, actually singled out the low profit margins in the sector as a contributory factor, telling the BIJ: 'There's been twenty percent growth in this sector year on year for several years now in terms of numbers of patients – that's a very rapid expansion. But profits in this sector are just two to four percent. That is a poor return given the extent of capital investment needed and the governance and logistics issues. As NHS budgets have fallen, all the slack has been cut out of contracts.' His statement was supported by the company's accounts: in its most recent published accounts Healthcare at Home reported a turnover of £1 billion, with pre-tax profits of just £15 million.[17] They're far from being the only company struggling to make ends meet in this sector.

The downfall of Hinchingbrooke

Most people familiar with the notorious story of the private company Circle Health's failed deal to run Hinchingbrooke Health Care NHS Trust in Cambridgeshire would probably know it took over thanks to a £1 billion deal. Beyond that, they're unlikely to know exactly how the company operates, and given how arcane the set-up is, you could hardly blame them.

Circle Health is owned by a parent company, Circle Holdings plc, which in turn is owned by a series of hedge funds. Nearly a third of the shares are held by Lansdowne Partners, founded by Sir Paul Ruddock, who has donated £692,592 over time to the Conservative Party. A smaller amount is held by Invesco Perpetual, set up by Sir Martyn Arbib, who's donated £466,330.[18] Another fifteen percent was previously owned by Odey Asset Management, set up by Robin Crispin Odey, who has donated £220,000, and Michael Platt, founder of BlueCrest Capital, which had a five percent stake in Circle Holdings, has gifted the party £125,000.[19] Take that alongside the *Mirror*'s point that 'Since the Tories' hated health reforms became law, [Circle's] profits have gone up from £64.6 million in 2010/11 to £170.4 million in 2011/12' and it would be easy to see a conspiracy.

But for a start, the majority of Circle's contracts – including Hinchingbrooke – were drawn up under Labour. When Andy Burnham, the former Labour health secretary, was asked by an MP in Parliament why he allowed Hinchingbrooke to be taken over by Circle, he told him to get his facts straight, saying the deal was signed under the coalition.[20] This was true, but it's also true that it was put out to tender in 2009, and that the only NHS bidder pulled out on cost grounds, whereupon Burnham allowed three private hospital companies – Serco, Ramsay and Circle – to compete.[21]

There's no doubt that under Circle Hinchingbrooke scored reasonably well in clinical ratings. Nor, for that matter, was there any doubt that ministers had been keen to trumpet this to the press – in 2014 the *Daily Mail* was happy to praise it for winning the CHKS award for 'best trust in England for quality of care', without mentioning that CHKS was a healthcare intelligence specialist agency recently bought by Capita, which was working with Circle to bid for contracts.[22] In reality, Hinchingbrooke's performance, according to NHS England's patient satisfaction survey, was only slightly better than the nationwide average.

There was always a question over what the Circle project was supposed to stand for. The original vision – still outlined on Circle's website – described a 'John Lewis-style' model. It would be half owned by clinicians through a British Virgin Islands-registered company (under its corporate laws the medics wouldn't have to pay for their shares). In return they'd channel work into the company. But by the end of 2013 the forty-nine percent of Circle held by the employees was acquired by Circle Holdings, because it was deemed costly to administer and overly complex.

The problem with introducing more shareholders is that they want to see returns. And how were they doing on that score? Well, in its last six-monthly results, Circle Holdings reported an overall loss of £9.7 million, or twenty-two percent of its turnover. However, it still managed to raise £25 million from shareholders to fund expansion – allegedly due to a pitch that between sixty and seventy NHS trusts were failing for financial reasons and/or due to the quality of services being provided.[23]

The wider context of the original plan was called into question. In 2013 a Competition Commission report into the private healthcare market sparked interest when Circle complained rival companies weren't allowing it to compete properly. The report found in favour of the company, but also said that clinicians shouldn't be able to own shares in private hospitals unless they paid the full market value. On top of that, it said they shouldn't be linked to any requirement, express or implied, to refer patients to the private hospital or conduct a minimum percentage of their private practice at that hospital. All of which rather undermined the original scheme.[24]

If Circle was the future, there were some pretty tough questions to ask on the transparency side of things, too. In 2014 *Private Eye* did some excellent research on the convoluted way in which one of the company's assets, its flagship private hospital in Bath, operates. Two thirds of its income comes from the NHS. The hospital is owned not by Circle Health but by a Jersey company called Health Properties (Bath) Ltd, which leases the building back to Circle. It has offshore status but the magazine found clues in Circle Holdings' accounts to suggest it had debts of around £40 million, on some of which it had already defaulted.

As the magazine went on to explain (and you'll be forgiven for not being able to keep up):

The Bath hospital is part of Circle's business and the amounts would be consolidated in its balance sheet, but this is where the off balance sheet trick comes in. Health Properties (Bath) is owned not just by the Circle Group, but by two other companies: one of which is called Health Estates Ltd. The structure means it owns just 38.7% of the property company and keeps it off its books. Closer scrutiny reveals Health Estates Ltd is managed by another company – Health Estates Managers Ltd, which is owned by Circle.

When it comes to voting on matters concerning Health Properties (Bath) Ltd, it will do what Circle tells it to do. Circle Holdings' latest figures show debts of around £55 million. Adding in the Bath debt would take that towards the £100m mark. It wouldn't look good as it regularly goes to the City to stay afloat while running vital health services.[25]

Welcome to the transparent world of privatized healthcare. As the magazine went on to point out, Circle had already had to pay off a loan from one hedge fund that was running up twenty-five percent interest costs: Circle Holdings' accounts showed debt of about £60 million, but there had to be almost that much supporting the Bath venture.

Like many major NHS providers, Circle operates as a loss-leader model in a restricted market: the likes of Care UK, Virgin Care and General Healthcare Group all make annual losses at the time of writing, surviving on funding secured from investors on the promise of more NHS work.[26] The most cynical explanation of their business model comes from the tax expert and anti-poverty campaigner Richard Murphy: 'I believe that what a lot of these companies are trying to do is to undermine any chance that an NHS organization can win contracts. Once they have squeezed out the state sector, and the third sector, we will then see prices rise; then we will see profits; then we will see these tax-efficient structures working.'[27]

But what would happen if this model failed before it succeeded? We already had some idea. In 2008 Circle took out a £42 million loan from Barclays to open a new independent sector treatment centre at Nottingham's Queen's Medical Centre. It was to be repaid through income from the local NHS buying its services. It seemed Circle couldn't meet the five percent interest rate, so the NHS paid the bill in full, as apparently the firm had an 'unconditional right' to compel it to do so.[28]

And things did go wrong, in the end. In January 2015, Circle put out a statement that 'its franchise to operate Hinchingbrooke Health Care NHS Trust is no longer sustainable under current terms and that it has entered into discussions with the NHS Trust Development Authority with the view to ensuring an orderly withdrawal from the current contract.'[29]

It was hard to argue with some of the points Circle made in its statement: the company had indeed invested in the quality of care, staff and facilities, had won awards and had hit outcome targets. And Hinchingbrooke had indeed faced closure and been described as a 'basket case'. What had gone wrong? As with many other stories we've already looked at, it seemed the problem was less the company than the contract itself. As the consultant Tom Levitt pointed out, the failure was most likely 'due to the failure of the NHS to deliver its side of the bargain, not least the over-demand on A&E which was well above what the company was told to expect'.[30]

Of course, it's hard to know for sure: large swathes of the contract had been redacted due to commercial confidentiality laws. There were concerns, expressed in a report by the CQC that was published days after Circle pulled out, about A&E and medical care. And above all, as the public accounts committee would conclude, the Department of Health had 'play[ed] down the high level of risk involved ... The total deficit incurred during the franchise will be well above the level that Circle is contractually committed to cover, leaving the taxpayer to pick up the rest of the bill.'[31]

You'll have noticed those last few words are becoming a familiar refrain.

Conflicts of interest

The Health and Social Care Act has been in operation nearly four years at time of writing, and the issue of conflicts of interest has become hugely concerning. For instance, in 2013 it was revealed that a multi-million pound deal with Hospital Corporation of America (HCA) – a US business that had previously been fined $1 billion for mis-selling in the States (and has been singled out by the Competition Commission for overcharging the NHS too) – was signed to let the company treat NHS patients with brain tumours, days before responsibility for cancer went to the new quango NHS England.

Since the 2010 general election, HCA had given the Conservative Party at least £17,000 in political donations. Labour MPs were angered at the decision to stop University College hospital from treating brain cancer patients (NHS England – it is alleged – wouldn't pay for their treatment any more), who were instead directed to the Gamma Knife Centre at Bart hospital – owned by HCA – alongside Bupa's private Cromwell hospital. A hospital source claimed: 'The radiotherapy community is very concerned about the way NHS England is handing out contracts for NHS patients. There appears to be no clinical logic to the decisions they are making. Asking patients with brain tumours to switch hospitals and doctors when they are reaching a critical stage in their cancer is nothing short of madness.'[32]

Freedom of Information requests thus far on the subject of the decision appear to have drawn a blank, with those submitting them being directed to Bart for further details of the contract. Nevertheless, Grahame Morris MP, who sat on the health select committee during the coalition government, has described it as 'shocking and scandalous'.

If there are already signs of the wrong companies winning contracts, they're liable to be exacerbated outside London. As one outsider, who didn't wish to be named, told me: 'Francis Maude and the Cabinet Office ... made edicts to [improve commissioning], but you'll struggle to get a market there. When ... world class commissioning [a procuring process brought in by the NHS in 2008] was brought in for PCTs it was supposed to stimulate effective markets, and no one got their heads round it.'

My source told me that there were a limited number of firms prepared to offer their services away from the capital: 'It's very tough for buyers to stimulate the market, you can pull it off around the south east, but building markets in Cumbria ... I don't know.' At the same time, he was keen to point out that such deals make up a very small proportion of NHS spending: 'If it's being sold off, it's being sold off bloody slowly.'

This is a huge and complex change to the health service. No doubt it will have some positive impacts, but they may not compensate for the fact that successive governments have failed to learn from mistakes made at other times and in other areas.

But we'd do very well not to underestimate the scale and pace of changes. In the year after the Health and Social Care Act came into force, £13.5 billion worth of contracts were on offer: the amount available to the private sector had trebled. According to an FoI request made by the *British Medical Journal*, of 3,494 contracts awarded by 182 CCGs in England between April 2013 and August 2014, thirty-three percent went to the private sector.[33]

As a result there have been some less well-reported flashpoints. For instance, in December 2014, Nottingham University Hospitals Trust announced that it wouldn't be able to provide acute adult dermatology, including emergency care, after losing six of its eight consultants. Why had they left? Five of them apparently opted to leave rather than transfer to Circle, which won the contract to provide dermatology services in 2013. They were believed to be concerned about their job stability, and also worried they wouldn't have the chance to do academic research or training.[34]

There are also claims that the freedom of local health commissioners to make the best arrangements for a huge number of patients is being undermined by the market. For an example of this, we could look at the ill-fated merger of Bournemouth and Poole hospitals, rejected by the Competition Commission after a referral from the Office for Fair Trading, under the advice of the new regulator, Monitor. The hospitals favoured the merger, but Monitor, which is supposed to encourage both competition and cooperation, chose only the former in this instance. Benefits put forward by the hospitals were dismissed, and administrative savings ignored, because they might have been delivered by 'a merger with an alternative [hypothetical] provider' – a private hospital. After £6 million in legal fees had been paid, the merger was eventually called off. It prompted David Nicholson, CEO of NHS England, to claim the service was now 'bogged down in a morass of competition law'.[35]

Indeed, the senior staff of the regulatory industries appear to know rather more about competition, and indeed big business, than they do about cooperation. Among the board members are Adrian Masters, formerly of McKinsey and PWC; and Stephen Hay, formerly of KPMG. The Care Quality Commission's chair, David Prior, used to be a director of Capita, while NHS England's CEO, Simon Stevens, was previously the president of UnitedHealth Europe – a private health firm.

This could only be a cursory study of a huge subject, but we've seen enough here to make us realize that the same sorts of questions over accountability, transparency, quality of provision and the possible malign influence of a profit incentive are set to dominate the debate here as elsewhere for years to come. We have one more outsourced sector to look at before we can start to take some clear views on these issues. And it arguably contains the most horrifying examples of what can go wrong.

6

The Trouble with Social Care

Private care comes in many shapes and forms – for people with special needs, for the old, and – more and more – for the young. During the recent reporting of the Rochdale abuse scandal, in which more than a thousand girls were abused over a period that lasted over a decade, a little-noticed detail caught my attention. One girl at the centre of the case was moved from Essex and placed in a one-to-one home, where she was the only resident. She never woke up with the same staff member in the home who had been there when she went to sleep.[1]

I found much the same when I reported on Operation Bullfinch, a similar case in Oxford: 'A girl, who had just turned 15, ran away from her children's home and upon her return, staff refused to pay her taxi fare so the driver took her back to Oxford, where the men abusing her found her and raped her for the next two days in various corners of the city's parks.'[2]

The care of vulnerable children costs a lot. There are around five thousand young people in residential care homes – and around three quarters of these homes are run by private companies. The stakes are high in this market, where a private firm can charge hundreds of thousands of pounds in order to care for a child. A Radio 4 report found that in 2011, the top five providers had turned a profit of £30 million. The chief constable of

Greater Manchester Police told the programme: 'We have had instances where young people go missing – sometimes hundreds of times. If that person has been found, the children's home has minimal staffing and they can't release a member of staff to collect the child, and then they ask us to do the collection. It's not really our job ... but we are the 24 hour service of last resort.'[3]

Charities used to bid for council contracts for childcare, but private equity firms took over. As the charity Social Enterprise UK pointed out in a 2012 report: 'Sovereign and 3i are the big contenders, but it is hard to pinpoint which firm owns what; their waters seem to be in perpetual motion, as they buy one another and take one another over, and offload assets.'[4] These companies operate by buying up cheap housing stock around the country, to which vulnerable children can be shunted. The charity's report found that two London boroughs now have no children's homes at all. There are 101 homes in Lancashire alone, even though Lancashire has a population of less than 1.5 million. London, the report claimed, has 130 homes, for a population of 7.8 million. Ann Coffey MP, quoted in the report, described the movement of children around the care system as 'the most terrible market failure'.

The report also highlights Ofsted figures published in May 2012 which show that children's homes in England – caring for 3,040 boys and 1,800 girls – had reported 631 suspected cases of young residents being sold for sex in the past five years. These are just the reported cases: the true figure is likely to be far higher. So as much as we'd like Rochdale and Oxford to be exceptions that prove the rule, they aren't. And it's not hard to see how the practice of moving vulnerable children around can exacerbate some of the problems they're suffering in their personal lives.[5]

The sector has responded to these criticisms, with the executive officer of the Independent Children's Homes Association claiming that 'the simple connection of cheapness isn't accurate' with regard to the shifting of children.[6] But it's still hard to disagree with Coffey's conclusion that the sector is 'murky to say the least'. As Peter Holbrook, the CEO of Social Enterprise UK, told me in an interview in 2012: 'There's no problem with upscaling if you're doing something like buying paperclips. But most public services rely on human relationships, so upscaling leads to a huge degradation in the quality of service.'[7]

In 2014 the *Guardian*'s Polly Toynbee noticed that Gravity International, a private equity firm, was promising an eighteen percent return on investment in children's care homes. She wrote: 'As soon as I applied online for a brochure, eager Luke, the portfolio manager, called to hard-sell the investment. Caring for these children is highly profitable, he said, with each child worth at least £2,500 and up to £5,500 a week for the multiply disabled, abused and damaged. "The naughtier children pay more," he explained, with a bit of a laugh – though "naughty" might not be in the official social care lexicon.'[8]

According to Toynbee, the brochure indicated: 'UK government restrictions on public spending have had an impact on already overstretched resources of many local authorities, yet they have statutory obligations towards children.' Gravity International seemed to be in a good position to cash in on the situation these authorities found themselves in. As they were unable to raise capital for new housing or repair existing stock, Toynbee claimed, 'the opportunity is there for the company to create new [homes] and buy up current council homes to sell their services back – at this high profit.' Whether offering these services in-house would lead to better or cheaper care is impossible to say and would depend, of course, on the individual council: what matters is that there are private firms whose business model relies on councils' inability to borrow to invest, therefore resorting to outsourcing – it's indicative of a growing trend towards corporate involvement in the sector.

In 2013 we learned, for example, that the government planned to let outsourcing firms bid for social service contracts for vulnerable children in England. One year later, the plans had been shelved, following a huge public outcry. A Department for Education statement read: 'The majority of responses raised concerns with the proposals. By far the most common reason given for this was an objection to the possibility of privatization or profit-making in children's services. The government recognizes the scale of concern in relation to the potential inclusion of a profit-making motive in the proposed range of additional delegable functions – in particular child protection.'[9]

When elderly care goes wrong

In 2012, a group of care workers raised concerns about the Old Deanery, a 93-bed residential care home mainly for the elderly in Braintree, Essex.[10] A subsequent investigation by Essex County Council and the Care Quality Commission found 'woefully inadequate' staffing levels, with residents waiting too long for call bells to be answered. Special measures had been put in place, and new admissions stopped.[11] The plan was for concerns to be addressed – but two years later the BBC went undercover in the home and found little had changed. The resulting episode of *Panorama*, which aired in April 2014, showed shocking scenes of abuse.

Working as a care assistant, the programme's reporter, Alex Lee, used a hidden camera to capture footage during thirty-six shifts at the home. She uncovered many of the same sorts of issues and behaviours reported earlier – some residents being roughly handled, calls for help and assistance being ignored, residents being mocked, shouted at and left in their own excrement for hours. Lee's film showed a woman with dementia, left partially paralysed after a stroke, being slapped by a care worker who had previously been complained about by other residents. The elderly woman was also repeatedly mocked and bullied by other care workers. Viewers also saw cries for assistance from a resident suffering a terminal illness being ignored as she sought help to go to the toilet. Seven employees were suspended.

Anglia Homes claimed that the complaints in 2012 'were made after weekend pay and hours were cut'. But Amy, one of the whistleblowers from 2012, who worked as a care assistant at the Old Deanery, told the broadcaster: 'It was horrible. There was one resident, there'd be a massive puddle on the floor, and the amount of time that people just used to walk past and shrug it off. You wouldn't wanna be treated like that, so why do you treat them like that?'[12]

Given the footage that had been captured, the company's response to the broadcaster was remarkably unapologetic. It said its 'broadcast of what is likely to be highly emotive material [would] give a wholly false view of the home', and that *Panorama* should consider 'the many positive views that have been expressed about the home by residents, their families, commissioners, safeguarding and the [CQC]'.[13] It said the worker who was captured slapping a female resident with dementia had already been demoted and given a final written warning after making inappropriate comments and added it was 'reprehensible that the BBC did not notify us immediately of this alleged incident', noting that some dementia sufferers can be difficult, violent and aggressive. It didn't believe the allegations about the care the woman received 'would be a fair portrayal of this lady and how staff provide care for her'. However, it would later issue an unreserved apology, suspend seven workers, sack one, and hire an independent law firm to carry out a full investigation.[14]

The Old Deanery remains open for business. Indeed, in March 2015 it actually received a relatively positive CQC report.[15]

Regardless of how far Anglia had been misrepresented, the truth is that complaints about Britain's elderly care system had been bubbling under for some time before this media flashpoint. In 2013, there were serious complaints concerning care homes in Scotland, but they received next to no press coverage.

Margaret Hall moved into the Eastbank care home in Glasgow in 2009, due to her dementia. Throughout her time there, her family were concerned. On one occasion they found her lying in a freezing cold bath, shivering, and had to warm her up with a hairdryer. They also said she wasn't given proper care for a mouth infection. They thought of calling the CQC but were worried about her being at the home while an investigation was underway.

Four years later, she died in the Bupa-run home's lounge in agony, at the age of seventy-eight, because the home couldn't provide end-of-life drugs for her. She was found by her daughter, Elizabeth Peebles, who told the *Daily Record*: 'I could instantly see the deathly colour of her. She was holding my hand really tightly, roaring with pain and clutching her chest. You could hear the crackle in her chest.' Peebles was told the necessary painkillers were too expensive to keep at the home.[16]

The Scotland Care Inspectorate had never rated the home better than 'adequate' since 2009, and Mrs Hall's wasn't the first death in similar circumstances. In 2007 Margaret Carroll died at the home after staff failed to notice she'd broken her hip and needed treatment – it was only twelve hours later, after her paramedic son visited, that an ambulance was called. Bupa would eventually write to the family and admit fault.[17]

There has been a surfeit of negative stories about Bupa's Scottish care homes in the past couple of years. In October 2013, the company had to meet with the Scottish health secretary, Alex Neil, after it emerged police were investigating four deaths at another of its homes, Pentland Hill. That year, the charity Compassion in Care (CIC), in partnership with *Private Eye* magazine, found that of the chain's thirty care homes, there were serious failings at ten, and nine more gave cause for concern. The magazine reported on complaints that included a former worker being jailed for 'dragging an 86-year-old across the floor, leaving her bruised and bleeding'.[18] One home, Kirknowe, had been rated 'very good', but the *Eye* found that six complaints from two people had been upheld in 2013, 'two of which related to hydration and nutrition, while there was another to oral care and another to infection control'.[19] As it happens, a year before, the *Daily Record* had reported that a member of staff at the home had been sacked after feeding a dog biscuit to a resident with dementia for a joke.[20]

Private Eye and CIC also looked at Darnley Court in Glasgow, which housed 120 residents. It found a vast array of problems – medication being used as a chemical cosh; a resident slumped over, unable to eat until they called for assistance; and no monitoring of residents at risk of malnutrition – along with seventeen cases of staff misconduct resulting in dismissal or warning. The magazine would go on to claim: 'Rather than properly address Darnley's serious failings, however, Bupa commissioned a glossy in-house "satisfaction" survey so it could claim on its website: "Darnley Court provides exceptional care and support for those requiring long or short term care."'[21]

After detailing a host of other complaints, the *Eye* pointed out that Bupa charges between £550 and £1,200 a week for this service to its care home residents, around seventy percent of

whom are funded by local authorities or the NHS. Bupa made
£637.8 million in profits in 2014.[22] In a statement, Bupa said
that twenty-six of its thirty care homes 'meet or exceed' inspection standards and that the other four 'all have robust action plans
in place and improvements continue to be made', adding that
'over 100,000 people with complex and challenging conditions
have been well looked after in our care homes.'

The problem with whistleblowing

According to the 2012 Adult Social Care Survey, one in three
adults who are in residential care or receiving help at home fear
abuse or physical harm — that's about half a million people.[23]
Many thousands of these people are being cared for in the private
sector — it's hard to get a clear estimate of how much of this
industry has been outsourced, but research suggests around sixty-
five percent of jobs come from the private sector.[24]

I'd been so stunned by the statistic regarding fear of abuse —
along with the CIC/*Private Eye* investigation – that I decided to
get in touch with Eileen Chubb, who runs CIC and helped
Panorama expose the abuse at the Old Deanery, for a piece for
BuzzFeed News. Her story has been told many times before: she
worked at a Bupa care home and lost her job in 1999 after speaking out about the abuse she'd witnessed – but not before she'd
been harassed by senior managers. As a result she set up CIC in
2001, which she continues to run using donations from the
public. She's visited hundreds of homes across the country since
then.

What I wanted to know was her view on whether it was the
increased role of the private sector that was responsible for these
issues. She thought that the same problems would no doubt
happen in the state sector – the real issue was over what happened
once they were detected: 'I believe a lot of the problems I see are

driven by the pursuit of profit, and I've concluded we need a publicly funded care system. I'm not saying that council homes – of which there are very few now – are better; I'm just saying that they have a clear line of accountability.'

She saw the 2011 collapse of care home provider Southern Cross as an example of this: 'I went into sixty of their homes, and could see that the staff had been cut to the bone. At the time of the collapse they were applying to the Department of Health for dignity grants to pay for bedsheets, yet the management got out with millions.'[25] In theory, the private sector rather than the taxpayer should carry financial risk. But there are many ways companies can sidestep this. Take, for example, Winterbourne View, a home for special needs people in which horrific abuse was exposed by *Panorama* in 2011. It was owned by Castlebeck, which was part of a group called CB Care, owned in turn, via Jersey, by a fund called Lydian, which is backed by some Irish billionaires.[26] CB Care makes healthy operating profits, but they disappear in interest payments, leaving the group with annual losses and liabilities exceeding assets by £14 million.[27] And this makes life rather difficult should anyone, say, wish to sue the company over abuse.

Though the company said it had taken out insurance for 'appropriate risks', there was actually no requirement for it to have insurance under the Health and Social Care Act. In 2013, Castlebeck went into administration. The compensation for the abuse uncovered by *Panorama* was paid by the NHS – though it was, according to the families' lawyer, a 'modest amount'. A statement from the lawyer said:

> The civil law system is woefully deficient when it comes to
> determining what is fair compensation for vulnerable people
> who have been injured, but who are unable to explain and
> recount their experiences or relate what impact abuse and

ill-treatment has had on them. It is impossible to translate their experiences into the types of financial losses you would normally recover for someone with capacity who has suffered a personal injury, such as loss of earnings.[28]

Chubb believes that abuse occurs because people are scared of the institutions within which they work:

> Around seventy percent of the whistleblowers who approach me come from the healthcare sector. They don't go public because they don't feel they have legal protection – they certainly don't feel they get it under PIDA [the Public Institution Disclosure Act, which claims to protect whistle-blowers from being mistreated by their employers, and under which Chubb's dismissal was the first case to launch]. You have to protect the protectors: we're living in a country where people feel it's not safe to speak out. I was assaulted at work and was in fear of what was to come. People deserve better than to know their credibility will be attacked.[29]

Chubb also claimed she'd been offered jobs by big care home providers, 'to get me off their backs. I don't believe you can take money from the industry. All our money comes from the public. Last year we survived on less than Maria Miller [the former culture minister who was sacked over her expenses] claimed. I didn't want this to be my life, but once I blew the whistle, I realized that no one else was going to do it.'[30]

And here's a story that illustrates why the introduction of a profit incentive means we need even more transparency. In 2013 the River View care centre in Reading, run by the European Care Group, saw people moved into community hospitals after an NHS nurse raised an alert that there weren't enough properly trained staff there. Devon County Council and Devon NHS put an embargo on sending residents to the home from the NHS and began working with police and the CQC. While this was going on, the centre was still taking on private patients – and charging £700 a week to do so. The issue was resolved, but the public was none the wiser.[31]

Concern surrounding what happens when the profit incentive is introduced extends beyond care homes to home visits. More than 300,000 care workers are on zero-hours contracts, tied to an employer essentially without any employment rights. As Vidhya Alakeson has written in the *Guardian*: 'Coupled with other features of domiciliary care, such as the growth in 15-minute visits and inadequate payments for travel time, the dominance of zero-hours contracts raises real questions about the extent to which today's insecure workforce can deliver care that treats older and disabled people with dignity and respect.'[32]

Just over half of local authority funded visits last thirty minutes, and workers spend twenty percent of their time travelling between homes, according to LaingBuisson, a firm of healthcare analysts.[33] In 2013 one only needed look at the jobs for carers advertised on the Universal Jobmatch website to see how much of an issue it is. There were hundreds of jobs which, while being advertised above minimum wage, didn't pay for travel. Due to transport costs, a carer could work from 7:30 A.M. to 12:30 P.M. (without being paid for a lunch break), providing thirty minutes of care for each of six clients, and end up being paid little more than £18 for their five hours.[34] There's confusion as to how the lack of minimum wage can be policed – the website is run by the Department for Work and Pensions, but the Department of Business, Innovation and Skills is responsible for enforcing it. It's clear time spent travelling on business counts as time worked for minimum wage purposes, if not to or from the carer's home.[35]

The UK Home Care association told *Private Eye,* which initially reported on the problem, that this was due to cost-cutting measures by local authorities pushing providers' charges down. But the issue was still unsolved in January 2014, when the magazine found that the DWP's website – which we'll look at in more detail shortly – had much the same problem.[36] It interviewed Sheila, an assistant in the north-east of England, who'd been twice sacked from a care job after she witnessed abuse.

The magazine reported that her £6.50 rate was theoretically 19p above the then minimum wage, but she wasn't paid for the time spent travelling. It said she was on a zero-hours contract, so she had no control over her working week or budget. She could work forty-two hours a week or twelve; she could finish one day at 11 P.M., but be back on call at 7 A.M. the next day. Another jobseeker, the magazine reported, rang Care UK about a position offering £6.75 an hour. This was 44p above the minimum wage, but journeys between homes could take half an hour – with petrol costs reaching 20p a mile, they could spend half a day working for nothing. Added to that must be the cost of six unpaid training days and a £44 enhanced Criminal Records Bureau check. This issue was brought into sharper relief in August that year, when fifty workers at Care UK, which took over services for people with learning difficulties in Doncaster from the NHS, staged 'one of the longest ever strikes in the history of the health service' (according to the *Guardian*) after wages were cut by thirty-five percent and a hundred workers were brought in on £7 an hour.[37]

Care and local government

Of all the cuts made by central government, those to social care are perhaps the hardest to quantify, because budgets are largely administered by local councils. In May 2013 the Association of Directors of Adult Social Services warned that a 'bleak outlook' was becoming 'bleaker', after its research showed £800 million was to be taken from the central budget that year.[38] But that central cut was only part of the picture. Around the country councils are looking for ways to make savings under the radar. And outsourcing is as much an option for local government as it is for the national one.

Five years ago, in a survey by *Community Care*, the journal for social care, respondents said the transfer of social care services from councils to private providers has been bad for the sector. Two thirds said the quality of adult care had deteriorated because of the amount of outsourcing since the early 1990s.[39] Of course, they would say that, and the champions of outsourcing would argue quality has been unaffected and money saved in the main. But what's perhaps more important is that while chipping away at local budgets doesn't generate the media coverage of a governmental department cut, it does have just as much impact on the people who use that service.

In 2013 I covered a story about one council's social care disaster, and it made me question whether there was an endemic problem in the way local government deals with these services. The tale begins in 2011, when Tory-run Barnet council in north London, as part of a radical experiment in privatization, put around £600 million of services out to tender. Residents and trade unions challenged it in the High Court, and lost their case in 2013 only after a judge ruled it had come too late to be considered; however, he also found that the council had 'never set out to consult about its outsourcing'.[40]

The *Guardian* gave us a glimpse of how this new-look council operated:

For those who live and work in Barnet, their local affairs are now handled remotely by people hundreds of miles away, who know nothing about them or the area. Payroll for what remains of council staff is done in Belfast, while for schools it's Carlisle. Pension queries go to Darlington. Benefits end up in Blackburn … Got a complaint? Then you have speak to someone you'll never see – that is, if you can speak to them at all.[41]

The council created a so-called local authority trading company called the Barnet Group, which would run housing and services for adults. The Barnet Group had two subsidiaries: Your Choice, which would offer disability services, and Barnet Homes, which would manage 15,000 homes across the borough.[42]

The journalist Kate Belgrave and I got in touch with a local, John Sullivan, who'd been campaigning against the results of the scheme. He felt his daughter, Susan, a young lady with Down's syndrome, had been left short-changed as a result. He told us the name Your Choice was deeply ironic: 'There was no consultation. We expected letters and so forth: in fact we never got a single phone call to tell us what was going on.' But hopes were high. The new company would apparently turn a profit. Kate showed me a series of business documents which presupposed the Barnet Group would have a surplus of £½ million by year four.[43] But there was very little detail as to how Your Choice would generate profits – the originating documents mentioned 'generating business from a wider group of services users including other local authority areas, self-funders, and other vulnerable people', but it seemed unlikely that disabled people around London would be travelling to Barnet to pay to visit the outsourced day centre and residential facilities.[44]

John told us he'd never been impressed with the plans: 'The first meeting for residents was a disaster. We asked what the plan was for the middle of winter. It was clear there was no structure – Susan would be dragged around a series of shops and garden centres. She needs two things – continuity, and her friends: the people she's been friends with since they were kids.'

It seemed the only group doing any risk assessment at all was the trade union local branch, which commissioned an academic, Dexter Whitfield, to look into the plan. The council dismissed his report as trade union propaganda. His conclusions were certainly favourable to the union. Whitfield wrote: 'The business plan concedes that the Your Choice company is financially vulnerable. There is no assurance provided on the quality or reliability of data and assumptions used.' There was no evidence that the plans to generate business from other service users would work, and even if there was, he pointed out, 'Ethical and moral issues concerning why adult services should be expected to have such high level of profitability are absent from the business case and the report to cabinet.'[45]

The trouble was, Whitfield's report was accurate. One year after it was published, unions and staff were presented with a redundancy consultation document by Barnet Council. Of course, the council's consultation language was rather muted: 'If no changes are made with regard to efficiencies, the change from a block contract to payment-by-actual would create a gap of approximately £1m. This does not necessarily mean that people have stopped using [the] service, but rather that the arrangements for the block contract did not accurately reflect day-to-day usage.'[46] It essentially seemed to claim that the reason behind the £1 million debt wasn't the business plan, but the high levels of wages. Barnet Homes would give Your Choice a loan, and in the meantime Your Choice proposed 'to radically change the structure, review its enhancement payment practices and review salary structure to be able to compete within the sector and to fully meet our aspirations of flexible, personalized and value for money services'.

This document was never shown to the people like John and Susan Sullivan who used the service. It described 'staffing' changes, rather than changes to the service itself. The company admitted, however, that workers in its supported living services were to be downgraded to an 'assistant support worker role', because the 'wide variety' of tasks they carried out were 'not complex'.

When we interviewed John Sullivan, he was furious:

> It's bloody immoral. I've had run-ins with politicians before. But they could see the reality in front of them. These guys have no integrity. They denied profit was a motive, then they predicated their plan on making profit, and now it's all about savings. In order to keep skilled staff it would cost a few pence every week. If someone asked the people of Barnet what they wanted I don't think they'd have a problem with that money being spent.

After Belgrave and I had written up our piece about the fiasco, we approached Barnet Council, who told us: 'We are pursuing a robust new business strategy, as detailed in the Operational Plan 2013/2014. We recognize that this process will take time to fully materialize.' But, as we responded, 'Parents and families, needless to say, have no faith in this claim of a viable business model at all. And after a year, who can blame them?'[47] We also asked what would happen if Your Choice continued to fail – would the services be brought in-house? The company replied: 'We would be disappointed if this were to happen as we believe we have a viable business model, quality services and can offer value for money.'

Barnet's trade union issued a statement: 'You can't downgrade staff jobs and cut staff numbers like this without causing real instability in the workforce.' Shortly after our article was published, Belgrave heard that residents and users were going to lobby the Your Choice board. She went to the meeting, and witnessed an extraordinary scene. Family members and carers were asked to leave the room because the board was about to discuss confidential items on the agenda. They asked what the titles of the items were, and were told they too were confidential.

A row kicked off, and the chair of the board walked out of the meeting. Belgrave caught him on camera saying, when asked why he wasn't listening to the families that were present, 'This is a board meeting of a company. It is not a local authority meeting and therefore that right does not extend.' At which point one audience member said: 'This is exactly our problem with our services being outsourced.' We made much the same point when we updated our story: councillors don't walk out of meetings or hide behind 'confidential' items on agendas, and they can be held to account at the ballot box.

A few weeks later, we were able to report that Your Choice had backed down and promised to consult with families and service users before going ahead with any changes. It was a testimony to the way that authorities can be pressured into rethinking the decision to outsource. One reason was that Susan Sullivan was eligible for legal aid. That was why her father had been able to make a legal threat on her behalf. [48]

The saga of Barnet's outsourcing project encapsulates four main themes that have emerged thus far in our journey through the industry. Two of them go hand in hand: accountability and transparency. Once a private company is brought in – or in the case of Your Choice, created – the entire dynamic in the provision of services is changed. It's simply impossible to apportion blame and seek justice when things go wrong if it's not possible to know who's responsible for a mistake: that can only happen when there's transparency. But transparency is more important than simply being a means to deliver accountability. It's about how we work out why the government has made the decisions it has, and about whether we as voters can judge those decisions as being good or bad. That leads to another theme: political influence. Are the motivations by which politicians make those decisions born of ideology, evidence or something rather more concerning – and do they have the best interest of the public at heart? And that leads to the final theme: market failure. Whatever their motivations, how far are politicians constrained in the decisions they make by the options available to them?

7

Accountability

So far in this book, we've consistently seen people – often vulnerable people – being let down by agents of the state. But the obvious question, which we've not really touched on until now, is: whose fault is it? Moreover, how does one determine whose fault it is? And it's obvious that the outsourcing process, by its very nature, often makes this a difficult question to answer.

Take immigration – we could point to any number of errors and mistakes within Britain's asylum system and it would be a challenge to apportion blame. We saw this when we looked at notorious cases like Jimmy Mubenga's death, but it's the same story regarding less well-known misdemeanours. For example, when in October 2013 we heard that 140 people had complained after receiving text messages mistakenly accusing them of being illegal immigrants and asking them to leave Britain (among them Suresh Grover, a veteran civil rights campaigner who has lived in the UK since 1966), it was initially hard to tell whether it was the fault of the Home Office, or Capita, the company that had been sending the messages on the Home Office's behalf.

It was later revealed that the company was given the phone numbers in 'regular data drops of information detailing applications with a negative outcome on the Home Office immigration database', and so in a familiar pattern the target of campaigners' anger was split between both government and contractor.[1]

And consider the work capability assessment (WCA), which we looked at in Chapter 3. We explored the issues with the way Atos approached the job, but we only really touched on the Department for Work and Pensions' (DWP) culpability. In February 2013 the House of Commons public accounts committee delivered an excoriating report on the debacle and revealed that, quite apart from the problems with the company, there had in fact been a huge failure of management at a governmental level. The committee concluded that the majority of problems lay with the DWP rather than with Atos.

In a statement it said:

> The Work Capability Assessment process is designed to support a fair and objective decision by the department about whether a claimant is fit for work, but in far too many cases the department is getting these decisions wrong at considerable cost to both the taxpayer and the claimant. Decision-making causes claimants considerable distress, and the position appears to be getting worse, with Citizens Advice reporting an 83% increase in the number of people asking for support on appeals in the last year alone.

The committee placed the blame for this squarely at the feet of the department, which it found 'unduly complacent' about how many appeals were upheld by tribunal – it was failing in its delivery of 'accurate decision-making' and in 'minimizing distress to claimants'.[2]

Committee chair Margaret Hodge gave an additional statement in which she singled out the fact that the DWP had failed to 'create a competitive market for medical assessment providers'

– so Atos had inadvertently become a monopoly supplier. On top of that, the DWP was simply accepting what Atos told it – in Hodge's words: 'It seems reluctant to challenge the contractor. It has failed to withhold payment for poor performance and rarely checked that it is being correctly charged.' And it was failing to hold the company to account for its poor performance: 'The Department also cannot explain how the profits being made by Atos reflect the limited risk that it bears.'[3]

Indeed, as the years went by and the negative stories mounted up, Atos itself was keener and keener to point out the DWP's role in designing the WCA, never more notably than in October 2013, when the BBC learned that Islington Council had written to ministers saying the assessment's performance had been 'shocking' after eighty-seven percent of appeals by its residents were won (the council's letter to Iain Duncan Smith, the work and pensions secretary, actually identified both the simplicity of the test and the inexperience of the Atos assessors as the main reasons for the figure).[4]

So the overriding impression is that blame for the WCA can be evenly divided between the government and Atos – with the proviso that the company isn't obliged to disclose any information about the contract, and commercial confidentiality laws restrict a great deal of potential information that could be released. A cynic would say it wasn't in either party's interests for all the facts to be made clear.

In other outsourcing fiascos involving the DWP, it seems unfair to blame the contractor at all. Take the Universal Jobmatch website. This is a website for jobseekers, who are compelled to use it under threat of benefits sanctions. But it has been littered with fake job postings that were put up in order to trick jobseekers into handing over money or personal details. Those wishing to prove how poorly regulated it is could point to the fake jobs discovered by the *Guardian* in 2012 – 'an MI6 "target elimination specialist", "international couriers" to work for CosaNostra Holdings, as well as listings for pornographic websites'. As the paper pointed out, this is pretty shocking for a project that apparently cost £17 million.[5] Following that report, we learned that the DWP had removed over 120,000, or one fifth, of all job adverts from more than 180 employer accounts, because the ads did not abide by the site's terms and conditions.[6]

The website is run by jobs firm Monster. However, in 2013 we learned that two other companies that bid for the contract, one called Steria and another called Methods, had complained to the DWP about the way Monster won. Steria's complaint was addressed by running the tender again, but Methods started a legal challenge. It transpires the company was eventually paid off to keep the whole thing from turning into a noisy public dispute.[7] Methods wouldn't say how much taxpayers' money had come their way, but Simon Jones, a government transparency campaigner, found that DWP accounts for 2012/13 included mention of a payment of £950,000 to 'compensate a supplier for reasonable costs incurred in connection with procurement activities'. In March 2014 we learned that the department planned to scrap the website when the contract came up for renewal.

Stephen O'Donnell, who runs the National Online Recruitment Awards, told the *Guardian* that Monster was 'exercised' with how the website had turned out: while the company had made 'very good money' on the contract, the fact it was a 'real mongrel of a website' wasn't the company's fault. He said:

> Monster . . . have real expertise worldwide in building spectacular job boards. They more or less invented the industry. So you do think 'How come it's so bad?' The reason for that is the

civil servants basically told Monster 'Forget everything you know about job boards, this is what we want' ... I think it's criminally unfair to sanction jobseekers for not using such a clumsily built website, rife with spammers ... identity thieves and anonymous job ads.[8]

There were still some problems with the site in August 2014: *Channel 4 News* obtained a ten-page document from the National Audit Office entitled 'The Universal Jobmatch System and Bogus and Non-Compliant Postings', which stated that there was 'still no formal guidance on the depth or nature' of the checks performed on firms advertising on the Jobmatch service.[9] The government, for its part, stressed that any problems came from a minority, that more than half a million employers had registered with the system and that there were almost five million job searches a day.

A couple of months before *Channel 4 News*'s revelations, we learned that plans had been drawn up to shut the website down in 2016.[10] As one campaigner argued: 'The appalling thing about this decision is that it shows that they intend to continue forcing unemployed people to use a hopelessly flawed system for the next two years, simply because they don't want to suffer the PR disaster of shutting it down early and having to compensate Monster for breach of contract.'[11]

So the answer is simple: sometimes things go wrong because of contractors, sometimes it's almost entirely the government department's fault, and most of the time it's a combination of the two. But what's most important is that if blame for poor performance often seems difficult to disentangle between state and private contractor, that's hardly helped by the mechanisms we have in place to assess such projects.

How do we try to find out where blame lies?

The issue of accountability and the question about what happens when the government introduces a profit incentive into state services are closely related: when mistakes happen, it's natural to wonder if they've been made because companies are trying to save money.

I interviewed Mark Fox of the British Services Association, a policy and research organization devoted to improving public and private sector projects, about this issue. I flagged up the cases of fraud in the Work Programme we discussed in Chapter 3.

'Where will you be having lunch?' he asked.

'I don't know,' I replied.

'You'll get a sandwich from Sainsbury's or something?'

'Probably.'

'Right, and will you care who made it . . .?'

I began to stutter an answer, but Fox continued:

This is the point. The point about the profit is, do you care how much profit Sainsbury's makes on the sandwich you eat? I doubt you'd give it a nanosecond of thought. What I do think you mind about is whether you've got the sandwich so you can eat it when you want it. The fundamental thing is about management – it's about managing these companies, rigorously and effectively, so they deliver what it is, when they've agreed to do it, to the budget they've agreed. The procuring person is responsible and accountable. Beyond that, you can't have inappropriate behaviour if you're managed properly. If you weren't managed, who knows what you'd get up to. This stuff is not at all complicated. It's rather boringly uncomplicated in that sense.

But is it? It's hardly Fox's job to account for the actions of government over the last decade, but recent history suggests that the quality of management has been hugely lacking in that time.

And when I interviewed Tom Gash from the Institute for Government, a think tank that aims to promote more effective governance, he told me that not enough money is spent by the government on oversight. It simply doesn't employ enough people to oversee the firms it's contracted: 'People don't factor in the cost, but the story of the last ten years is that the government hasn't spent enough,' he said.

We've seen numerous examples – think of the Olympics scandal described at the start of this book – of how false the savings can be when things go wrong. Gash expressed his concern, in that regard, over the probation contract: 'If I'm sitting in the Ministry of Justice, how will I really know if these providers are doing a good job, and once I've worked that out, are the costs of oversight going to be proportionate to the gains I get from people competing?'

And the truth is that the government generally seems less worried about the answers to such questions than you might think. Above all, there's very little by way of systems in place for when you have a catastrophe of Olympics 2012 proportions. While the Treasury will approve the business case for an outsourcing project, it doesn't really provide any kind of ongoing scrutiny based on its performance.

That task generally falls to the government's Major Projects Authority (MPA), a body that has been created to give 'assurance' to big projects like the Work Programme by assessing their progress. It has a risk register where it grades the projects on a traffic light system of red, amber or green, depending on how well they're going – according to the Cabinet Office website, a red ranking means: 'Successful delivery of the project appears to be unachievable. There are major issues on project definition, schedule, budget, quality and/or benefits delivery, which at this stage do not appear to be manageable or resolvable. The project may need re-scoping and/or its overall viability reassessed.' At the time of writing, there are 188 projects in the MPA's portfolio, and barely a third of them are rated green.[12]

As Gash put it to me:

> This narrative about the government being risk averse is untrue. It's risk averse about small-scale risk. In terms of wider systemic risk it's quite risk loving, it does all these huge, complex programmes. Look at the MPA risk register – what company would have a portfolio with a whole bunch of projects in red or amber? So who is managing this risk? Who's managing our learning process? Well, no one ... There are all these projects that are red getting approved, so what's the point?

He went on to point out: 'Look at Tesco – every change to store format is tested. If we're going to have the most centralized system of government in the world – as we do – why wouldn't we test different working models?'

Gash singled out the Department for Transport – in spite of the various criticisms that have been made of its various rail franchises – as managing this risk better than some other departments: 'They do rolling cycles. If you look at the deal on which they lost £100 million [the East Coast Main Line] – if they'd done every region at the same time they'd have lost £600 million, so at least they're managing certain types of risk.'

I suggested to Mark Fox that there is simply no way to give effective oversight of a complicated human activity like probation and that the risk – of fraudulent behaviour by the companies on the one hand and of a bad service on the other – is impossible to quantify. He defaulted to his previous point: essentially, responsibility always had to come back to the government:

I would say to you, outsourcing is fine as far as it goes. You can take the view everything can be outsourced. I would say it's about quality and effectiveness of management. If you've worked as a freelance journalist, you're working for a news editor. Their job is to manage you to deliver copy. Whether you're staff or freelance is immaterial to the quality of the copy. I'd say the same – we obsess about who it is, whether it's charity or state or private. The question is about whether it's managed effectively and that actually the customer – in this case the taxpayer – is getting what they want in a way that they find acceptable. Now that's what we wrestle with, all of us, in the private, voluntary and state sectors. So do you know how many bins are collected by the state across London? None. Do we care? No, because we're not wading through rubbish.

Fine, I said, but bin collection is rather different to, say, probation. Fox said: 'When dealing with probation you're dealing with tricky, sensitive stuff ... We're talking about sensitive areas that aren't delivered perfectly as they are. We have to be really confident we've got the right management processes in place.'

I took issue with this, and told him that the probation service had always met the targets it had been set. Fox replied:

I'm not going to argue – people with experience tend to do the same jobs in the private sector and bring their experience to bear. Myself, I'm not in an argument with people who deliver services. My members will only offer services in areas where they've been asked to bid for contracts. We can, and I can, go to people and say 'Look, if you're interested in outsourcing this we can offer it across a range of services'. But I can't make anyone do it, I can't strongarm government, at local or national level, to do these things. There's no compulsion, it's a political will or desire.

Fundamentally, the only difference between Gash and Fox – and this is something I would find fascinating as I looked back over my notes – was that the latter seemed to have rather more faith in the workings of government. Gash was keen to highlight flaws in its management of contracts. Fox's only real professional responsibility as far as his interview with me went – and even then, it was hardly an obligation – was to portray the firms we've read about thus far in a favourable light. So it was interesting how many positive things he also had to say on the political process:

> The responsibility government has to deliver a range of complex services is absolutely awesome. Amazing. It's easy to knock public sector procurers and ministers and it makes good copy and it's good fun. But the truth is most services, most days of the week, most weeks of the year are delivered in a way most people most of the time find useful. Do we get instant response to everything we want? No. But we know it's OK. We experience it. You've travelled on a bus or tube run by a mixture of private and state companies, you've walked on clean streets. You live your life with a range of services provided by all sorts of people.

Of course, the thing that's left out of all this is that while outsourcing itself isn't an ideology, the decision to outsource most assuredly can be born of one. Fox acknowledged this: 'You can't take away the political dimension unlike when it's a procurement by a private sector firm; you always have the political dimension to it ... to pretend that you can make these things neutral is wrong, it seems to me.' But what we've seen so far over the course of this book is that the political ideology among our main parties when it comes to outsourcing is strikingly homogenous. That's why our politicians rarely have an answer when things go wrong – indeed, find it particularly hard at times (the WCA being a prime example) to mount effective cross-party criticism.

But then perhaps that doesn't matter so much if you're willing to take Fox's view that many problems in the outsourcing process are the result of Britain's innovation in the use of outsourcing: 'In this country we're doing these things for the first time. We're working out how we do this stuff. It's obviously the case as you're doing things for the first time you make mistakes. You won't write your copy for this interview and say "Bang, first time". You'll sit and work at it, and this is what needs to happen. You go through processes.'

I asked him about the fact that, outside the political divisions, government can still be impotent, as when it gets tied into long-term contracts. I gave the WCA as an example. 'Well, it is what it is, isn't it? Anyway, if government's determined to not do a thing it won't do it. Government is an almighty power. If government is set on doing a thing, it will do it, and thank God because they're the only thing between us and the chief of the general staff. They may not do everything that I like. But that they are entitled to do this on my behalf I do not dispute. Government will have its way.'

But this isn't always true. Did government have its way when it had to draft in troops for the Olympics, or when it had to replace the companies it had wanted to work on, say, WCA or tagging? It may well have eventually recouped any lost money, but it's a long way from a positive result. And this gives rise to another simple question.

Why do we outsource?

The honest answer to this question, so far as politicians go, is obvious. We outsource because it saves money. Of course, you will hear other reasons from politicians about bringing in expertise and increasing innovation and all the rest, but the most common explanation you'll hear from them is that it has saved money.

But does it? However absurd this might sound, it's pretty much impossible to say. One researcher, John Seddon at the consultancy Vanguard, thinks not. His work draws on public and voluntary sector studies, tracking individuals who are using outsourced services. In the words of Richard Vize from the website Public Procurement Insider, this means it 'encourages service providers to think in terms of individual needs and underlying causes – debt, relationship breakdown, mental illness and so on – rather than the big numbers of standardized transactions'.[13] As a result of his research, Seddon believes a scheme like the Work Programme will never address the root cause of a problem; it'll only generate more and more transactions. He's not alone; the academic Dexter Whitfield has found much the same.

I asked Mark Fox if 'his guys' could conclusively prove they can save money. No, he replied:

It's not just about saving money, it's about how you make use of people, it's about configuring them in different ways. [Your question about savings] is unprovable – because you can't tell me how much the public sector spends on delivering a service. Why? Because records aren't kept . . . What I can show you is that often at the point a contract has begun, money can be saved – or not, because it's not the *raison d'être* of all contracts, to save money . . . Sixty percent of what my members do is business to business – there [are] plenty of things there where they're being asked to deliver things in different ways. If you use the voluntary sector, say, to deliver services, they can do it in ways that [the] government might find interesting use for.

Fox was, like many champions of outsourcing, keen to stress that saving money was only one part of the equation, but there's still no doubt that it is *the* major selling point for the government. As one insider, who didn't want to be named, told me: 'Money's bloody tight. You can have sophisticated discussions about value but above all, you've got a legal requirement on the part of politicians to balance the books.'

A number of insiders will tell you that, rather like the stock market, the outsourcing project depends just as much on confidence as it does on hard data. The same source told me:

It's really difficult with this stuff to demonstrate value for money. With transactional stuff you can demonstrate savings but with any part of public services it's devilishly difficult to prove you've taken money from the system. Staff cuts are really the only way you can. My belief is that it absolutely does save money on things like, say, environmental services, but it's much more difficult to nail that conclusively for other things.

Tom Gash was inclined to take a similar line:

When you're talking about government outsourcing and doing a deal for the first time, you've got this easy-to-measure thing, cost, and this hard-to-measure thing, quality. It's not just hard to measure, it's a bit invisible. You've got a bunch of professionals who know their careers will advance if they can prove they've saved a certain amount of money – irrespective that it could end up costing a lot more in the long run.

The focus is a cheap initial deal. And then [on the companies' side] to make your money over time through change requests [i.e. asking for more money by modifying the contract or adding additional services to it] and also just knowing that focus is on the initial deal but the value-for-money oversight over time is weaker. You've [also] got the problems around political cycles: projects become orphaned, as you saw with E-Borders.

E-Borders, it's worth noting, was a true fiasco. In 2015 the Home Office was forced to pay the IT firm Raytheon more than £224 million for the breach of its contract after sacking the firm from the project in 2010. Ministers had said that 'key milestones had been missed and parts of the programme were running at least a year late,' and that they had 'no confidence' in the firm. The decision had been made by the London Court of International Arbitration (LCIA) – a private court set up by the City of London and distinct from British state courts – which doesn't publish its findings. The Home Office managed to get the decision overturned, but Raytheon appealed by saying the British courts should not question the LCIA's judgments, and in the end a settlement of £150 million was reached.[14] Home secretary Theresa May would later describe this horror show as 'a mess with no attractive options', and told us that all 'other alternatives available to the government would have led to greater costs'.[15]

Gash described how political accountability becomes dissipated as a result: 'You get this dynamic where politicians like to lock in the party that follows them in. In practice that doesn't factor in the fact that politicians will often pay a high price to do what they want and still might cancel the contract. If you spent more time proving these things actually worked and created the flexibility to allow people to change it in the way they wanted, that would be better.'

His organization has carried out research on when government should and shouldn't contract. He said:

> We looked at the characteristics of services and asked if it was possible to do it. I'm more and more convinced that in services where it's easy to observe quality, where there aren't natural monopolies, where you have a degree of policy certainty . . . and demand stability – it's reasonable to outsource provision. Where that doesn't apply, and you've got all sorts of different types of problems, it becomes difficult to create anything like a complete contract.

So why do we outsource? Consider Mark Fox's closing words on the industry:

> People get vexed and heated. But outsourcing is a mechanism. It's not an ideology, it's not a philosophy, it's not a noble enterprise: it's a mechanism . . . It can happen in a variety of ways, in partnerships in all sorts of things, and it's a useful tool for private and public sector procurers. Is it a platinum bullet to solve all ills? No. Is it just a cost-cutting measure? I would resist that interpretation and understanding. Can it deliver good things? Yes and it does. Will things go wrong? Yes of course, but they already do.

It's possible to agree with that interpretation, and still feel that there are serious flaws in the way the mechanism he described works, and that it's too easily used to dodge accountability. It also neatly dodges my aforementioned point that there's an ideology behind the decision to use this mechanism – an ideology that always assumes savings can be made, even when there's evidence to the contrary. It's also a school of thought that has become accepted political wisdom under Thatcher, Major, Blair, Brown and Cameron. All have run schemes, such as payment by results, that deep down assume individuals working in these sectors are more likely to be motivated to deliver a good service by money than any other incentives.

You'd be amazed by how virulent the government can be in its desire to insulate the process from media criticism. In July 2014 the work and pensions select committee delivered a new report on the WCA and employment support allowance system. It said the problems were so grave that simply 'rebranding' the assessment by appointing a new contractor would not solve the problems. Dame Anne Begg MP, the committee's chair, said: 'We know that the redesign can't happen overnight, but the current system needs to be improved now, because it is clearly causing claimants considerable distress and anxiety.'[16]

The report also confirmed that a backlog of 700,000 assessments had been allowed to build up: in large part it seemed this was due to the system of face-to-face assessments, which had finally been scrapped in April that year following a review (the fourth independent review commissioned by the government since the policy's inception). It made clear that it wasn't just the test itself that was failing: it was the whole process of assessment.

Upon the report's release, I wrote a feature for BuzzFeed News about the history of the WCA. A press officer from the DWP emailed my news editor and claimed: 'The journalist clearly has a political agenda (quoting at least six Labour MPs).' It struck me as a remarkably aggressive intervention from a government (rather than a political party) press office: they'd sought to portray me to my boss as some sort of left-wing activist purely for questioning whether the ideology behind the scheme was misguided. And as it happened, most of the quotes I cited were from a debate in 2013 where there were complaints aired across the board: I could have used lines from a number of Liberal Democrat or Conservative politicians if I'd wanted. I told the press officer that if there was a robust defence of the WCA out there from a minister I'd have included it. There wasn't one, and there still isn't.

There's another question about why we outsource. Given that the profits seem to be lower when working for the state and there's a danger of hugely damaging media coverage, what's the attraction for the companies? Mark Fox said:

You'd have to ask them. But sixty percent of this sector – and growing – is business to business. But that's not the bit people take notice of. There's also an international sector, which Britain happens to be good at and leads development and technique round the world. In the public sector it's interesting because the state delivers incredibly complex and difficult services and does things no other provider could do and that's important and we're lucky. But it's a human activity. Provision of services will go wrong as they go right.

He cited a recent scandal that had broken around the time we carried out the interview – the failure to protect children in Rotherham from abuse over a decade – and compared the accountability in that situation:

No one's resigning. If it had been a private provider people would be going down like ninepins so we just have to be a little bit careful about this. The primary deliverer – in your case the state – has a huge responsibility to procure effectively and to manage robustly. And it doesn't matter whether the people they're managing are employed by the state, a charity or a private company. It's immaterial, it seems to me. And do not run away with the idea that charities make any less money than private sector companies. They may call it surplus, it may run into administration costs, but it's exactly the same principle. They do it because it's a commercial activity.

There are a couple of things to note here. First, his assertion that private providers would see people 'going down like ninepins' seems a little questionable: did the head of G4S face the sack over the Olympics scandal? More to the point, had he faced the sack, would the electorate have had any direct part to play in the decision? His second point about charities is intriguing, however. Anyone who has spent time dealing with the sector knows that there's some truth to what he said: it has in some areas become monopolized by 'big beasts': five percent of the UK's registered charities receive eighty-five percent of the money that British people donate.[17] And in terms of how certain projects operate – like, for example, probation – hiring a huge charity could be just as problematic as hiring a huge outsourcing firm. How much innovation would they really bring to the table? Do they really, for example, understand the local area and the specific social pressures that increase the risk of a client committing crime again?

On the whole, however, the biggest concern is over the private companies. Part of it comes out of the way they've evolved. As another Whitehall insider, who didn't wish to be named, told me: 'What was interesting about early transactional companies is you had these huge companies, mostly French, who really knew their stuff. Now they think they can turn their hands to anything, and you're massively ramping up the risk. How do you measure that risk and how do you balance off the risk and rewards?' But at the same time, as pro-outsourcing commentators repeatedly told me throughout the research for this book, Britain's use of private companies is pioneering. It means all sorts of things can go wrong. And at present, when they do, they take place in an environment where there are questions over accountability that make the entire system seem corrupt. Is it? Perhaps not, but it's far harder to say than it need be.

8

Transparency

The question of accountability goes hand in hand with the issue of transparency: it simply isn't possible to have one without the other; both are absolutely central to good governance. In our initial survey of the asylum industry we looked at the death of Jimmy Mubenga. We saw how there was muddiness over the question of who, exactly, was to blame. There was another question we didn't ask: what form would the news of his death have taken had the *Guardian* not picked up on a few tweets?

One would certainly hope, in a functioning democracy, that all of the details would eventually come out in the manner they did: through official inquiries. But think also of the details we still aren't allowed to know regarding that story – in fact never mind us: the details that frontbench politicians aren't allowed to know.

Several years after Mubenga died, shadow justice minister Sadiq Khan would reveal a detail about the case that had not been reported. Announcing a new Labour policy on Freedom of Information, he wrote:

The inquest [into Mubenga's death] prompted me to write to G4S, Serco, Sodexo and GEOAmey – the four companies responsible for most of the Home Office and Ministry of

Justice work involving detaining and transporting suspects and criminals. I sought information on their staff training in the use of restraint. In my correspondence, I asked for the information under the provisions of the FoI Act.

The range of responses I received was eye opening. Serco responded in the most detail, closely followed by Sodexo. GEOAmey refused to divulge any information, instead directing my request to the Ministry of Justice. G4S did not provide any information directly, instead mentioning that the Ministry of Justice and Home Office would respond formally. Unfortunately, neither did.[1]

This lack of transparency is particularly true in the case of Yarl's Wood detention centre. Of course, it would be very difficult to have a standard of detention that was found acceptable by those held in it. And we should also note there has never been – if we are to believe repeated inspections – any kind of endemic culture of sexual abuse there. As we saw, many problems – such as the fact that women are held in detention for unduly long amounts of time – are due to chaotic governance, not the agents of the state.

But look at all the stories we heard in Chapter 2 regarding the centre and female detention – in particular, look at how they were revealed. In the case of Roseline Akhalu's treatment in a Reliance van it was through a social media campaign later reported on by journalists. A combination of journalists and campaigners were the people who brought the mistreatment and sexual assault of women in detention to light. The standard process of state inspection had little part to play in how the public found out about these issues.

Experts I spoke to about the aura of secrecy surrounding asylum detention were divided on why it exists. As one pointed out to me, it simply wouldn't be in any contractor's interest to offer a service that was entirely inhumane, because there's a threat of losing contracts if there's too much unrest or too many protests. The fact that the outsourcing process adds an extra layer of confidentiality (for example, Serco's internal report on the sexual abuse in Yarl's Wood would, in a public institution, be instantly viewable) was – in the eyes of most experts I spoke to – a convenient coincidence.

And in the case of this centre, what we can see is an institution that has had many problems and which has been incredibly slow to improve. It really shouldn't be that difficult to run an institution in which the male guards don't enter into sexual relationships with the vulnerable women they're supposed to be guarding, yet this seems to have happened since at least 2011. It's terrible management – and yet Serco has been told to continue to run the centre, because the treatment of the vulnerable people inside it simply isn't a political priority.

There's such an odd dissonance about this. In 2014 the Foreign Office proudly invited me to report on a summit at the ExCeL centre it was hosting on sexual violence in war zones: the swanky stalls and engaging words from charities, along with an appearance from actress Angelina Jolie, were somewhat at odds with the group of protesters outside the venue giving speeches about how we actually treat these victims when they arrive in Britain.

The cumulative impact on thousands of vulnerable women's lives has been vile, while the level of secrecy surrounding institutions like this is breathtaking. It's simply staggering that the UN's special rapporteur on violence against women should end up censuring the British government for refusing to give her access to the centre, as she said she would in January 2015.[2] How bad is the problem of sexual abuse in Yarl's Wood? We simply don't know, because it's not deemed important enough for an independent investigation. According to Serco, there have been thirty-one complaints and ten sackings since 2010, but according to a Home Office FoI answer it's four complaints of which only one has been substantiated.[3] Confusion reigns.

The truth is that as far as successive governments have been concerned, it doesn't matter. Asylum seekers are the last people the British public cares about. 'Out of sight, out of mind' just about sums Yarl's Wood up. And there's a wider reason this matters: outsourcing works perfectly well when it's applied to something transactional, like the ordering of office supplies, but for vulnerable people a certain level of dignity must be maintained. Yet the priority is rather more about protecting the public perception of the companies' work than maintaining quality of service. Here's a personal tale that encapsulates this.

In March 2012, the Home Office felt the price of housing asylum seekers was too high. At that point there were 23,000 asylum seekers in Britain – who were housed by thirteen different suppliers – and the department decided £140 million had to be taken out of the cost of housing them. It scrapped the existing agreements, and gave the contracts to G4S, Serco and Clearel, only the last of whom had housed asylum seekers before (G4S must, in retrospect, have been delighted the deal was done shortly before the Olympics fiasco broke). As Ian Dunt, editor of politics.co.uk, pointed out: 'This is against government policy, which is supposed to be encouraging small and medium-sized companies to supply government services.'[4]

In 2013 I wrote a short blog for the New Statesman on this issue.[5] I questioned whether security companies would have the infrastructure to carry out emergency call-outs, cyclical repairs or maintenance. I argued they owned few properties themselves, so subcontractors were employed, many of whom would in turn be expected to find private landlords. I also pointed out that while the state has a duty of care under international law, there was a gender imbalance in the system for asylum applications – many of the people trying to get into Britain could have been trafficked or have suffered rape, but the system, which emphasizes a speedy decision, is at odds with a situation in which these women are hesitant to speak out about the traumatic and distressing reasons for which they're trying to seek asylum.

I cited the example of Sarah, a woman who suffered years of physical and mental abuse after being trafficked in the UK thirteen years previously and whose story was revealed by *Private Eye* magazine using the work of the researcher John Grayson. She had recently won refugee status and the right to stay with her eleven-month-old son.

In the months leading up to the story she and her baby had been uprooted four times away from medical and social support systems. She even spent four weeks in a damp house riddled with cockroaches and slugs, until local authority inspectors condemned it as unfit. According to the magazine, the day before Sarah learned she was to be granted refugee status, she also learned she was to be moved out of her latest house because Cascade – the subcontractor – hadn't paid the rent, so the private landlord wanted her out.

To my surprise, the blog led to the outsourcing giant that was ultimately responsible for Sarah's case calling me up and asking for an off-record meeting in a cafe in central London. They defended their performance in the sector, pointed out a couple of inaccuracies in my piece, and revealed some troubling things about the behaviour of one of my sources. The message to me was clear: there was no story here.

But there was. They hadn't lied to me at the meeting; but they had distracted me from the bigger picture. In April 2014, a report by the public accounts committee (PAC)[6] branded housing for asylum seekers 'unacceptably poor'. 'The knowledge of experienced specialist providers has been lost and there are fewer alternative options available to the department if the contractor fails,' chair Margaret Hodge concluded.

It was, contrary to what I'd been told, a horror show. As Ian Dunt would write:

> [In asylum services] where there is a diversity of supply [as there was before the government changed the contract], there is a limit on how many people are affected when something goes wrong. Once you're down to just three suppliers, it will affect many more asylum seekers. When it comes to housing for the most vulnerable people in the country [the lack of supply] can have severe repercussions, from homelessness to forced prostitution.[7]

According to the PAC, there was a staggering catalogue of errors. For a start, the PAC felt there was no business case for changing the contract, nor had any risk assessment been undertaken (the contractors didn't even inspect or carry out due diligence on the properties they'd inherited) for the new contracts. The Home Office didn't share information about predicted inflows of refugees. 'This lack of information contributed to delays, additional cost, and disruption and confusion for a very vulnerable group of service users,' the report found. The contractors complained about the data they were getting on the housing stock – but at the same time, they didn't bother to check it for themselves.

The Home Office had rushed the entire procedure, standing back and failing to facilitate information sharing between the old and new providers. The report said the three-month-long 'mobilization' period for the contracts was problematic given the tight time frame and the contractors' lack of experience. It meant the Home Office incurred additional costs, needed to extend existing contracts during the transition period and then had to start inspecting property itself.

Hodge said:

> The standard of the accommodation provided has often been unacceptably poor for a very fragile group of individuals and families. The companies failed to improve quality in a timely manner. None of this was helped by the department's failure to impose penalties on contractors in the transition period. It is disturbing that over a year into the contract the accommodation is still not of the required standard and the department has only chalked up £8 million in savings.

All of which put my friendly chat over a coffee in some perspective. Had I been investigating a government-run project, it's unlikely they'd have attempted to head me off at the pass quite so aggressively (though in recent years there has certainly been a shift in how some departments operate, as we saw in the last chapter). But I was writing about business, and the rules of engagement are different.

Once again, there was a grim, human side to this story. A year before the PAC report, the charity Freedom from Torture had interviewed asylum seekers staying in these places. A lady called 'VA' provided testimony that epitomized all of the case studies. She couldn't speak English when she arrived in the UK in 2006 to claim asylum. According to the report, she was not interviewed about her asylum claim for a year after her application, in part because of the problem of finding an interpreter who spoke her language. Her asylum claim and subsequent appeal were refused.

What this meant was that her financial support was stopped

and she was evicted from her accommodation: she stayed in various centres that were frequently raided by Home Office officials. She found a lawyer in 2011 who allowed her to make a fresh appeal, which – after months – was successful. Five years after arrival, she was allowed to live in the UK and given accommodation. However, according to her:

> I never ever feel safe and secure where I live. I can't leave things in my room. Two bedrooms were ransacked – the police came but nothing happened. For one month I have lived with a broken window just covered in cardboard, with glass on the floor outside. They have not sent anyone and my bedroom is very cold. There are also cockroaches and mice. There are seven women and five children in a six-bedroom house. My room is the smallest of all the rooms there. How can I describe it? I go to the room and I sit on the bed, there is not even room for a chair.[8]

There were scores of stories like this. This was how we'd elected to look after people fleeing torture and persecution – something we are bound by international law to do. The negative headlines hadn't gone away by 2016. In February that year, former employees of one of Serco's contractors, Orchard and Shipman, told *The Times* that their colleagues had humiliated and threatened asylum seekers in Glasgow, and that they had been housed in dangerous and dirty homes. Days later, the Scottish government asked for a Home Office enquiry into the allegations.[9]

Transparency in the justice system

We have heard how Sadiq Khan expressed his concerns over transparency regarding the Jimmy Mubenga case. He's had far bigger worries about the justice system. The department's programme is dominated by two companies: as Richard Garside of the Centre for Crime and Justice has pointed out, around £300 million is spent on G4S and Serco respectively by the National Offender Management Service, which manages Britain's jails.

However, the closer one looks, the more one sees the figure is far higher than it seems. Bridgend Custodial Services, which runs HMP Parc, and Fazakerley Prison Services, which runs HMP Altcourse in Liverpool, are the next two companies on the list of spending – but they're owned by G4S. As Garside asked: 'What about Moreton Prison Services, Lowdham Grange Prison Services, Pucklechurch Custodial Services and BWP Project Services? These companies are responsible for, in order, HMPs Dovegate, Lowdham Grange, Ashfield and Thameside. All are part of the Serco empire.'[10] In fact, three quarters of the contracting budget is spent on these two companies.

And so – whether our politicians like it or not – there's no doubt a political incentive to protect these companies. This is not about Conservative policies: the privatization of our justice system is, like almost every theme in this book, merely part of a political trend. But there have been worrying developments concerning the government in recent years. In February 2014 the *Guardian* reported that Sadiq Khan had written to justice minister Chris Grayling's permanent secretary and to the cabinet secretary, Sir Jeremy Heywood, to complain that parliamentary answers from the Ministry of Justice (MoJ) were being 'deliberately manipulated for party political purposes'.

This happened because someone in the MoJ got in touch with Khan to describe their frustration at the way that political staff from Grayling's team had apparently tried to draw civil servants (nominally impartial) into 'the spin machine'. The paper reported that the whistleblower wrote:

> I am sure you will have noticed the increasingly tardy response of the MoJ to PQs [parliamentary questions] from you and your shadow colleagues. This is because the SoS [secretary of state] has instructed SpAds [political special advisers] to review every single response to ensure a favourable reply is presented. As you might imagine this has infuriated officials at all levels with their constant requests for redrafts of accurate answers and dragging them into the spin machine.[11]

The civil servant was so outraged they even offered tips to Khan on how to stop it happening, suggesting he demand answers to questions on particular days: 'It seems to me that a judicious and co-ordinated use of named day and normal questions, with swift follow-up when the late response occurs, would effectively paralyse the MoJ, turn officials against ministers and destroy what is left of SpAds' wafer-thin credibility. A complaint to the parliamentary authorities too would undermine the SoS's weak grip on his department.'

An MoJ 'background note' advised officials preparing the answer to the question about the detention of prisoners in police cells to bear in mind that Khan had 'regularly tabled PQs in relation to prison population'. The note asked officials to answer twelve questions in a 'PQ action list' before drafting the reply. The first question asked: 'Why do you believe the MP has asked the question?'

Khan wrote to Grayling, complaining that he'd received no answer to twenty-two questions he tabled between 18 November and 20 January. The *Guardian* reported: 'Khan says four questions received "holding" answers, three were answered incorrectly, one answered a different question, four were not answered and one was answered after two months but handed to journalists first. He said there was a trend in the subject matters that are not being answered correctly. These include the performance of private companies, such as G4S at Oakwood prison and on other private contracts.'[12]

Here is an example from December 2013:

> **Sadiq Khan:** To ask the Secretary of State for Justice how many staff at HM Prison Oakwood have less than one year's service at this establishment.
>
> **Jeremy Wright [then parliamentary undersecretary of state for justice]:** Staff working at HMP Oakwood are employed by a number of providers to deliver a range of services. These include, for example, probation services, education and healthcare, as well as custodial services. While G4S, the main provider, is not able to provide information covering staff employed by all these providers, within the last 12 months 385 people have been cleared to work at the prison. Most of these are employees of the various providers, but the figure also includes volunteers, such as Independent Monitoring Board members and lay visitors.[13]

While the answer included information on staffing, it didn't directly answer Khan's question. There was another example in February 2014 – rather than answering 'what' experience, the question of 'whether' was answered:

> **Sadiq Khan:** To ask the Secretary of State for Justice what relevant prior experience each member of senior management working in HM Prison Oakwood possesses.
>
> **Jeremy Wright:** All senior staff at HM Prison Oakwood

have appropriate qualifications and experience relevant to their positions within the establishment.[14]

And if it's tough for politicians to get straight answers about the outsourcing process, consider what it's like for journalists. In August 2013, I was struck by a Twitter discussion between Nicola Savage, then head of press for G4S, and Frances Crook, of the Howard League for Penal Reform. Crook was outraged by a story that had appeared in that week's *Daily Mail* about G4S-run HMP Oakwood, the opening lines of which read:

> Prisoners are earning £20 a week phoning householders and quizzing them about their valuables. Burglars and other criminals are asking unsuspecting families if they would like to save money on their home insurance.
>
> The inmates get paid to read from a script which includes asking potential customers their names and postcodes. They also inquire about the total value of their possessions – including details of any worth large sums.[15]

As Crook put it: 'Prisoners should be employed on work repatriated from exploitation not as cheap labour to enhance G4S profits.' Savage responded: 'We believe it's better to prepare prisoners for life on release and so help to keep them from reoffending. Do you agree?'

This went on for a while. I, separately, provided a link to the discussion to my own followers, which was spotted by Savage. As I'd done so I'd alleged that G4S was making money on the contracts, but Savage corrected me and asked me to apologize, which I did.

But then I began to wonder – if G4S weren't employing prisoners for a few pounds a day in order to boost their profits – then who was? The news report cited 'insurance companies', but didn't name them. Savage would later clarify that a 'consumer lifestyle survey', whatever that is, was also involved. I asked a question to which I already knew the answer: 'Can I assume you're unable to name the insurance companies for whom they're working because of commercial confidentiality?' She didn't respond.

The point here is quite simple: you may think that the companies employing these prisoners are doing a valuable service by preparing them for the world of work, or you may feel that they're simply exploiting prisoners by getting them to do work for them at low wages. Either way, you should be allowed to know which companies are benefiting from what is essentially a government scheme.

And if you search for long enough on the internet you will find examples of members of the public having similar struggles. Here's a Freedom of Information (FoI) request to the Ministry of Justice I spotted in the course of researching this book. It reads: 'Anya Hindmarch the designer handbags and accessories maker has dustbags made for her hand bags under a "rehabilitation project" at HMP BRONZEFIELD. While these handbags cost often over £1000, women prisoners, working under the auspices of A Stitch in Time, a Blue Sky Development project are not paid properly or even the minimum wage.' It asks for the terms of the contracts between Anya Hindmarch and Blue Sky Development, a company which provides work for prisoners in jails. It has been declined. The response reads:

I should begin by explaining that the contracts relating to the work of both Pimlico Opera Productions and Blue Sky Regeneration are held between Sodexo Justice Services and the respective providers. The Ministry of Justice is not a party to these contracts, we therefore do not hold this information.

As regards the information requests I have identified above:

I can inform you that no funding was provided by the Ministry of Justice or any other public-sector source. The remainder of the information requested is not held by the Ministry of Justice. This is because there is no legal or business requirement for us to do so.[16]

The person who made the request is invited to direct their query to the prison, which has no obligation to respond. In 2016 I decided to do some digging of my own and contacted Blue Sky Development, the multi-million-pound social enterprise behind the project, to find out exactly what was going on. It was public knowledge that three designers – Sue Bonham and Brora as well as Hindmarch – were using their products. I asked them to confirm whether any other designers had made use of their products. They told me some had, but despite repeated requests from me, they refused to name them. The three named designers were, they told me, their major clients, and while these designers were public about their use of prisoners' work, none of them actually named their suppliers on their websites or elsewhere. Blue Sky Development also all but confirmed that the prisoners were paid around £9.60 a week for their work, but did not tell me what the designers were paying for it.

Blue Sky did present compelling evidence that the project was of use to the prisoners – giving them work experience, qualifications and in some cases finding them jobs once they left prison – but did little to answer the uneasy questions of transparency surrounding the project.[17] Indeed, they seemed shocked that I was even asking them. 'It sounds like you're writing a hit job,' one member of staff told me.

When commercial confidentiality doesn't get in the way, the government itself does. In March 2015 Frances Crook posted on social media a letter from the National Offender Management

Service explaining that she would not be allowed to visit Birmingham and Oakwood prisons because 'there is appropriate independent scrutiny in place', and so G4S – which had expressed on the same social network that it was happy for Crook to be allowed in – had been advised to 'withdraw the invitation'. The letter said it wouldn't be 'appropriate' given her 'comments about private prisons'. But the Howard League passes comment on both private and state-owned prisons. Certainly, it has been critical of outsourced jails from time to time, but not without good reason. What possible purpose could be served by not allowing Crook to visit? Surely – to quote the government on internet surveillance – if you have nothing to hide, you have nothing to fear.

Often the lack of transparency seems born more of cluelessness than any kind of conspiracy. When shadow justice minister Andy Slaughter asked the MoJ how often Serco, G4S and Capita had tendered for contracts since May 2010, he was told a response would 'incur disproportionate costs' due to the searching required. This is, to quote Ian Dunt of politics.co.uk, 'basic information which shows what kind of contracts the firms are interested in and how interested they are'. He added: 'It's small wonder the taxpayer is so often the loser in the financial agreement which follows. It's equivalent to a high street brand not bothering to do any market research.'[18]

Other questions of transparency

In the justice sector, the monopoly of giant outsourcing firms is somewhat masked by the number of subsidiaries related to them. In the health service, the extent of private firm involvement is unclear for a slightly different reason. In May 2013, Barry Sheerman MP asked the government for the value of contracts the Department of Health held with G4S, and was told that it amounted to a mere £790. This wasn't quite accurate – because, as junior health minister Dan Poulter had earlier pointed out in Parliament, 'the department does not centrally collect information on the contracts which individual National Health Service bodies hold with private sector companies.'[19] And as OpenDemocracy has found, the company has 'tens if not hundreds of millions of pound's worth' of contracts with the NHS. Most of the contracts are for auxiliary things like cleaning, security and portering. Among them is a £12 million, six-year contract at Liverpool women's hospital, a £4.5 million-a-year contract with South Warwickshire NHS Trust, and a £56 million contract (over five years) with four hospitals in the Pennine Acute Hospitals NHS Trust in Manchester.[20]

There's much more, not least its involvement in the Private Finance Initiative and various health schemes which allow it to run health centres across London and some other parts of the country. It's also moving into counselling for rape victims, with a contract to provide services for West Midlands NHS. OpenDemocracy also alleged that NHS Torbay has seen mental health staff being replaced by security staff on night shift since the company began to provide health services for children who have survived sexual abuse.

Again, there are questions over transparency. OpenDemocracy asked: 'How much are Barking, Havering and Redbridge paying G4S for facilities management services? They won't say. [Because] "this could prejudice the commercial and/or financial interests of the Supplier ... and become a barrier to fair trade". So how do we know we're getting value for money?' The website pointed out that in April 2012 the company won a five-year contract to provide non-emergency patient transport to embattled Lewisham hospital. A local wanted to find out how much the contract was worth and submitted an FoI request, but was told that to reveal the value would 'breach commercial interest'. We would later find that Lewisham was paying between £127,000 and £146,000 a month for these services.[21]

Another area within which G4S operates is patient transport services – it receives £2.7 million a year from St George's University Hospitals NHS Foundation Trust in south London, and £3.5 million a year from Epsom and St Helier University Hospitals NHS Trust. *Private Eye* published a chastening write-up of the St George's scheme after being approached by a whistleblower, claiming that there was insufficient training and low morale. Similar problems manifested themselves at Epsom and St Helier. Retired newsagent Palaniappan Thevarayan, 47, died in 2011 as a result of the lack of training. He suffered fatal head injuries when his wheelchair came loose from the floor clamps in the back of the vehicle taking him to St Helier hospital, in Sutton, south London, from a dialysis centre in Epsom hospital. The inquest jury found the driver had not received sufficient training to move him safely.[22] The point here is less about the quality of service G4S provides, however – it's about the fact that it took investigative reporters to get any kind of insight into the full extent of its involvement.

And in the disability sector, there are a great many questions about the failed Atos contract we looked at in Chapter 3. How far was its failure due to the previous administration, and how far was it due to the company involved? Did Atos outmanoeuvre the Labour administration, or did the government simply draw up a bad contract through managerial incompetence? The laws surrounding the information that can be made public regarding such deals make it impossible to say, but those in the know will tell you both explanations are equally likely.

And what did we ever really know about the work of Atos?

It was difficult to gather information on its UK operations – quite apart from the fact that its work was shrouded in commercial confidentiality agreements, it used legal threats to defend itself; in 2011 it did so to silence online criticism by disability rights campaigners. After warnings of legal action, web host myfreeforum.org pulled the plug on the website CarerWatch, a closed forum. The site's users were not initially informed of the nature of the complaint. However, it turned out that the company had taken exception to a five-month-old post that contained a hyperlink to another article it deemed defamatory.[23]

Mike Harris of the Libel Reform campaign told Index on Censorship: 'This case demonstrates the inconsistencies in our libel laws. Because Atos Healthcare are outsourced work by the public sector they are allowed to sue for defamation, whereas a public body performing the same services can't. It's unacceptable. The work that Atos are undertaking is paid for by the taxpayer and as such taxpayers, in this case a group of carers, should be able to express a strong opinion on this.'[24] Such activity seems to have died down on the part of outsourcing companies: it's rather untoward that a company in receipt of public money should choose to devote funds to it.

In June 2014 the *Evening Standard* revealed Atos was fined £30 million for errors in its welfare tests. It was a diary entry, and it made fascinating reading:

'They are paying us a financial settlement but we can't disclose the amount for commercial reasons,' says the DWP spokesperson. Perhaps Atos would like to confirm or deny the figure. 'It's all legally bound up, I can't comment,' said its company spokesperson. But is the £30 million correct? 'Will you tell me who gave you the figure?' was Atos's only reply.

The real question is not who blabbed but why it's all coming out now. Could it have anything to do with the fact that senior Atos staff spent Monday complaining to a Parliamentary Select Committee that they had been 'vilified' for the government's mistakes and someone felt this might have been a whinge too far?[25]

It took me over a year to get to the bottom of this story. The political team at my employer, BuzzFeed News, had first investigated that year, because the implications seemed fascinating: would those who'd done the tests be liable to compensation? They didn't get far, as no one would comment. Eventually, in 2016, I received confirmation from sources at both Atos and the DWP that the company had indeed paid the department a 'substantial' sum, but the *Evening Standard* was mistaken: the money was part of a settlement that would allow the company to exit the work capability assessment contract early. How much had it paid? The Atos source revealed it was a sum in the millions of pounds, but FoI requests on the subject have been refused. The story didn't seem to have any impact on Atos's relationship with the government – a few days later the company was chosen by the Department of Health to manage the NHS's new data-sharing project.

And regardless of accusations of duplicity, of spun figures, and of the risk posed to smaller institutions by the interests of larger ones, the Department for Work and Pensions' (DWP) commitment to outsourcing continues apace. While we can say that fraud is fraud and the ultimate responsibility for such practice lies with those who do it, the major issue is the grey area over accountability. At worst, a lack of transparency incentivizes fraud and at best means honest mistakes end up looking like corruption.

In the case of the Work Programme, for example, look what

happens when charities sign up to it. As Roger Singleton, an ex-Barnardo's chief executive, wrote in the *Guardian* in 2013:

> Voices are being directly silenced in the Work Programme through so-called 'gagging clauses' that prevent voluntary sector contractors from doing anything to 'damage the reputation' of the Department for Work and Pensions, or giving out their own data publicly – data that might highlight problems for specific groups. Is it right in a democracy to prevent whistleblowing about things that might be wrong with public services or public policy?[26]

One government transparency campaigner told me she couldn't even get charities to sign an open letter her organization had written to national newspapers over the issue – not because they disagreed, but because they thought it might jeopardize their contracts.

In the light of what happened with A4e, we should note that *Private Eye* magazine managed to obtain minutes from July 2012 in which Chris Grayling, then a DWP minister, visited the company. His words to the directors were recorded:'Keep up the good work – you will move on. Crises come and crises go. In six months it will be all forgotten. Storms crop up. They are a pain and as an individual maybe you've had a tough time from your friends and it seems like there's been a cloud following you. I'm grateful that you have done what you needed to get done and that's getting people into sustainable jobs.'[27] Hardly stern words for a company where fraud was taking place.

The magazine had also obtained a 'short feedback' email from minister Mark Hoban to Maximus, another of the major contractors, in which he asked how 'we all sell' the Work Programme. The Centre for Social Justice, a think tank which was co-founded by Iain Duncan Smith, has repeatedly championed the Work Programme – yet it previously declared funding from the parent company of Working Links (which was accused of fraud in Chapter 3).[28] It's not exactly alone in this regard: most right-wing think tanks don't reveal their funders but the fact they receive large sums from outsourcing companies is hardly a well-kept secret.

One of the most staggering examples of this was uncovered in August 2015, when it was revealed that Sir Martin Narey, the former director general of the prison service, had been receiving tens of thousands of pounds from G4S in a consultancy role, yet had recently written an 'independent' report for the Youth Justice Board website claiming that significant improvement had been made at Rainsbrook secure training centre, only months after a joint report by Ofsted, the Care Quality Commission and the chief inspector of prisons into the centre had condemned it for a series of failings. Narey had even advised G4S with its bid to continue running the centre in 2016.[29]

When I interviewed Tom Gash from the Institute of Government about the issue of transparency, he pointed out a further problem:

> The lack of transparency is shocking, but it's true of the public sector too. Do we have excessive use of force, name scandals – charging for things that aren't happening? Yes – so . . . this is why [the debates around outsourcing are] ideological rather than evidence based. You get the individual case that can be proof of whatever preconviction you've got, whether it's high public sector wages or something going wrong in the private sector. This lack of objectivity is quite damaging but no one seems to want to address the gap.

The government has made considerable noise about opening up public services. The Cabinet Office has declared that improving the transparency and accountability of government and its services is a policy. On the web page for its open data white paper, produced in 2012, it states: 'From the Prime Minister down, central government is committed to making open data an effective engine of economic growth, social wellbeing, political accountability and public service improvement.'[30]

In March 2015 it set out plans to publish a clause requiring suppliers to agree a schedule with the government for releasing information to the public and requiring all government contracts to be subject to audit; the National Audit Office is to be given access to the contracts. It doesn't appear to be willing to open these contracts up to FoI requests, yet. To say it has taken time is an understatement: this issue of transparency is the biggest failing in the outsourcing industry's evolution over the years. Not only does it muddy the waters around accountability, it's actually stifling debate around how, and when, we should outsource. It's central for two reasons: because there are the question marks over accountability we saw in the previous chapter and because, as we'll now see, there are far bigger concerns over the way state and contractor interact.

9

Lobbying and
Conflicts of Interest

If the issue of transparency when it comes to the actual business of outsourcing is shady, then the question of how one lands a contract in the first place only adds an extra layer of murkiness. Lobbying is, of course, huge business – and it regularly provides rich fodder for journalists. However, the business of how outsourcing firms approach politicians has been somewhat under-reported. One wonders if it might one day be the next big scandal. After all, can any business have a greater interest in forcing the government's hand than one that is looking to secure work from it?

We've certainly seen plenty of headlines about conflicts of interest between outsourcing companies and the government offices that contract them. In probation, for example, the media went into a frenzy when it was revealed in early 2015 that Paul McDowell, the chief inspector of probation, was married to the deputy managing director of Sodexo Justice Services, which won the largest number of probation contracts in England and Wales when they were put out to tender. McDowell said he and his wife had maintained their professionalism, but the media had a field day; he eventually resigned, and little changed.

Arrangements that appear to show a conflict of interest provide rich fodder for news desks. There are in fact deeper, more interesting variants, which we'll come to later – but let's start by looking at lobbying in the same sector, about which we've heard rather less. In Chapter 4 of this book I revisited the concerns I'd heard from people working in the probation sector about the way that big companies were creeping into the market. Now comes the other side to this story: what were those big companies up to while the government was laying the ground for the privatization to take place? They certainly weren't sitting by and waiting for the market to open up: behind the scenes, they were already jostling for their position at the head of the table.

In October 2013 *Private Eye* magazine obtained documents under the Freedom of Information Act that showed how A4e used the Liberal Democrat party conference in Brighton to get around civil servants and arrange an official meeting to lobby justice minister Lord McNally over the contracts that would soon be on offer.[1] The magazine reported that in 2012 A4e wrote to all Ministry of Justice (MoJ) ministers asking for a meeting. At the time A4e was facing the allegations of fraud over the Work Programme we mentioned earlier. Senior MoJ civil servant Jenny Giblett wasn't keen on a meeting and sent an email stressing this: 'From our perspective there would be no specific need for a meeting,' she wrote. She highlighted 'presentation and media handling' issues since A4e had suffered some 'reputational damage in connection with the earlier allegations of fraud'. She also pointed out that meetings with ministers 'are declared, and are the subject of repeated parliamentary questions and Freedom of Information requests'. It seems likely that's why Chris Grayling and two of his ministers declined to meet the company.

But, as the magazine went on to report:

An anguished civil servant revealed 'Lord McNally has let me know this morning that he agreed whilst he was at Lib Dem

conference to meet with ██████████ for A4e.' The firm's
lobbyist had already used the conference, where ministers are
free of their civil servants, to extract a promise of a full meeting with the minister in his office. Though Lord McNally was
advised of the minister's position and the possible pitfalls, he
made 'very clear that he is going to meet with ████████, as
he promised'.[2]

Another civil servant wrote: 'He's going to need some very
robust advice if we think he shouldn't proceed with a meeting.
Lord McNally has been chased directly by A4e twice already.'
And a third added: 'If we're going to convince him not to do it
(which it seems to me we should!), I'm going to need to give
him some more robust arguments. Do you think you could
outline in an email the reasons you think such a meeting would
be ill-advised.'

As it turns out, the official Whitehall meeting went ahead. It
makes for a rather strange entry in the department's transparency
return for that month (McNally's other meetings were with official bodies such as the Personal Support Unit, Citizens Advice
Bureaux and the Bar Council and Law Society).

A4e was able to overcome the concerns civil servants had
about the fraud scandal it was facing and gain official access to
the MoJ ahead of other companies because it nabbed the minister at a conference. At the meeting the lobbyists described their
'concern that the level of risk organizations are being asked to
take, at least initially, should not be too burdensome' for probation contracts – they also tried to advise against 'the risk of huge
penalties for initial failure to meet targets' on contracts.[3]

And the fact that this sort of stunt can be pulled means that
when it comes to transparency regarding political influence, one
could be forgiven for finding prevailing attitudes confusing.

Compare the previous story with this one: in August 2014, Simon Hughes, the then justice minister, was barred by his civil servants from visiting women's community centres where community sentences are worked out as an alternative to custody. Why? According to MoJ civil servants, it was because it would jeopardize the probation plans: if he visited a provider seeking to bid for a contract (or one that might in future), it could be construed as showing favouritism. Yet ludicrously, part of Hughes's responsibility in the MoJ was to reduce the number of women in jail.

Moreover, while it took use of the Freedom of Information Act to uncover the background to the McNally meeting, only a few months later, in early 2013, Chris Grayling announced that probation officers faced the risk of disciplinary action if they publicly criticized on Twitter or other social media his plans for the service. The order included 'any comments that are made in criticism or designed to undermine the justice secretary's policy or actions', and even warned that retweeting others' comments would be taken as 'incitement or approval'.

'He advised that the government are unhappy with CEOs and other senior managers being critical of government policy, regarding Transforming Rehabilitation on Twitter,' one senior probation trust manager told the *Guardian*. 'He told them to behave like civil servants as they are being paid by the government. So much for free speech and democracy. It seems government policy cannot be questioned in public arenas. I am furious that staff and managers are effectively being gagged in asking questions and objecting to the direction of travel.'[4]

One probation blogger pointed to a now-deleted tweet by Heather Munro, the London Probation Trust chief executive, as an example of the government's desire to keep a tight lid on any bad news. Munro had questioned a claim by Grayling that the

London community payback contract with Serco had delivered savings of forty percent. She described it as 'pure fantasy' and said savings were 'nearer 20%'.

For what it's worth, it was hardly the first time we'd heard criticism of this scheme. Serco and the London Probation Trust were awarded the four-year £37 million contract in 2012, under which they supervised offenders on probation doing unpaid work in the community: it was in fact the first private probation scheme. A year later, there were media reports questioning whether probation computer codes and records that log offenders' community work histories, and their reasons for attendance or non-attendance, had been altered to remove any direct reference to Serco being at fault for a breakdown in a work placement.[5] Serco denied that it had attempted to mislead the MoJ and claimed that the changes were 'minor administrative' ones. If it wasn't conclusive proof of a scandal, it certainly had echoes of many of the others we've read about.

Shortly after these reports, *Newsnight* found that some of the projects weren't properly supervised and uncovered further inaccuracies in reporting cases of offenders not attending such schemes. A Serco employee told the programme: 'There are not enough projects and there are not enough staff. The projects we have are oversubscribed and anything oversubscribed causes problems.'[6] Early in 2014, buried in the footnotes of an MoJ press release, the news was made public that the scheme would be scrapped. The MoJ was clearing the decks for what was to come.

Conflicts of interest in the health service

In Chapter 5 we touched on the conflicts of interest that have arisen since the health service was reformed, but there's plenty more to say. In April 2013, Sir Bruce Keogh, the medical director of the NHS, announced that some of his colleagues had been using the NHS to further their personal interests: a staggering admission that, for some reason, did not create much of an outcry. He told the health select committee: 'I am not denying that it happens. I am saying that professionally, as the most senior doctor in the NHS, I regard it as utterly abhorrent.'[7] This came after a survey by the *British Medical Journal* found around a third of doctors in charge of the new clinical commissioning groups had interests in private medical companies.

Even before the Health and Social Care Act had passed through Parliament, MPs on the health select committee were being warned that doctors were trying to get people to go to their own private practices rather than use the NHS for free. Ian Swales, the MP for Redcar, described his own 'personal experience' of a doctor telling him to pay for a private procedure.

There's also the issue of companies attempting to ingratiate themselves with medical leaders. One only needs to look at the sponsorship section on the NHS Confederation's website for more details – £7,000 will buy you dinner with NHS leaders, while £5,500 will buy you access to a non-executive directors' lunch ('an opportunity for delegates to debate some of the key challenges and opportunities of patient and public engagement, share best practice examples and network with peers').[8] The conference has not published its listing of corporate partners for the 2016 conference at the time of writing, but Pfizer, General Electric and Bupa among others have 'supported' the conference since 2013.

And the concerns extend far beyond individual doctors and managers: there's a political dimension. In February 2014 the *Daily Mirror* revealed that private healthcare firms with links to the Conservative Party had been awarded NHS contracts worth nearly £1.5 billion. It singled out Care UK, whose chairman,

John Nash, had donated £247,250 to the party (including £21,000 to Andrew Lansley, the prime architect of the Health and Social Care Act), pointing out that its healthcare revenue rose by 63.2% from £189.7 million a year in 2012 to £309.5 million in 2013 thanks to the Act.[9] One can trawl through the register of members' interests and find scores of MPs with various connections to private health firms – many have received political donations, while others have held directorships or been majority shareholders, and others have been paid for consultancy work.

Here's a typical story that comes out of this arrangement. Early in 2015 BuzzFeed News discovered that NHS England had awarded Alliance Medical (a private company which pays Conservative MP Malcolm Rifkind £60,000 a year to sit on its board) a contract to provide cancer scan services across the north-west of England. It had beaten an NHS consortium that allegedly offered to do the work for £7 million less. When BuzzFeed News asked why it had won, NHS England offered a generic statement:'NHS England is currently running a procurement process to ensure people who require medical imaging continue to receive a high quality sustainable service.' Ian Syme, the campaigner who uncovered the bid, told BuzzFeed News that it was evidence NHS England had a 'privatization agenda' which it was enacting 'by stealth'. He said: 'There's little or no openness or transparency in these tendering processes, no public debate, no meaningful public scrutiny. Ask for details and you get obstructed by the "commercial confidentiality" excuse.'[10]

The entry of such players into the market provides rich fodder for journalists. Take Care UK, one of the country's leading private medical providers. It's owned by Bridgepoint, a private equity firm. One of the men sitting on its advisory board is Lord Rose of Monewden (Stuart Rose), the former boss of Marks and Spencer and a committed supporter of the Conservative Party, taking a seat on the Conservative benches in the House of Lords in 2014. That year the government announced: 'Sir Stuart will particularly look at the problems faced by the 14 trusts currently in "special measures", the programme to turn-around failing hospitals introduced last year, where strong leadership was identified as key to improvement.'[11] One of those hospitals would be George Eliot in Warwickshire, at the time subject to a takeover bid from Care UK.

Political funding

This is not a book about the actions of the present government. It's a book about a political trend. When we talk about recent events that call into question the acceptability of politicians' relationships with the companies they're ultimately responsible for commissioning, we need to be aware that what we're talking about has gone on for a long time. Back in February 2009, for example, *Private Eye* ran a story about outsourcing company A4e. 'Critics wonder if it's a good idea to chase single mums and the disabled off benefits but work and pensions minister James Purnell can create jobs – for former officials and ministers,' the magazine reported. It said that in September 2008 the former Cabinet Office minister Sir Richard Mottram joined a company called Employment Service Holdings. It claimed the move 'may have increased the employability of David Blunkett who became a £30,000 a year adviser to A4E, which already holds lots of New Deal [New Labour's welfare to work programme] contracts.'

As *Private Eye* noted, Blunkett had recently written about 'empowering the third sector' in a paper for the Fabian Society – which the magazine, with some foresight given the recent stories we've looked at, took to mean 'using charities as a cover for A4e'. In that paper, Blunkett actually described the company as a 'social enterprise', in other words a business that reinvests all profits into the community or the business itself. Rest assured, A4e is no such thing.[12] This was the second time his relationship with the company had attracted interest: earlier that year he'd amended his entry in the House of Commons register of interests to include a trip to South Africa paid for and organized by A4e, but only after he was told to by the Office of the Parliamentary Commissioner for Standards.[13]

So this kind of concern is nothing new. It encompasses the NHS, security industries, and – particularly worrying given the state of some homes – the private care market. As the *Birmingham Mail* has discovered, the current business secretary, Sajid Javid, received an £11,000 political donation from Moundsley Healthcare in 2013. The company's main business is a care home called Moundsley Hall, which was found in 2013 to suffer from care, staffing, management and compliance problems.[14] According to the Care Quality Commission's report: 'It took until 12 p.m. each day to get people washed and dressed; there was no training for staff in health and safety, food, hygiene, and infection control and dementia care.'[15]

Private Eye has also remarked that the then deputy prime minister, Nick Clegg, accepted £10,000 from the owners of Caretech, which has a £114 million turnover – in part helped by reliance on zero-hours contracts. As the magazine pointed out, there's a tension between this fact and Clegg's own pronouncements on the subject – in summer 2013 he talked about the 'worrying insecurity' of these arrangements. Such scandals were still being uncovered the next year – in 2014 the *Independent* reported: 'Ravinder Gidar [the owner of Gold Care] gave £50,000 to the Conservative Party after making hundreds of thousands of pounds from Gold Care's nursing homes where residents have been found lying naked in their own urine and have not been helped despite being "in visible distress".'[16]

G4S staff can regularly be seen at each party political conference. In her speech at Labour's 2012 conference shadow home secretary Yvette Cooper even made reference to the Olympics scandal only a few months earlier: 'The staff of G4S who have been professional and helpful at conference entrance, it's not your fault the company's senior managers let everyone down, and we say thank you.'[17]

The relationship between the Labour Party and outsourcing firms has quietly continued apace even while the party has remained in opposition. At the 2012 conference in Manchester, shadow ministers actually stood on platforms paid for by Working Links, despite the fact that, as we saw in Chapter 3, the public accounts committee had heard evidence of fraud and poor performance at this firm. Nevertheless, at that conference, Stephen Timms, then shadow employment minister, spoke in front of a Working Links banner with Mike Lee, the company's director, who argued in favour of more apprenticeships organized by firms like his.[18] Such stories even seeped out during the party's 2015 leadership contest. Caroline Flint, one of the candidates for deputy leader, was revealed to have a member of staff working on her campaign who was paid for by Sovereign Strategy, corporate lobbyists for – among others – Maximus.[19]

Again, it's the lack of transparency above all regarding such relations between the private and political that so concerns campaigners. When an off-duty soldier, Lee Rigby, was murdered by Islamic extremists in south-east London in 2013, viewers of *Newsnight* might have been slightly confused to see former New Labour home secretary Lord Reid of Cardowan on the programme switching the discussion away from, say, the thorny issue of dealing with Islamic extremism and towards the importance of biometric data.[20] He was introduced as a former home secretary, but no mention was made of the fact that he was earning £50,000 a year from G4S – which sells biometric security technology – as a consultant.[21]

Twice that year, in the House of Lords, Reid had managed to talk up the importance of biometric security. You may or may not believe the issue is something about which the politician feels strongly: the point is that such interests are often missed by reporters, buried away as they are in the register of members' interests. There are scores of these little clashes, and that's only looking at the Labour Party. They plague all the parties: on the Tory side, for example, Carillion organized a dinner with local government minister Greg Clark at the 2015 Conservative conference. In previous years Jeremy Hunt, the health secretary, has had a private round-table discussion on NHS reform, paid for by private provider BMI Healthcare, while Sir Peter Fahy, the former head of Greater Manchester Police, has spoken courtesy of G4S.[22] Reform has been responsible for organizing some of these meetings and, like many right-wing think tanks, receives funds from many of the companies it champions – for example, in June 2014 it claimed that most of the work the NHS does could be carried out by private or voluntary providers within a decade. Most of these think tanks do not reveal on their websites exactly who funds them, but leave enough of a trail through public sponsorship at events.

Just as there's a huge question over the lack of transparency in political interests, so there's a huge worry over the 'revolving door' whereby civil servants leave their jobs and join the firms they were, until recently, responsible for commissioning. For example, Alan Cave, a central manager of the Work Programme as a civil servant, left to join Serco, one of its main beneficiaries, in 2013.[23] It means civil servants who are thinking about their next career move might be tempted to cosy up to possible future employers while they are being paid to serve the public interest – a clear abuse of office. Alternatively, having left office, they might exert undue influence on their old colleagues or exploit information that they gained when they were on the inside, to the benefit of their new employer. There's a little-known government-funded body that's supposed to deal with this issue: the advisory committee on business appointments (Acoba). But it's weak and under-resourced and has no monitoring powers, so it can't check if people are abiding by its rulings. It has been the subject of numerous stories whereby former ministers and civil servants have taken jobs that seem to involve clear conflicts of interest – the latest was in December 2015, when David Laws, the former schools minister, took a job with the free schools sponsoring-charity Ark, which he had spoken warmly about in 2013 and whose chair of trustees, in the run-up to the 2015 general election, had given him over £15,000.[24]

There's a very good example of the problems this creates that dates back to 2005. Back then, the government planned to outsource the search-and-rescue service in the UK. A competition between several consortia started that year, led by a joint project team from the Ministry of Defence and the Department for Transport, and a bidder was chosen. However, in 2011, it transpired that the winner, known as Soteria, had owned up to serious irregularities in its bid team. Transport secretary Philip Hammond told the House of Commons: 'The irregularities included access by one of the consortium members to commercially sensitive information regarding the joint project team's evaluations of industry bids, and evidence that a former member of that project team had assisted the consortium in its bid preparation, contrary to explicit assurances given to the project team at the time.'[25] It meant the collapse of the procurement, the waste of years of work on the government side, and the loss of tens of millions of pounds invested in the competition by the various bidding consortia.

What do outsourcing firms really care about?

What we've heard about so far is the more secretive side of the lobbying industry. There are, of course, more official channels through which the companies can attempt to gain influence with ministers. What, exactly, are they attempting to achieve when they use them? Tom Gash of the Institute for Government told me that the companies try to contact ministers rather than their civil servants: 'That confuses me because I thought it was an official-driven process. When I speak to those officials it seems it's them making the decisions based on a set of rules and procedures ... I've always found it confusing. I think, if you think about the way our systems work, a lot of policy choices have an impact on who can win the contract.'

This rather suggests that the firms are more interested in trying to change the direction in which a policy is heading, and thereby appear the best candidates for the job, than simply selling themselves as being the best. Gash added: 'You see a lot of occasions where one thing companies can do is stay in the bid as long as possible and then start engaging with what they're going to do. You go through a compliance process, the other providers get burned out by the hoops they have to jump through – it strikes me the biggest strategy is stay in the bid [as long as possible], and then put all your cards on the table.'

The outsourcing researcher John Grayson articulates exactly how far the web can spread:

When, as in G4S's case, over a quarter of your business depends on revenue from state contracts, then you need to be part of the political process ... But G4S's lobbying power is not simply about the wholesale buying of politicians and former civil servants. It is embedded in the regulatory process and sits on the very bodies that licence and regulate its markets. G4S is in on UN debates on regulating private security, involved in EU advisory bodies, and UK industry bodies and lobby groups.[26]

One wonders whether the companies have attempted to influence the government's policy on taxation. It would hardly be surprising. In November 2013 the National Audit Office (NAO) found that, despite holding government contracts worth around £4.5 billion, Atos and G4S paid no corporation tax at all in the UK in 2012 (Capita only paid between £50 million and £56 million, while Serco paid £25 million).[27] It hardly marked them out as unusual – that year the tax affairs of a whole range of private companies dominated the news agenda. Paymaster general Francis Maude made all the right noises in response, telling the *Today* programme there had already been quite a lot of progress in improving the process: 'We are turning the supertanker around but a lot of this is about change of attitude and culture and mindset, and that does take time.'[28]

How odd to note, then, that only two months later Maude invited G4S and Serco to a meeting in Whitehall to talk about 'how to develop the government's commercial reforms', as part of a delegation invited, along with John Cridland, the head of the Confederation of British Industry, to tell him 'how government can continue to deliver savings for taxpayers'.[29] Both companies were at the time under investigation by the Serious Fraud Office due to overcharging for electronically tagging offenders who were dead or in prison – a scandal we'll look at later.

G4S's chief executive, Ashley Almanza, and Serco's corporate affairs director, Clive Barton, spoke with Maude, Treasury officials, chief procurement officer Bill Crothers and government chief operating officer Stephen Kelly. Maude's round table discussed 'greater openness and trust between government and its suppliers'. This might seem rather positive, in the light of what we've seen about the Cabinet Office's white paper on the subject. But *Private Eye* was rather more cynical: 'Instead of demanding that contractors be open with the facts, however, the government was simply following the CBI's lobbying on transparency,' it alleged. It pointed out that 'Cridland has "proposed a range of transparency measures" drawn up by the CBI's "public services board" which includes . . . Serco and G4S. The firms are making their own pitches to head off more serious demands.'[30] On the subject of transparency, it's worth noting the Cabinet Office named neither company on its press release and only admitted they'd attended the meeting after further questions from journalists.[31]

Some individuals involved in the outsourcing business are certainly making serious money. There's no doubt the pursuit of profit can create poor incentives. But what's also true is that there's no cash bonanza here. The recession and subsequent dampening down on public spending may have instigated more outsourcing, but they haven't created a gigantic surge in profits: Serco's, for example, are set to fall from £95 million in 2013 to £50 million in 2016 – not helped by the media coverage of the aforementioned out-of-hours GPs and tagging scandals.[32] This has been a steady decline: in 2013 it had to ask shareholders to add emergency funds in a share placing.[33]

Indeed, according to the NAO, the profits made by outsourcing giants average around five percent, which is slightly lower than the typical margins of FTSE 100 companies. That said, the NAO also pointed out that they 'work on the basis of highly valuable, stable and often much longer-term contracts'. There is also a wide discrepancy in terms of how much profit could be made: G4S made an overall loss on some of its public sector contracts in 2013, giving an overall return ranging from minus eight percent to plus sixteen percent.[34]

So why go into the market at all? It's very hard to get a definitive answer on that. But from the outside looking in, the obvious answer seems to be that it's an easy one to dominate, with a risk/reward balance that's firmly in the firms' favour. In other words: it's broken.

10

Market Failure

Supporters of outsourcing will tell you that one thing it brings – which isn't available in the state sector – is competition. If companies don't do their jobs properly – or don't provide value for money while doing it – they'll be replaced by ones that can. And with the addition of payment by results, there isn't just a fear of failure as motivation – there's an incentive to do one's job well. But it just doesn't work like that. The first reason is the fact that contracts are drawn up in such a way that – disregarding the gigantic fines and reputational damage that companies have occasionally suffered in recent years when things have gone wrong – too often the balance of risk and reward seems unfairly tipped in favour of the firms.

Not only does the government often lose such cases, but the public doesn't realize when this has happened. In 2015 BuzzFeed News revealed an unpublished London Court of International Arbitration (LCIA) judgment relating to the National Programme for Information Technology, a scheme to create electronic patient records. The government scrapped the scheme in 2011, but three years before then, it had sacked one of the main contractors, Fujitsu, from the scheme. As BuzzFeed News reported, according to the National Audit Office (NAO), 'only nine of 41 acute hospitals were running the IT systems Fujitsu was meant to have installed – and it wasn't even working properly in those'. However, the LCIA awarded Fujitsu more than £700 million out of the £896 million it would have won for completing the project. Neither the Cabinet Office nor the contractor would give BuzzFeed News a comment – indeed, the only confirmation that the website could find that the case was even heard by the LCIA came from the online CV of a lawyer at a City firm.[1]

Such losses are frequent. In May 2014 we discovered that Clinicenta, a subsidiary of Carillion, picked up £53 million when the NHS was obliged to 'buy out' the remaining three years of its contract to run the Surgicare service at Stevenage's Lister hospital. The Care Quality Commission was in the process of suspending its licence after three patients had died following routine surgery, six had lost their sight due to delays in treatment, local GPs had boycotted it, and patient records had been lost. However, a Freedom of Information request revealed that the company had still received £6.7 million from the Department of Health towards staff redundancies, winding the service up, loss of earnings in the three years its contract still had to run, and the breakage cost of a loan Clinicenta took out to fund the 26-bed unit's £31 million construction costs in 2011.[2]

It wasn't the first time the company had benefited from failure: in 2011 it picked up an £8 million pay-off from NHS London to terminate a contract for out-of-hospital care in north London which was marred by a series of failures, including one fatality.[3] But in 2014 Carillion still managed to pick up a £200 million, five-year management contract at Nottingham University Hospitals NHS Trust, promising expected savings of ten percent in the first year and beating the in-house bid from the staff employed in the various services. In August 2015 a report from the trust revealed that the number of beds out of action due to outbreaks of viruses as a result of poor cleaning

had almost doubled under Carillion's watch. A special decon-
tamination unit had to be set up and some wards had to be deep
cleaned.[4]

Nor was it the first time the company's healthcare services
had made the headlines: in August 2012 there were 20 strike
days by 150 Carillion cleaners at Swindon hospital. An internal
investigation acknowledged there was some bullying and racist
remarks ('but not a racism problem'), and that managers
demanded bribes from low-paid Indian staff in return for holi-
days and other requests – in one case a supervisor even drove a
cleaner to Argos and demanded gold jewellery. Amazingly, the
company attempted to discipline the low-paid cleaners for
giving the gifts, claiming: 'It was appropriate that Carillion
carried out disciplinary processes with employees who admitted
giving or facilitating gifts for advantage.' The report suggested
that the bribes were due to their Goan background.[5] Two years
later, a judge would rule that the GMB union, on behalf of the
workers, could air their complaints at an employment tribunal.[6]

In 2016 I came across another curious story involving a
government department being taken to court by an outsourcer.
I had read that Concentrix, a Belfast-based firm owned by an
American conglomerate, was planning to take the Ministry of
Justice to court because it had rowed back on plans to outsource
the collection of court fines.[7] The really curious detail about this
story was that no contract had been signed between the firm and
the department.

Concentrix was widely known to be the preferred bidder, but
it was apparently suing purely because it had been led to believe
the contract was in the bag. I phoned the MoJ to find out exactly
how much Concentrix were attempting to sue for, and they told
me they'd try to pin down a figure. I then called Concentrix,
who said they would do the same. A few hours later, I received a

call from the MoJ to tell me the company had dropped its claim. When I called Concentrix back to verify this, they refused to comment.[8] It's impossible to say whether the escalation of this dispute into the public domain had persuaded the company that the bad headlines that would undoubtedly be generated were worth less than the money, but it seems a reasonable assumption to make.

The weighting of contracts is only one small way in which the outsourcing market has failed. If you want a full understanding of how basic competition has broken down, of how we reward failure over and over again, you need to look at what happened over tagging in 2013, and in particular, at what happened afterwards.

The 2013 tagging scandal

In November 2013, the Serious Fraud Office (SFO) said it had opened an investigation into the government's contracts with G4S and Serco for tagging criminals.[9] It came after an audit suggested the firms had been charging for tagging criminals who were either dead, in jail or never tagged in the first place. The BBC reported: 'The audit by accountancy firm PricewaterhouseCoopers, launched in May, alleged that the charging discrepancies began at least as far back as the start of the current contracts, in 2005, but could have dated back to the previous contracts in 1999.'[10] In December 2013, justice secretary Chris Grayling stripped G4S and Serco of responsibility for tagging criminals – the contract instead went to Capita, which would continue to use the other companies' equipment.

In March 2014 G4S agreed to repay £108.9 million plus tax to the UK government. Serco had agreed to repay £70.5 million plus tax the previous December. What had gone wrong? We're still waiting for the official version from parliamentary reports, but some clues can be given by two whistleblowers who both worked for G4S in the south-west of England. In March 2014, they alleged to the International Business Times website that convicted offenders wearing faulty tags were being hauled back into custody because the equipment would wrongly show they were in breach of their curfew.

One of them, Paul Wakeman, said G4S cut its costs by having the tags made in Poland. G4S said that everything had to be independently tested to meet Ministry of Justice specifications – and where it came from wasn't relevant. But Wakeman claimed the cost-cutting had in fact affected the quality of the equipment, with batteries that died and straps that didn't fit. He told the website: 'You've got not just the actual equipment for the tagging, but the equipment that the staff use – ie, the PDAs (personal digital assistants), the satnavs, the vans – is so out of date that the stuff they've got is just not fit for purpose.'[11]

The other whistleblower, Sarah Bamford, described 'the amount of times we would go round to see people and the families would go absolutely berserk because they were in the house and our equipment just didn't work'. The website said: 'She recalled a man who was on bail. G4S had been alerted by their equipment that he was in breach of his curfew and issued a section 9 breach notice to police. The police went to the man's house during the alleged curfew breach – and he answered the door. "The police were right there on his doorstep and we're telling the police he's not in," Bamford said.' G4S, in response, told International Business Times: 'We receive a small amount of complaints all of which are thoroughly investigated. Our equipment is well tested before use and is robust and reliable, with a failure rate of less than 1%, with any malfunctions very rarely interfering with the actual monitoring of subjects. Our equipment performs far better than comparable systems elsewhere.'[12]

The pair made a number of other allegations: they claimed G4S was visiting the homes of offenders it knew were in prison, waiting for official confirmation from the courts before they stopped charging. International Business Times also reported on the case of a man called William Allen, who broke his tag on some stairs, called G4S immediately – five hours before his curfew began – was told no one could fit a new one in time, and was still sent to court. He told the site:

> I find this strange and a waste of time and money. The tag guy told me not to worry as it happens and is no big deal and he could see how I did it. Now I am thinking that G4S could be on to a potential never-ending supply of their own business. I have been told I could have time added to my curfew when I go to court. This seems stupid to me . . . why . . . would [I] take my own tag off and then ring five hours before curfew for a new one.[13]

The legal investigation is still ongoing. But it tells us everything that however badly this contract may have turned out – and it could hardly have turned out any worse – the only option left to the MoJ was to commission another of the outsourcing giants – Capita – to oversee the tagging contracts. That's the very same Capita responsible for the court translation fiasco you read about in Chapter 4. By the end of 2015, there was some evidence to suggest that the company had overtaken its competitors to become the biggest supplier to British government.[14]

But here's the question: where else could the government have turned? How many other companies out there could even have pretended to have expertise in operating a niche contract like this? Indeed, as *Private Eye* discovered by looking at contracts filed with the European Union, the MoJ dealt with 'preferred bidders' because of the 'complexity and technical nature' of the task: due to the different specialisms involved, it concluded, 'it has not been possible to set an estimated overall price.' The magazine felt this meant G4S and Serco essentially wrote their own contracts.[15]

Since the story broke, the SFO and City of London Police have launched inquiries into five contracts with the two firms, worth more than £200 million. They include G4S contracts involving tagging (and two for the management of 'invoicing, delivery and performance reporting'), and a Serco contract for the escort of prisoners to and from courts. Early in 2014, the government announced that G4S was to be barred from negotiating for new contracts pending an independent review.[16] And in April that year, the Cabinet Office said G4S had taken 'positive steps' to change its practices and engaged 'constructively' with the government and it would be considered for government business again.

But the claim that the company had been barred from negotiating for new contracts was called into question. Only three weeks after it was deemed to have been rehabilitated in the government's eyes, the company announced that it had landed most of the Department for Work and Pensions' (DWP) £300 million community work placement (CWP) schemes. The *Financial Times* reported:

> G4S is the biggest winner of Help to Work contracts, which involves providing 'intensive' coaching for the unemployed in six regions including west and east London, the East Midlands and the Southeast. Other companies to win work include Seetec, Interserve and Pertemps.
>
> The Help to Work programme – worth a total of £300 million over two years – will mean that G4S will be at the

frontline of far-reaching change to benefits for the workless, providing community work placements, tailored coaching and help with preparing CVs.[17]

The paper didn't mention – though left-wing blogs certainly did – that the plans involved people working for free for community organizations: if they failed to do so, benefits sanctions could be applied. Indeed, a year later, there were protests in Finsbury Park over the fact that there were about thirty wardens in high-visibility jackets patrolling the area for six months without pay in order to receive their unemployment benefits. When the *Guardian* journalist Shiv Malik tweeted about the story, writing 'Of course, G4S is getting paid', the company responded through its official account: 'It's DWP & government policy that determines the structure of the programme.'[18] *Private Eye* magazine would later notice that while the eighteen nationwide contracts under the Help to Work programme were actually awarded on 10 April, the day after G4S got the Cabinet Office all-clear once it had paid back £109 million due to the tagging fiasco, the deadline for sealing the deals was originally mid-March – when G4S was still officially not allowed to bid.

As it went on to report: 'Moreover, in February the firm was advertising job vacancies for contract directors, coordinators, monitoring officers and validators "in preparation for the launch of community work placements". Its website said: "G4S is looking to recruit key members of staff to join our team for the mobilization and delivery of this programme." It had picked up contracts in six of the eleven areas for which it advertised.'[19]

Private Eye asked to see the correspondence from the DWP concerning the effect of the ban on G4s's right to bid for Help to Work, but – and this will be of no surprise given many of the other cases we've now encountered – was told it was 'exempt from disclosure' due to 'commercial interests'. However, the DWP claimed in a statement to the magazine that it wasn't uncommon for bidders to advertise vacancies ahead of competition, and that the contract deadlines were moved to April because 'due diligence' took longer than expected.

However, in September 2014 it emerged at a public accounts committee (PAC) hearing that G4S and Serco had indeed been bidding for further contracts while potentially facing fraud charges. Margaret Hodge told the executives of both companies: 'I am . . . shocked that this can carry on. I think you should be dropped until the SFO has finished its inquiries. I do wonder what on earth the government is doing dealing with you if you are not, as you say, too big to fail.'

Rupert Soames, the group chief executive of Serco, told the committee: 'I understand that part of the problem around an outright ban was a ban under EU law which we would not have challenged anyway.' (He was later proved correct – the Cabinet Office confirmed that EU procurement restrictions meant the firm couldn't be blacklisted.[20]) It also turned out that existing contracts to run prisons had been expanded, which led to Hodge claiming Chris Grayling had 'misled the house'.[21] The companies' executives said that they hadn't won any business while under investigation, but in December the PAC reported that the firms had in fact been awarded work worth £350 million by five government departments during this period.[22]

In June 2015, research by the Centre for Crime and Justice Studies revealed that, in fact, the contract hadn't entirely ended: both companies had continued to receive payment for tagging equipment over the previous twelve months. G4S had received £8.7 million and Serco £4.5 million over the course of that year. Why? Because the MoJ had failed to find a suitable firm to provide the equipment after it had hired and then dropped technology firm Buddi: there simply wasn't a suitable replacement company. The MoJ described the payment as a 'necessary interim arrangement', but the original agreement had been for Capita to use the new tags at the end of 2014. They hadn't been able to find another provider in time, unsurprisingly, since the manufacture of electronic tags is hardly something offered by thousands of companies. We return to a question we asked at the start of this book: if not G4S, then who?

Tom Gash from the Institute for Government told me that however the saga eventually plays out, the end result has been disastrous: 'It's catastrophic. You have two incumbent suppliers gone, so you've brought in a supplier with no experience in an uncontested bid process.' But then there's an answer to this problem. It's incredible to note – yet few media outlets seemed to pick up on this at the time Andrew Selous MP announced it (as part of a written answer to Sadiq Khan) – one of the companies Capita subcontracts in order to do the tagging is . . . G4S.[23]

It was all rather at odds with the aims of ministers and industry leaders in November 2013. Back then John Cridland from the Confederation of British Industry had told the PAC that politicians and the media should dampen down their criticisms of the companies: 'The rhetoric risks damaging a market which is hugely important to the future of this country and a fast-growing part of Britain's economic renaissance. I'm proud of these companies that have grown out of nowhere and exported that to the rest of the world.'[24] A day later the *Financial Times* reported that ministers had 'toned down their rhetoric against the outsourcing companies despite the ongoing Whitehall investigation . . . A government aide said senior ministers were determined to ensure investigations were "appropriate" and "not excessively punitive".'[25]

Before drawing any conclusions on what seems a shocking tale of complicity, we should consider another side to this story. A number of insiders to whom I spoke were keen to point out that the narrative of misbehaving private firms pulling the wool over the eyes of the government was an oversimplification.

One said:

G4S and Serco were probably underperforming on these contracts, but at the same time the MoJ had forgotten about them, cut the staff monitoring considerably, and then [the companies] were the ones who signed up to monitoring and assurance processes. The requirement was G4S and Serco had to contact local authorities, send them a fax confirming someone wasn't on the register to remove them – they chased the local authority, and stopped chasing, probably because they had better things to do. The government signed up to that process but didn't specify where the liability lay or what the checking process was.

Indeed, it even seems that G4S tried to raise concerns with the MoJ as far back as 2009.[26] Furthermore, a cross-government review of the process, published in 2013, found 'no evidence of deliberate acts or omissions by either firm leading to errors or irregularities in the charging and billing arrangements' on twenty-eight contracts investigated.[27]

I put this case to Mark Fox of the British Services Association. Did the media misrepresent the firms? Though he didn't explicitly say so, he seemed to agree in part:

Don't blame the media. I used to be a journalist. They're commercial enterprises with space to fill. Very few reporting the story are lucky enough to be in possession of a hundred percent of the facts. It's profitless to blame the media about anything. What I think is that when you outsource or privatize . . . you don't outsource political responsibility for things. It doesn't matter who's running prisons or building roads. You don't outsource responsibility.

For all the fire, thunder and strong words in Parliament, the tagging scandal certainly didn't put the government off working with Serco. In November 2014 the Home Office decided to renew Serco's contract to run Yarl's Wood for eight more years, for which it would be paid £70 million. One has to ask, in the light of the sexual misconduct and harassment claims outlined in Chapter 2, and given the tremendous outcry at the time over the tagging scandal, what would have constituted a poor enough performance for Serco's contract not to have been renewed. Anger came from the usual quarters; Julian Huppert, a Liberal Democrat member of the Commons home affairs select committee, told the *Independent*: 'I think this calls into question the entire process for private management of establishments like this, especially given how few companies bid for these contracts.'[28]

What a basket case the industry appears to be when one looks at these two stories together. An investigation is underway to establish whether Serco committed industrial-scale fraud on tagging. If found to be the case, one would think it should never be handed another contract. If Serco is cleared, however, that will mean it quietly took an excessive hit over a fiasco for which the government was at least partly responsible (to what end we can only speculate). Either way, once it was 'rehabilitated' it had the Yarl's Wood contract renewed, a place that by any reasonable measure appears to have been mismanaged at great cost to inmates for years.

Four months later, *Channel 4 News* went undercover in Yarl's Wood, and as we've heard, found workers describing inmates as 'animals' while threatening violence against them. Yet another investigation was instigated by the Home Office. The findings will hardly be surprising given what we've seen earlier in this book: numerous instances of self-harm among inmates, workers describing them as 'bitches' while threatening violence against them, and serious concerns over healthcare standards. One member of staff was suspended, and the Home Office instigated yet another investigation.[29]

What market failure looks like

How does this sort of market failure come about and what does it look like when it's happening? Earlier in the book we looked at the background to payment by results, which suggested that the government understands the problem, and is taking steps to deal with it. But at the same time, there's a sense in which, behind the scenes, it's perfectly happy to contract to providers that are seen as the least bad solution. For example, in March 2014, a story broke that pointed at the degree of complicity that often exists between companies and the government in the tender process. This time the issue was Atos's contract, awarded in summer 2012, to provide personal independence payments (PIPs), a benefit paid to help with costs incurred by a disability or illness, replacing the old disability living allowance.

In its tender document, submitted to the DWP, Atos suggested that more than seven hundred healthcare providers – fifty-six of them NHS hospitals – had agreed to provide accommodation where assessments for PIPs could take place.[30] It claimed the 'hyper-local' network would mean that no disabled claimant would have to travel for more than sixty minutes to attend an assessment, with 'over 90 percent of claimants able to reach the centres in 30 minutes'.

Atos claimed in its tender it had an 'extensive network of 16 NHS trusts, two private hospital chains and four physiotherapy providers – 740 assessment centres in total'. Four months later, both the private hospital chains and all but four of the NHS trusts had dropped out, leaving just ninety-six assessment centres – meaning, for example, that there was only one for the whole of Suffolk, one for all of Cambridgeshire and one for all of north London. The PAC heard that, since the scheme was launched, more than forty percent of claimants had to travel for more than an hour to reach an assessment centre. Under half of them were able to reach a suitable location within forty-five minutes. Atos had, the *Independent* revealed in March 2014, 'in fact contracted fewer than 100 healthcare providers to provide accommodation – and a miscalculation by the DWP over how long each session would take meant that some severely disabled people were waiting longer than six months to be seen'.[31]

An Atos spokeswoman subsequently denied that the company had made misleading claims in the tender document. 'We had the written agreement of every single trust named in our tender document that they could be named. The department was fully aware throughout the process where we were.'

The PAC hearings were fascinating. Most of all, this was because after Margaret Hodge accused the company of misleading Parliament, she put a quite different allegation to the DWP's permanent secretary, Robert Devereux – she claimed he knew Atos didn't have the required commitments, but told them to put them in anyway because it would make them look better.

Devereux said he'd be 'astonished' if that allegation was true. But Hodge felt it was clearly irresponsible to let the company take a contract at a time when the work capability assessment, which we also looked at in Chapter 3, appeared to be in meltdown. Replying to Devereux, she said: 'What on earth was going through the brain of people in DWP responsible for advising ministers on who to give contracts to, that you think Atos, who were failing in one area of work … would then be ready to provide an effective service [on PIP assessments], which they clearly haven't, on another area? What went through your brain? I just don't get it.'

Devereux replied that the DWP had assessed the bids on 'quality and price' and had decided that the Atos bids were 'better' than those of its competitors, and he added: 'We were making a judgement based on the bids in front of us.' But Hodge said: 'It is the worst advert for using private contractors to deliver a public service. It's awful, it's awful. It's a real dereliction right the way through.'[32]

It's not the only story involving the department that suggests its relationship with contractors could be a little too close for comfort. Here's another involving the department's Work Choice scheme, which helps people with disabilities and long-term health issues claim jobs. Two whistleblowers told the Disability News Service (DNS) in 2013 that Seetec, a small-scale contractor that specializes in employment services, had been artificially inflating the number of jobs it was finding. The DNS claimed the company was offering its clients as 'free' labour to charities and other organizations, would pay their wages for the next six months, and lied to the DWP about where the salaries were coming from. This allowed it to claim money from the department for doing the job, and the payment it received was far more than the salary paid out (Seetec only had to pay for twenty hours a week at minimum wage to secure payment from the government for a successful outcome).[33]

The DWP investigated the claims and exonerated the company, but neither whistleblower was interviewed. A DWP spokesman told the DNS all the information had been supplied in emails, but no evidence had been put forward by them besides a 100-word statement. And what's particularly noteworthy about

Seetec in terms of the issue of competition and market failure is this: almost all the company's turnover comes from the DWP. It lost its Work Programme contract in the east of England due to its poor performance, but then picked up five new contracts under Help to Work, another scheme designed to help people who've failed to find jobs under the Work Programme. It meant the people it had failed to help would be passed back to it. Interserve, another firm which had been similarly punished for its Work Programme performance in Yorkshire, was also awarded a set of contracts.

The reason it's worth flagging little tales like this is that they feed into a greater truth, which is that the government's ability to negotiate and manage outsourcing contracts is highly questionable. In February 2014 the PAC delivered a report into contracting out public services to the private sector. It brought together evidence from two hearings, held on the basis of reports by the NAO. In the first hearing, the committee heard from four major government suppliers: Atos, Capita, G4S and Serco. Between them, they held government contracts worth around £4 billion in 2012/13. In the second hearing, it took evidence from the Cabinet Office, the Department of Health, the Ministry of Defence and the Ministry of Justice.

The committee concluded: 'Government is clearly failing to manage performance across the board, and to achieve the best for citizens out of the contracts into which they have entered. Government needs a far more professional and skilled approach to managing contracts and contractors, and contractors need to demonstrate the high standards of ethics expected in the conduct of public business, and be more transparent about their performance and costs.'[34]

It flagged up various issues we've looked at – the Olympics security failure, the work capability assessments, court translation, tagging contracts, Serco's out-of-hours GP service in Cornwall – and said: 'These high profile failures illustrate contractors' failure to live up to standards expected and have exposed serious weaknesses in government's capability in negotiating and managing private contracts on behalf of the taxpayer.'

Contracts, the committee said, 'have been too large and too complex'. It described how experts in contract writing were being 'rushed in' by the MoJ to negotiate the private probation contracts, 'shoring up a depleted civil service that is usually outsmarted by the private sector'. It warned also that 'large companies such as Serco and G4S hold major contracts, creating the problem of over-dependency', so a few contractors risk becoming 'too big to fail'.[35]

The report found that while companies like Serco and G4S had grown, often by buying up smaller competitors, the government hadn't given any thought to what that really meant for the rest of the market. It pointed out that many of the markets we've looked at already in this book, such as prisons or detention centres, are 'dominated' by just a few contractors, and 'the government is exposed to huge delivery and financial risks should one of these suppliers fail.' What this means is that taxpayers aren't getting the best possible deal from these firms, in the words of the committee, 'at the very least'.

Once again, the subject of transparency was of high concern for the committee: 'Government spends an estimated £187 billion on goods and services with third parties each year, around half of which is estimated to be on contracted out services,' yet 'too often the government has used commercial confidentiality as an excuse to withhold information, often in response to Freedom of Information (FOI) requests from the public and MPs'.[36]

It was perhaps the first time the shadow state as a whole had really been at the top of the media agenda. Radio 4's *Today* programme interviewed a number of small business owners about the report. One, Sara Murray, founder of Buddi, the tracking equipment company, summed up the prevailing mood: 'The words that we heard the most often were "high risk". "It's just too high risk to contract with you." Civil servants are just not used to dealing with small companies,' she said.[37]

Rewards for failure aren't the only problem: it's the fact these companies are forcing smaller competitors out of business. We've already seen how the Eco-Actif case went wrong, but these problems even apply to outsourced work that directly concerns the government. Back in 2012 the Cabinet Office signed a £250 million contract with Capita to provide civil service learning and development training. Capita took over responsibility from departments for procuring the training, but was supposed to deliver the work through 'an open and competitive supply chain' of small and medium enterprises.

Fast forward to 2015, and twelve companies involved in the scheme formed a group to complain to both the Cabinet Office and the NAO: they claimed Capita routinely paid invoices late, included 'non-compete clauses' in contracts that stopped them getting further work from the government without Capita's say-so, and took excessive fees for administering contracts. One said working under Capita was like 'working while being sat on by an elephant'.[38]

How to fix market failure

At a media briefing in 2014, Margaret Hodge said smaller companies wanted to compete for many of the contracts, but the costs of bidding, excessive bureaucracy and the complexity of the contracting process were putting them off. She also wanted fewer rewards for failure, with tougher sanctions on underperforming firms: '[The likes of Atos and Serco are] good at winning contracts, but they are less good at running services.' Hodge said that private companies that wanted a 'sustainable future in the public domain' needed higher ethical standards.

Above all, she wanted proper policies to protect whistleblowers and a test to make sure companies were 'fit' to deliver public services, citing the tagging scandal. The PAC called for three basic measures: extension of Freedom of Information to contracts with private providers, access rights for the NAO, and a requirement for contractors to open their books to officials.

It seems a consensus is beginning to build on both sides of the political spectrum. Mark Wallace, executive editor of conservativehome.com, was even moved to write in the *Guardian* in 2014: 'For far too long, a small number of huge firms have won vast numbers of government contracts with huge price tags attached and delivered relatively poor value for money.'

Wallace said he wasn't 'against private sector involvement in public services', but wanted to see public servants 'playing hardball' on behalf of the taxpayer. '[It's] assumed (by people on both sides of politics) that being on the low-tax, free-market centre-right must make someone an automatic fan of private companies,' he added – but said that anyone who wanted taxes cut should 'campaign against taxpayers' money being wasted regardless of whether it is private sector or public sector organizations doing the wasting'.[39]

Part of the problem is that government lacks confidence. When I spoke to Tom Gash from the Institute of Government he said that we could learn lessons from outsourcing areas that don't have a social element. He was keen to bring up the subject of HM Revenue & Customs' (HMRC) 'Aspire' ICT contract, under which 650 ICT systems are provided by Capgemini and its subcontractor Fujitsu to enable HMRC to collect tax. The contract's cost has risen from £4.1 billion to an estimated £10.4

billion by the time it expires in 2017, according to the NAO, which found that the companies had achieved average yearly profit margins of sixteen percent on the contract; this is twice as much as the £500 million forecast when the contract was originally set up back in 2004.[40]

Gash told me: 'Government got into a situation where it lost its confidence about its capacity to deal with technology. It started to rely on a number of providers, but increasingly got persuaded it should hand over responsibility across a related range of IT services ... government became completely reliant on the provider of the contract. It had no intelligence. No ability to challenge back [over the change requests].' Much the same, Gash felt, could be seen in the Barnet contract we discussed in Chapter 6: 'It combines everything into a mega-deal, because people claim they can find efficiencies. Then they say they'll subcontract different bits of work to different technology providers, who can do the different bits, and it'll be a fantastic offer.'

He argued that the government has learned some lessons from the Aspire fiasco – it's trying to become 'a more intelligent customer and break the contract into different bits'. And he felt that the dynamic of primes and sub-primes that we're beginning to see develop in projects like the Work Programme and probation service was the government's attempt to do this. But it isn't clear that competition drives innovation, while at the same time, as Gash said, 'you have to take a lot of risk'. There is, bluntly, a higher risk of the money being wasted on unknown charities or businesses who have no track record.

At the same time, government doesn't articulate precisely what it's trying to achieve when it introduces new providers. And in fact, Gash feels that this lack of coordinated leadership is the single biggest problem with the outsourcing culture. When I asked him for examples of this, he mentioned the probation service. Gash felt that the probation set-up, in which the National Offender Management Service is essentially the distant contractor to both the public and the private sector, was flawed. 'Instead [the government] should say [to the probation service]: "You used to do this, we'll change the nature of what you do, we'll give you commercial expertise and you commission."' He sees benefits in the potential diversity this model would provide:

> You could, for instance, have co-commissioning between prisons and the local probation service.
>
> There's not a mature market, they're changing policy around it, changing the geography, creating a split, but lots of what they're doing has been done by other bits of government. Do you get people to bring their skills over? Nope. How is it we've ended up with a strategy where in IT we want government to be more intelligent, we don't want ... other people doing procurement for us, and yet someone in MoD is saying we need to outsource our defence procurement. What theory is government working on? I'm not saying I want uniformity across the piece, but it would be nice to know there's someone in government working out which bits worked and which didn't, and the reality is absolutely nobody is.

Given the lack of systematic knowledge being shared across government, it's no surprise that Gash and others would like to see major outsourcing projects subjected to early scrutiny by the Major Projects Authority, and departments showing that they've conducted market studies before they release budgets for projects.[41] His organization has recently been looking into other countries around the world and how they use institutions at the top of government to oversee such deals, in a bid to stop the public sector bias of working around electoral cycles and focusing on attention-grabbing announcements. Politicization makes it very tough to manage these projects as one would a business. If any of the projects we've looked at were deemed so disastrous that the prime minister had to intervene, the only way he could do so would be to fire the minister running it. And as Gash pointed out: 'Unlike in a business, that person will then hang around and cause them pain. So all these dynamics tie in to why government struggles with all sorts of things.'

11

Conclusion – What
Is to Be Done?

In April 2014 an anonymous Serco employee published a blog to the *Guardian*'s Public Leaders Network. Barely anyone noticed: it was tweeted a few dozen times and received a few hundred Facebook shares. Which was odd, as it was one of the most damning summaries yet written of what's gone wrong with this industry. The author wrote:

Anyone from team manager level upwards constantly repeats the mantra that 'commercial targets must be met', leaving customer service by the wayside. We are fully aware that profits must be made, so why are the individuals who carry out this complex work treated as schoolchildren? It is common knowledge among the lower ranks that the work we produce is only to enable Serco to be paid. Customer service is a secondary requirement. Staff fear being 'managed out of the door' if they fail to comply.

Case workers are set impossible targets to satisfy the terms of our contract with our government body, which leads to unrealistic expectations that cannot be met. Many of these contracts put out to tender are ripe for abuse. Customer service is repeatedly ignored because targets are seen as the biggest single priority. We fully understand that productivity is necessary but, at the cost of customer services, is this really the ideal way?[1]

The author attacked the 'folly' of top executives, who had received pay rises in the face of a three-year pay freeze for staff, and concluded by saying: 'Little of this reality gets through to those in government.'

This point of view is not representative of every employee. When the writer Sam Knight interviewed 'nurses, porters, cleaners, swimming teachers, train managers and prison guards' for a long essay about the company's travails, he found that 'at its best, they described a company that made steady profits delivering public services with more care than the state ever did.' One employee, who had been a trade union official, told Knight he was proud that Serco had never faced a strike on its contracts. 'They had this mindset that public sectors were good people surrounded by bad systems,' he said. 'It was a brilliant paradigm.'[2]

And this is outsourcing in a nutshell. The industry is huge, complicated and difficult to generalize about. But however far you agree with the various opinions you've heard over the last few chapters, you'll probably have concluded that some sort of change needs to happen in terms of the relationship between the state and private sectors.

In 2015 the Conservatives won the British general election with a majority. Shortly after the result was confirmed, the FTSE 100 rose 2.3%. Some sort of rise was only to be expected, since weeks of wrangling between the political parties over the shape of a coalition government had been avoided. But few noticed quite how much the outsourcing firms' share prices had risen. Serco's went up by 5.95%, Capita's by 6.72%

and G4S's by a mighty 7.35%.[3] Welfare-to-work provider Staffline saw its shares skyrocket by more than a fifth.[4] The shackles had been taken off the government's impetus to outsource.

The outsourcing firms will tell you that they have cut the government's costs. But there's evidence to suggest that they are responsible for wages falling across the country, thus ultimately harming the British economy. According to the Trades Union Congress, residential care workers, for example, earn £9.45 an hour in the public sector versus £7.23 in the private sector.[5] John Philpott, from independent consultancy the Jobs Economist, has said that the protections placed on the pay and conditions of former public sector workers still translate to cuts in the long term: 'Once you get natural turnover in the outsourced organizations, new people can be hired on separate terms and conditions.'[6]

For an illustration of how such firms can treat their employees, let's return to the first story we looked at: the 2012 Olympics. One issue which slipped under the radar involved the treatment of G4S's staff, and the potential employees who had been guaranteed work.

Cameron Wauchope was a student at Warwick University when he saw an advert in the student newspaper for a summer job at the Olympics. He'd never heard of G4S, the company advertising it, but 'it seemed a good opportunity,' he told me. 'You didn't need experience, you were well paid, you were working at the Olympics, and you got a basic security qualification.' He went to a large hotel in London and did a basic interview and aptitude test, and was told a few weeks later that he'd been successful: he received a letter promising him work ('Not, as I now realize is a crucial distinction – an actual job contract').

Then things went cold on G4S's part. He struggled to get in touch with them, generally spending hours on hold when he called. He was eventually told that, once a background check had been completed, he'd have the job. But he heard no more. One week before the Olympics was due to start, he phoned again, and this time he had his dad on the line, because he'd been trying every day for a few weeks prior to the event:

I didn't feel there'd be time to train me as had been promised. I knew there was a big problem, because of the chaos at the other end of the phone. It's hard to describe but you could just tell everything was going wrong. The call centre sounded in uproar. They were stressed, but it was more than that. And the only answers we got was the girl on the phone saying 'I don't know' to almost all our questions. You could tell from the background noise at the other end of the line [that] people were stressed in the office. My dad was really annoyed about the whole thing: he told them it would look bad if it ever got in the press. One day later, it did.

Wauchope felt that initial media reports, which suggested the company hadn't been able to find enough staff, weren't telling the full story – at least not judging by his experience. And as it turned out, he wasn't alone. Many were promised work, training and the chance to serve the country during the Olympics. They were instead left on the scrapheap by the company, which for a long time failed to acknowledge their complaints.

Shortly after the revelation that G4S had failed to deliver on the contract, the BBC contacted some of the workers. Geoff Munn, from Orpington, told them he had yet to find out whether he would be working at the Olympics: 'I've been given the run-around. I have contacted G4S on many occasions, only to be passed from one person to the next. No one had any idea what was going on and couldn't even tell me if I was still on the books. I'm reticent now to work for G4S even if they do sort themselves out. I'm going to be looking into my rights and investigating whether they are in breach of contract for not honouring my employment.'[7]

However, the BBC's story was swiftly forgotten once the Olympics got underway. So Wauchope set up a Facebook group, in his words, to find other people in a similar plight to himself – people who had lost out on work they were counting on for money, lost out on the promised training, lost out on other work they had turned down for this opportunity, paid to travel to supposedly successful job interviews all over the country, or spent hours on hold to G4S 'helplines'.

He said: 'There was no number to call and complain. I wasn't really sure who I was supposed to go to. I had been posting complaints on the official company Facebook pages, which got me banned, so someone suggested I set the group up and posted links to it in groups complaining about G4S. Within a couple of days about fifty or sixty people had joined. At its peak, it had about four hundred members.'

The Facebook group still exists. It's now achieved its aims, but they are still outlined on the page:

Firstly, to raise as much awareness of this scandal as we could, to ensure G4S could not get away with such mistreatment of employees on this occasion, and to ensure they received deserved media scrutiny looking at this failing so in the future they could not get away with such an action.

Secondly, to achieve from G4S a public apology, personal apologies to those affected, compensation for money spent to get the job (travelling, phone bills, etc) and a return of all sensitive documents G4S had taken in the application (such as passports) and had hung on to sometimes for months on end. To achieve this we collaborated on an open letter to be sent to the board of directors, and the media, and engaged in publicizing this group and its aims far and wide.

As a result of his campaign G4S publicly apologized for casting aside thousands of willing workers. It sent a personal letter to all signatories on the letter to them in which it apologized for 'inconvenience and frustration' caused, and admitted it was a 'less than acceptable experience for which we are very sorry'. It also tracked down personal documents for immediate return and sent a compensation form with which to claim for expenses incurred during job interviews or during attempts to find out what was going on when G4S was ignoring queries.

Most impressively, the Commons home affairs select committee noticed the group. While the committee's main focus was on the cost of having to call the military in, and how that would affect the image of the Games, it ensured the group's story was heard too: a question was not only put to CEO Nick Buckles, but the group's letter and its cause was included as evidence in the committee's findings. Wauchope said: 'This means that our cause, our complaints, and how G4S treated us is forever officially on the permanent record so they cannot cover up our story, and also means our group had an effect on how Parliament ultimately dealt with G4S in response to their monumental failing.'

Over the summer, the committee received dozens of submissions sent by and on behalf of those who had applied to work for G4S. It noted that they were 'remarkably similar'. It described how 'some applications were dropped with no explanation, even after the candidate had given up several days for training passed successfully. Candidates also weren't reimbursed for training until they worked their first shift, so some people ended up spending several days training, foregoing other opportunities in some cases, for no reward.' One applicant from Northern Ireland, the committee reported, arrived in Glasgow for work but was sent home because the company had run out of uniforms, one of many sent to difficult locations without accommodation.

The committee concluded that a 'clear and consistent picture' of poor communication between G4S and its prospective staff was apparent. In fact, it transpired that LOCOG was so concerned about the situation it had declined G4S's offer to help with its own staff communications. The committee actually felt that G4S's failure on this score was 'no doubt a contributory factor to the overall failure of the company's Olympic contract'. It also added:

> We were told that some experienced individuals, including former police officers, took up other employment because they were not sure whether G4S was going to make use of their services. While this may be a part of the general failure which this Committee is investigating, it also points to extremely poor management and personnel practices within the company. We have no means of knowing whether this was specific to the Olympic contract or reflects general practice in the company.[8]

The truth is that Britain has been hijacked by a group of companies that don't offer the value they say they do. They operate in a broken market, squeezing out or sitting on smaller providers who could bring more expertise to the arenas in which they operate. They are given an easy ride, because government offers no effective oversight, and consistently draws up contracts with generous terms.

But if not the outsourcers, then who?

Why don't we encourage social enterprises?

In 2012 I took a little time to catch up with Neil Johnston, the chief executive of the Paddington Development Trust (PDT). He told me: 'When the residents set up the PDT, the area of north Westminster was a colossal failure. You could see it through so many indices: housing, unemployment, mortality rates.'

In 1998, the PDT won £13.5 million of funding, through the government's Single Regeneration Budget programme, which ran from 1994 to 2001. Johnston told me how the trust distributed the money to various local organizations: 'We formed an interface between the public and the private sector – since then we've distributed £40 million over fifteen years and have been influential in the spending of another £120 million. The money's come from various sources – the great and good, local government authorities, the Department for Work and Pensions, and others.'[9]

And the trust now runs youth services, health centres and academies, has refurbished community centres, and has been involved in many more projects, most of which are designed to create employment and business opportunities for residents. The PDT funds start-ups, and anyone driving on the Westway will see the large, purple block of Westbourne Studios, which he told me the PDT was a lead partner in building: it charges a peppercorn rent to make sure assets are distributed through the local economy. It's currently one of Britain's most imaginative office and studio complexes, home to over a hundred small businesses.

PDT staff are genuinely happy in their work. It has a low rate of employee turnover: that helps it to pay acceptable wages. But Johnston told me that the PDT was becoming squeezed in the market, because 'social enterprises are often limited in size, partly because their purpose is often built around the needs of a particular area, and partly because they don't have the same will to grow as a purely profit-driven operation.'[10]

Johnston's trust has been commissioned by Maximus to engage with the Work Programme. He actually believed the commissioners save money when they outsource to organizations like his. As he said: 'The question for government is – do you let the money out through companies, or inject it into local organizations? There seems to be a belief that you can economize through upscaling and contracting to the big organizations. But Maximus know what they're doing on that side too – they won't give away any more profit than they have to.'

Organizations like the PDT can offer extra insight a large company can't. Johnston told me he wasn't surprised at the Work Programme's early struggles. He told me that his organization had managed to get five hundred people into jobs over the course of two years, but it was 'bloody hard work'. He said he'd had to work in partnership with 'a lot of community enterprises', and said it had taken 'neighbourhood-based advisers, who were going around knocking on doors'. He added: 'With the Work Programme there's a disconnect – I recently heard a story about one woman being interviewed and asked why she hadn't found a job sooner, even though she was blind.'

In Johnston's view, the fact his organization existed was proof it was needed: 'If communities weren't crying out for power, they wouldn't set up things like the PDT. So the challenge for the government – and it's something all governments *want* to do

– is how far they can drive down the democratization of budgets.'[11]

The future for social enterprises is looking relatively bright, in no small part thanks to the Public Services (Social Value) Act, which came into effect in January 2013. It requires all public bodies in England and Wales to consider the wider social or economic benefit to an area of any contract they award, over the value of £113,000 for central government and £173,000 for other bodies. As Social Enterprise UK has pointed out: 'Commissioners have told us that the Act finally gives them the justification to commission in ways that they have previously wanted to, but could not.'[12] The organization has made a number of recommendations with regard to the law, including establishing an independent body to scrutinize contracting, and previous performance being weighed up as part of the process.

Nick Hurd MP is quoted in Social Enterprise UK's report:

You could do really smart stuff. In my area, Hillingdon Council, BlueSky do the landscaping. Their motto is, "we're the only company in the country where you have to have a criminal record to work". It's the first chance to prove yourself, to prove that you can be trusted. From Hillingdon's perspective, they get a good service at a good price. But they also reduce reoffending. For me, that's smart commissioning.[13]

And as Neil Johnston told me: 'Part of the reason for the upscaling [i.e. commissioning big firms] has been the assumption among commissioners that everyone will try to rip you off. But we've seen things like A4E recently – you will always get people who cheat.'[14]

Charities and social enterprises delivering public services was a much-repeated promise in the argument for David Cameron's 'big society' vision: the title may have fallen by the wayside, but is the idea dead? As Social Enterprise UK's report concludes: 'Public debate in the wake of the financial crisis has centred on whether public spending cuts must be made or avoided. But who benefits and who loses because of the way that public spending is done, is a much bigger question.' We can make savings – but at what cost?

Improving transparency

In the course of researching this book, I met up with Cat Hobbs from We Own It, an organization that campaigns for greater transparency about outsourcing. She was one of many who took issue with the classical defence of the industry:

> There's not really evidence for outsourcing; the line is that the outcomes matter, not who's providing it. But people do care [who's providing the services] – there's polling data showing that. The other thing is that there are structural reasons why private companies are less appropriate. They're natural monopolies – in that context a profit-making body has power and there's a conflict between the fact they're providing a service and making a profit. It's about caring for people – it takes time and attention, it'll always come into conflict with the profit motive. In private care for example, where you get fifteen minutes per person, and don't get paid for travel – that's the most stark example, but there are others.

Hobbs's organization is trying to make the case for more public ownership, 'but in the medium term we're trying to get a public service users' bill, which gives people rights and say over the process. The ideas came out of conversations with our advisers, who come from trade unions, Social Enterprise UK, academics and journalists. The idea is to try and build a coalition.'

She's keen to stress that outsourcing and privatization are two different things, in her eyes:

We're starting with outsourcing rather than privatization as a whole. The point is to show what public services have in common, and make the case private companies aren't best placed to run public services, whether you're talking about the Work Programme, water, energy or the NHS. We start with contracts because you can create legislation that would do something about them – when they come up for renewal the legislation can kick in.

Hobbs is a young woman, and what the champions of outsourcing often describe as a path to innovation she sees quite differently:

Even though the past thirty years have been a story of people going on about how the private sector's more efficient, what we have seen is that the system isn't democratic, accountable or transparent and doesn't give the people who use the services a say. It's really old fashioned. It's got to shift because unaccountable bureaucracies which don't give people a say isn't compatible with consumer power, or decentralized knowledge or any of those other things we think about now. The Cabinet Office talks about open data in the public sector, and they seem much more interested in that than the private sector.

Hobbs said her organization is aiming to put public service users at the heart of contracting: 'It's a closed-box process at the moment – local and national government in smoke-filled rooms taking decisions that affect millions of people. It's not the way we should be doing things. There's ... not much talk about actual democracy in the local process – of course not everyone wants to get involved but some people do, and they should be able to hold companies accountable.'

It's a dream somewhat at odds with the current state of affairs, splendidly encapsulated by the writer Sam Knight:

> The government chivvies its contractors to do a thousand things correctly. Private companies seek to minimize their risks, and ensure a quiet profit at the end of the day. Everyone covers their arse furiously. The documents that emerge are hundreds of pages long, dense with KPIs (key performance indicators) and SLAs (service level agreements) and kept secret from the customers – us, the public – whom they are supposed to benefit. Once they are signed, they are rarely looked at again.[15]

So what is Hobbs's proposal?

> We're saying that for any contract over £50,000 people should be consulted about what they want from that service and whether it should be privatized or outsourced. Public owner- ship should be the default – government should explain why they're opening things up to tender and put forward a realistic bid. They may not have the capacity to run things in house but there should be a requirement to consider it rather than just handing it over to Serco or whoever.

At the same time she wants to make social value more of a prior- ity and place a stronger incentive on the contractor to explain why social value is going to be a factor:

We think contracts should be publicly available – there'll need to be something online, not that everyone's happy going online but it's a start – performance and financial data so they can see how the provider is doing. It's a useful tool for campaigners – it's public money to provide a public service. We think people should have the right to recall companies who did a bad job. There'd be a break clause, at which point the authority would have a chance to start the contract again.

Her organization has carried out polling research that backs up their ideas: 'We asked the public what they thought about Serco and G4S being barred for fraud and about seventy percent thought they shouldn't be allowed to bid, and fifty-nine percent said they shouldn't bid again.' She feels that the buzzword 'localism' can often be used as a way to mask more insidious motives: 'It's great if local people can bid for assets but if it triggers a procurement exercise that big bidders are set up to win it's not really a net gain for communities. It feels politically motivated that it's been set up that way.'

I put it to Hobbs that all the Bill could eventually result in is the loss of, say, Capita, only for Serco to take over. What would it really achieve? She said: 'That's why we're trying to promote the in-house option. It's saying "OK then, let's have other options, if the government is reliant on Serco, G4S and they're too big to fail, but they're defrauding the taxpayer" – it's why we need to develop more capacity in house.' Hobbs didn't have much of an answer when I responded that it's incredibly hard for departments to extricate themselves from rolling contracts even if they want to ('At least we'd have something in place?'), but she's a firm believer in the wider benefits of her plan: 'Politicians in general are talking about integration of public services and smart ways of working – that's all a dialogue going on at the moment. You can't do that work if different private companies run different contracts. Integration means collaboration, which is easier to do in the frame of public ownership.'

Hobbs is one of those people I spoke to (though opinion was very much divided) who believed the motives for outsourcing could at times be slightly more insidious than they first appear: 'The fact [that] the government's outsourcing the reputation on the work is more of a reason to bring those services in house. The government's best placed to make those delicate decisions where welfare is at stake. The government should be making those decisions because it can be held accountable. It's double sided because outsourcing firms are doing work that the government doesn't want to do.'

In spite of the fact she's essentially championing the public sector, she doesn't consider her scheme any kind of left-wing campaign: 'Rebranding is important – we're saying these aren't options for the modern world, and people have more and more power over their lives in other walks of life, [but] in public services they have less power than they did before. We don't try to use those terms like "renationalizing", it's not a good news story.'

And she's right to think there's evidence of a growing appetite for more thoughtful commissioning. In October 2012 the Cabinet Office awarded contracts for the National Citizen Service – a project to teach teenagers life skills – with management fees capped and payment made in advance, so that smaller charities and community groups without large capital reserves could afford to bid. Apparently, ninety percent of organizations involved were locally based.[16] The government has also, as of 2013, set up a Commissioning Academy to improve public service commissioning – it aims to teach public servants the value of 'outcome-based commissioning', behavioural insights and new models of delivery, while the Department for Communities and Local Government has a number of initiatives to encourage communities to take control of their local services, including the MyCommunity website.

How to fix the outsourcing market

There are, I believe, several major issues on which some sort of progress needs to be made.

The first issue is that there's market failure. Failure is constantly rewarded. As it happens, outsourced failure is even sometimes rewarded in the private sector: for an example, Boeing lost billions of dollars after attempting to outsource the production of engine parts.[17] But I believe there is a severe lack of competition, to the extent that it almost renders the process pointless. As Tom Gash of the Institute for Government put it to me: 'If government is trying to get a service no one else provides then you've got to create your own quasi market and competitive forces – you might use public and private elements but you've got a range of different institutions who can develop different strengths and weaknesses. You've then got to balance that equilibrium carefully. What you can't do is just say: "We'll give it all to these guys, it'll be fine."'

He went on to cite the court translation failure we looked at earlier as an example of how the wrong people do get rewards they shouldn't: 'You've given the job to someone who can't do it, but what's interesting is who pays the price of the failure. The person who had that company made a lot from it. Large providers take over and extract more through transition costs [in which the terms of the contract are changed], financing and more leeway in terms of performance.'

So how much competition, I asked him, is too much? He replied: 'These are sort of semi-empirical questions.' He explained that it was easier to regulate private markets: 'It's much easier to do, you can see it in prices, whereas in these sort of things there's not so much visibility on prices, the goods aren't really comparable – all this kind of thing makes it really hard. There are ways of thinking about it – I don't know what not enough competition is. The Work Programme, for all its faults – providers are competing.'

In the case of Eco-Actif and our discussion of payment by results, we saw why there are concerns about excessive consolidation of the market, but, as Gash explained:

> At the same time I don't think the right model is thousands of tin pot organizations with no structure, no HR processes, quality control – that's not the right model either. The question you have to ask is who wins the consolidation games. Is it the providers providing the best value for money for the taxpayer or the ones playing the system most effectively? You'll get fraud if you launch a programme before you have assurance processes in it, which is what they did [with the Work Programme] because they made a political commitment.

Perhaps the reason for that is that a structure existed before the scheme was designed. As Gash told me, the only way that providers met the timescales for Work Programme bids was because it was a continuation of Labour's Flexible New Deal – they resubmitted offers for that. This means it's rather unlikely there was much innovation in what they offered. It seems the only way any kind of competition could be created was to shuffle the providers around the country. As Gash said: 'The question is why you'd want to curtail a bunch of existing contracts and get companies to move location when you're dealing with the highest demand you've had for some time. That seems odd.'

The second issue where progress must be made – and swiftly – is on the issue of transparency. Gash was keen to point out that transparency is not always as simple as it looks. He felt that what we have now is an illusion of transparency, which is actually damaging for all parties in the outsourcing process.

He said:

Take tagging. The rhetoric that [cut] through from Chris Grayling – he [said] 'You've been charging for dead prisoners' – it [set] off a chain reaction of public accounts committee inquiry, with four of the big contractors in the news – not even the biggest by revenue. Journalists follow the story, they go and find out about Serco. Serco and G4S, meanwhile, are forbidden from saying 'Look at my contracts [in other areas] relative to other providers', because they'll create stories elsewhere and make other departments look bad.

He described the result as 'this weird form of accountability. It looks like a witch hunt, the effect of which is actually quite damaging.'

And what's the end result of this process? Contracts may end up being given to companies that don't deserve them. It's hardly a nuanced assessment of how the companies are performing. And Gash – like myself – doesn't believe there's any benefit in simply hammering companies that fail when there's no genuine competition in the marketplace: 'Companies need to make money. If every time they make losses they have to swallow it and you take away their gains it becomes a bit problematic. They become cash-starved, bargain basement organizations dealing in high-value low-return work, because you're only looking at the cost side of the equation.' The truth is that in services that have traditionally been the preserve of the state, those usually involving people, quality should always matter more than profit margin.

As we heard, there will now be a clause requiring information to be released to the public, but one has to raise a sceptical eyebrow regarding the fact that outsourcing companies still won't be subject to Freedom of Information requests. In March 2015 the government set out plans to publish a clause requiring suppliers to agree a schedule for releasing information to the public, with government requiring all government contracts to be subject to audit: the National Audit Office is to be given access to the contracts. According to the Institute for Government this will mean that 'suppliers of taxpayer-funded programmes will be required to publish information about contracted services – such as the fees charged to government and top-level performance indicators – and details of major subcontracting arrangements.'[18]

But what's important is what's left out: will we be given data on how savings are made, on how bids were won, and the answers to any questions that could be asked? The government will tell you that this is part of an ongoing process to 'push' all the data out to the public: the former Cabinet Office minister Francis Maude said he wanted to remove the need for Freedom of Information by using open data. His successor, Matt Hancock, has argued that open data not only gives more transparency and accountability, but can be used to improve the performance of public services, citing the way that publishing contract data allowed one of his officials to spot '£4 million in savings in just ten minutes'.[19] Hancock may be optimistic about open data, but he has a lot of vested interests – both in government and business – to overcome. No doubt his travails will make rich copy for journalists.

Mark Fox of the British Services Association, for his part, said that there's little resistance on the companies' side: 'We've got to agree what's genuinely commercially confidential so that politicians, journalists and civil servants can have confidence that when we say "This is commercially confidential" you know that's true. Then we say, other than that, as long as we're happy it's a level playing field, we're sort of relaxed about publishing contracts online, spot checks by the National Audit Office, open book accounting and all the rest.'

One of the reasons that contracts have saved money in the past is, according to Tom Gash, 'through the commercial process government realizes it's doing things that are unnecessary'. Well, this is hardly ideal – it's a little rich for politicians to rage at 'wasteful' public services when they have inadequate internal processes to generate efficiency, but in his view that's what has happened. If anything, it's another reason to support transparency clauses.

Gash was unclear as to whether such clauses would see issues elevated to the level of government ministers; he felt senior officials in departments wouldn't be interested in enforcing them. But if they were to come in, and were to work, it would lead to greater accountability. I asked dozens of people over the course of writing this book a simple question – did they feel the government chose to outsource as a way of absolving blame? – and I rarely got the same answer twice.

It ranged from one Whitehall insider's pithy 'My suspicion is it's not a big consideration – they don't waive responsibility, the shit still lands on their heads' to campaigners' belief that it was a primary motivation. Gash, for his part, felt it was sometimes true, citing the decision to outsource the Work Capability Assessment as at least carrying the implication that the bill was supposed to be reduced: 'They created the test and it's kind of convenient to say Atos is the bad guy. I'm not entirely unsympathetic to the argument that there are ways of dispersing blame.'

The majority of people to whom I spoke – from the lawyers and campaigners fighting immigration detention to government insiders like Gash and Fox – did not have a problem with the fundamental idea of outsourcing. Gash felt it was possible to 'make a very strong defence of outsourcing, but just of certain things'. But he was less confident that outsourcing can be justified in many of the areas I've covered in this book. He agreed with me that on things like waste collection or stationery, where the quality of service provided is much easier to measure, it seemed to work best. He felt there were plenty of other areas where we simply don't know if it's the correct option.

Fox felt that the process is always improving:

I think this government [the 2010–15 coalition] has done a lot, as has been recognized by Mrs Hodge, to address weaknesses in public sector procurement. It takes time. I think they've done a lot with how to get to grips with contracts . . . I think that means that Mrs Hodge and her committee and the NAO have been clear about where they see responsibility. I think, regardless of the industry, public interest and accountability, rightly, is a fast-increasing fact of life. So if your business is to provide a service in the public space you have to be increasingly comfortable with explaining publicly what you do, how you do it and why.

But right now, we don't, I told him. He replied:

We're on a journey. I happen to think, because I work with these guys, that they're a bit more flexible and adaptable and faster round the pitch than many business sectors, but I think we're on a journey. That's encouraging because whoever's elected to govern, whether you like it or not – and I appreciate the arguments on both sides – the use of the private and voluntary sectors to deliver services at local and national levels is simply going to go on increasing. So we've all got to find ways of getting our heads round how we get what we want, how will we get it, and when things go wrong we need to say 'Look, it's a human activity, things do go wrong, we're going to explain what happened and put it right as quickly as possible'.

The future of outsourcing

Outsourcing disappeared from the headlines in the period after the 2015 general election: cuts and a rapidly imploding Labour Party dominated the attention of journalists for whom the industry would have been a subject of interest. But the industry did make the front page of one publication within months of the result: *Investors Chronicle*, which advised its readers to 'tap into Britain's outsourcing boom'. The magazine predicted that outsourcing could rise by a third under the newly elected Tory government, with '£1 in every £3' spent on delivering public services going to outsourcing companies. The only threat to their margins, according to the magazine, was the introduction of the national living wage, which the Chancellor had brought in earlier that year. The magazine said that 'a shortage of social housing' along with care providers being 'squeezed at the margins' could make Lakehouse, an 'outsourcer carving its way in the social market', and private care provider Care UK sensible firms to buy shares in.[20]

If it's the case that outsourcing is only going to increase, there are a fair number of people fighting to clamp on the brakes. As the outsourcing researcher John Grayson has pointed out, the anti-outsourcing camp is something of a broad church:

> Private security corporations that mix welfare with warfare and union busting with border control can expect, and have got, resistance from the most unlikely of allies. On a recent demonstration in Birmingham, against police privatization, UNITE was joined on the picket lines by the Police Federation and the Palestine Solidarity Campaign, which was protesting G4S servicing of Israeli and West Bank prisons. In Yorkshire politicians, churches, academics, lawyers, workers and tenants have united to get the G4S asylum housing contracts stopped.[21]

As we mentioned earlier, prior to the 2015 general election, the shadow justice minister, Sadiq Khan, announced that Labour was going to fight for more transparency. Committing the party to extend Freedom of Information legislation to cover the delivery of public services by private companies or anyone else running them, he commented: 'Shining a torch into the dark corners of public spending is a crucial check and balance on those in positions of authority. Along with judicial review and human rights legislation, it forms a vital part of our constitution that fetters the power of governments, holds them to account and helps prevent abuses of authority.'[22] Now that Labour has been defeated, that vision is in tatters.

But then how likely was Labour ever to deliver on most of the things it promised? Khan also made plenty more nebulous announcements regarding outsourcing which, in this author's opinion, felt more like headline-grabbing soundbites than constructive policy announcements. In December 2013 the *Independent* reported: 'Controversial public sector outsourcing firms such as Serco and G4S face being stripped of their lucrative government contracts if Labour wins next general election. Senior party sources told the *Independent* that they would have a "long, hard look" at the contracts, which are worth more than £6 billion.'[23] Beyond probation, it was hard to see which contracts he was referring to (apparently those contracts that had begun by 2015 'would be "forensically examined" by an incoming Labour government in an attempt to find ways to "unpick" them',[24] whatever that meant). It's indicative of political announcements on a subject that is held out of view from much of the public.

There are ministers in situ who have yet to begin outsourcing projects, but moves in government suggest that this mechanism will only spread. Prior to the 2015 election, on the board at the Department for Education there was a corporate lawyer, a banker turned barrister and a hedge fund chairman, providing 'strategic leadership' as part of 'a drive to improve governance across Whitehall'. As the journalist Clare Sambrook asked: 'Whom does [former education secretary Michael Gove, who made the appointments] serve? Our children? The taxpayer? Or his other present and future paymasters?'[25] It's a fair question. And yet the imperative to outsource will only ever become stronger, on the (by no means assured) assumption that it does actually make savings. Indeed, one Whitehall insider was far more concerned about how the companies could respond to austerity than councils: 'Is private sector capable of responding to changes in need in 2015? There've been about 28% local govt cuts since 2010 and another 20% by 2020.'

The general public barely knows this industry exists.[26] Yet it's an industry that has been responsible for such poor quality service that lives have been lost, that the nation was embarrassed on a global stage in 2012, that the government has been defrauded, that vulnerable people, young and old, around the country, have been repeatedly let down by the state, and still it remains one of the things on which the political class pins its hope for the delivery of public services. Without true transparency, accountability and a market that allows a proper diversity of providers to flourish, the same horrifying stories will be generated, time and again. Until then, the shadow state continues to thrive.

Notes

Prologue: The 2012 Olympics Security Fiasco

1 Tammy Hughes, 'Whistleblower Sacked after Speaking Out about G4S Cutting Corners when Vetting Security Staff for the Olympics', *Daily Mail*, 2 June 2012.

2 Mike Sullivan, 'Security Scandal at the Olympic Stadium', *The Sun*, 22 June 2012.

3 'How G4S's Bungled Olympics Security Contract Unfolded', *Daily Telegraph*, 21 May 2013.

4 'Jimmy Mubenga Death: Timeline of the Case and G4S Guards' Trial', BBC News [online], 16 December 2014 (http://www.bbc.co.uk/news/uk-england-london-28153863) (accessed 9 December 2015).

5 'How G4S's Bungled Olympics Security Contract Unfolded'.

6 House of Commons home affairs committee, *Olympics Security*, 7th Report of Session 2012–13, HC 531, 18 September 2012.

7 Deloitte briefing paper for LOCOG, 11 May 2012.

8 *Olympics Security*.

9 Ibid.

10 House of Commons public accounts committee, *Preparations for the London 2012 Olympic and Paralympic Games*, 74th Report of Session 2010–12, HC 1716, 9 March 2012.

11 Jacquelin Magnay, James Kirkup and Paul Kelso, 'Olympic Security: The Firm at Centre of the Shambles "Has Seen Fee Rise by £53m"', *Daily Telegraph*, 12 July 2012.

12 *Olympics Security*.

13 Ibid.

14 Ibid.

15 Ibid.

16 Ibid.

17 Vicky Wong, 'Live: Nick Buckles at Home Affairs Committee', Total Politics [online], 17 July 2012 (http://www.totalpolitics.com/blog/ 324527/live-nick-buckles-at-home-affairs-committee.thtml) (accessed 9 December 2015).

18 *Review of London Olympic and Paralympic Games Security Contract*, G4S plc, 28 September 2012.

19 *Olympics Security*.

Chapter 1: The Story of Britain's Outsourcing Revolution

1 Sam Knight, 'Can Winston Churchill's Grandson Save Serco? And Is It Worth Saving?', *Guardian*, 2 July 2015.

2 *The Size of the UK Outsourcing Market: Across the Private and Public Sectors*, Oxford Economics, April 2011.

3 'Q1 2014', Arvato Bertlesmann [online] (http://www.arvato.co.uk/ whats-new/press-releases/outsourcing-index) (accessed 10 December 2015).

4 *The Size of the UK Outsourcing Market*.

5 Stuart Weir, 'UK Becomes Second Largest Outsourcing Market', OpenDemocracy [online], 29 March 2013 (https://www.opendemoc-racy.net/ourkingdom/stuart-weir/uk-becomes-worlds-second-largest-outsourcing-market) (accessed 10 December 2015).

6 Ian Dunt, 'The MoJ Doesn't Even Know Who It Has Contracts With', politics.co.uk [online], 19 June 2014 (http://www.politics.co.uk/ blogs/2014/06/19/the-moj-don-t-even-know-who-they-have-contracts-with) (accessed 10 December 2015).

7 *The Role of Major Contractors in the Delivery of Public Services*, National Audit Office, HC 810, 12 November 2013.

8 'Our History', G4S [online] (http://www.g4s.com/en/who%20 we%20are/history/) (accessed 10 December 2015).

9 Andrew Hill and Gill Plimmer, 'G4S: The Inside Story', *Financial Times*, 14 November 2013.

10 John Grayson and Ed Lewis, 'G4S and the Corporate State', New Left

Project [online], 2 August 2012 (http://www.newleftproject.org/index. php/site/article_comments/g4s_and_the_corporate_state) (accessed 10 December 2015).

11 R. I. Mawby, *Policing across the World: Issues for the Twenty First Century* (London: UCL Press, 1999), p. 230.

12 Ibid.

13 Hill and Plimmer, 'G4S: The Inside Story'.

14 Ibid.

15 William Langewiesche, 'The Chaos Company', *Vanity Fair*, April 2014.

16 'Our History', Serco [online] (http://www.serco.com/about/ataglance/ history) (accessed 10 December 2015).

17 Knight, 'Can Winston Churchill's Grandson Save Serco?'

18 'The Shadow State', Social Enterprise UK, December 2012.

19 Ibid.

20 'The Thatcher Years in Statistics', BBC News [online], 9 April 2013 (http://www.bbc.co.uk/news/uk-politics-22070491) (accessed 10 December 2015).

21 Knight, 'Can Winston Churchill's Grandson Save Serco?'

22 House of Commons environment, transport and regional affairs committee, *Implementation of the Best Value Framework*, 11th Report of Session 1997–98, HC 705-I, 31 July 1998.

23 Margaret Thatcher, Nicholas Ridley memorial lecture, 22 November 1996.

24 'Transportation Planning Casebook/London Bus Deregulation', WikiBooks (http://en.wikibooks.org/wiki/Transportation_Planning_ Casebook/London_Bus_Deregulation) (accessed 10 December 2015).

25 'The Local Right', 1988.

26 Steve Davies, *Politics and Markets: The Case of UK Municipal Waste Management*, Cardiff University, November 2007.

27 Danny Bradbury, 'Capita: The Story of Where UK Public Sector Outsourcing Began', ComputerWeekly.com [online], December 2011 (http://www.computerweekly.com/feature/Capita-the-story-of-where-UK-public-sector-outsourcing-began) (accessed 10 December 2015).

28 Ibid.

29 Knight, 'Can Winston Churchill's Grandson Save Serco?'

30 'Outsourcing: The Terminator Meets Mr Complacent', *Investors Chronicle*, 12 January 1996.

31 Matt Weaver, 'PFI: The Issue Explained', *Guardian*, 15 January 2003.

32 Andrew Cave, 'Aviva creates jobs in India but cuts in the UK', *Daily Telegraph*, 3 December 2003.

33 Archived at http://www.labour-party.org.uk/manifestos/2001/2001-labour -manifesto.shtml.

34 David Harding, 'Political Origins', *Local Government Chronicle*, 4 May 2001.

35 'Outsourcing: The Quiet Revolution', *Newcastle Journal*, 26 June 2002.

36 Grayson and Lewis, 'G4S and the Corporate State'.

37 Graham Ruddick, 'Meet Serco, the Company Running the Country', *Daily Telegraph*, 27 August 2009.

38 'Up to the Job?', *File on 4*, 5 November 2013.

Chapter 2: The Asylum Industry

1 Jerome Phelps, 'The Lonely Death of Jimmy Mubenga', OpenDemocracy 50.50 [online], 10 July 2013 (https://www.opendemocracy.net/5050/ jerome-phelps/lonely-death-of-jimmy-mubenga) (accessed 10 December 2015).

2 Paul Lewis, Matthew Taylor and Cécile de Comarmond, 'Security Guards Accused over Death of Man Being Deported to Angola', *Guardian* [online], 14 October 2010 (http://www.theguardian.com/uk/2010/ oct/14/security-guards-accused-jimmy-mubenga-death) (accessed 10 December 2015).

3 Ibid.

4 Ibid.

5 Matthew Taylor and Paul Lewis, '"Jimmy Was a Good Man. Everyone Liked Him"', *Guardian*, 15 October 2010.

6 Phelps, 'The Lonely Death of Jimmy Mubenga'.

7 Ibid.

8 Ibid.

9 Oliver Wright, 'Security Officers Accused of Racially Abusing Asylum Seekers', *Independent*, 6 September 2011.

10 Clare Sambrook, 'The Racist Texts. What the Mubenga Trial Jury Was Not Told', OpenDemocracy UK [online], 17 December 2014 (https://

www.opendemocracy.net/ourkingdom/clare-sambrook/racist-texts-what-mubenga-trial-jury-was-not-told) (accessed 10 December 2015).

11 Quoted in Alan White, 'Why the Jimmy Mubenga Case Won't Be a Watershed Moment for Government Outsourcing', *New Statesman*, 6 August 2013.

12 Ibid.

13 Birnberg Peirce & Partners and others, *Outsourcing Abuse: The Use and Misuse of State-sanctioned Force during the Detention and Removal of Asylum Seekers*, July 2008.

14 Amnesty International press release, 9 July 2013.

15 'Jimmy Mubenga Inquest – G4S Statement', G4S United Kingdom [online], (http://www.g4s.uk.com/en-gb/media%20centre/viewpoint/press%20articles%20and%20statements/jimmy%20mubenga%20inquest%20-%20g4s%20statement/.aspx) (accessed 10 December 2015).

16 Paul Lewis and Matthew Taylor, 'Security Firm Was Warned of Lethal Risk to Deportees', *Guardian*, 9 February 2011.

17 http://blog.cps.gov.uk/2012/07/cps-decision-on-death-of-jimmy-mubenga.html (web page now taken down).

18 Matthew Taylor, 'Coroner's Damning Verdict on Deportations after Death on Plane', *Guardian*, 5 August 2013.

19 Matthew Taylor and Paul Lewis, 'No Prosecution of G4S Guards for Deportee's Death on Plane', *Guardian*, 18 July 2012.

20 If you want an indication of how common such controversies are in this industry, the CPS change of direction on Mubenga came the day after *Channel 4 News* had disclosed another case involving the death of someone during Home Office immigration procedures.

Alois Dvorzak, an 84-year-old Canadian citizen, was in transit from Canada to Slovenia. Having landed at Gatwick, he was removed from his flight to Slovenia by officials and taken to Harmondsworth Immigration Removal Centre. Three weeks later, he died there. He had been in handcuffs for hours. He was an elderly, frail, demented man, who wasn't seeking to emigrate to the UK, and unfit for detention or deportation. And that was all we knew about him: a throwaway line in a report by HMIP after a surprise inspection of the centre, which is run by contractors GEO.

But little by little, more details began to emerge. The doctor who first looked at him would eventually be interviewed on *Channel 4 News*. Remaining anonymous, she told the programme: 'This person was extremely vulnerable, he was frail, he should not have been there in the first place, let alone to be detained for such a long while. He was the sort of person you see and immediately identify with as a sort of grandfather figure.'

She asked her manager why he was there, and was told: 'UK Border Agency are not giving us this information because it's none of our business.' According to her notes, she asked: 'What do I have to do to get him out of here?' As a result she phoned both the UK Border Agency and the Canadian High Commission, and was assured he'd be put in appropriate care. He wasn't.

Soon more details emerged about who Alois Dvorzak actually was. He was a Slovenian man who, as a young man disillusioned with the communist regime that had taken over after World War Two, had emigrated to Canada, worked as an engineer, and had lived a happy life there for many years with his wife, whom he'd met before he departed. She eventually died and so, in his final years and with Alzheimer's setting in, he'd decided to reconnect with the life he left behind all those years ago. He never made it there. The HMIP report said he was one of a number of 'shocking cases where a sense of humanity was lost' at the centre. They included a victim in a wheelchair who was handcuffed on a journey to hospital for no obvious reason, and another of a dying man who was handcuffed during an angioplasty operation at hospital.

Reports into what happened with Alois Dvorzak are ongoing at the time of writing. There will no doubt be the same questions over where the allocation of blame lies. And this will complicate the fundamental questions about the dignity with which our asylum industry treats our fellow human beings.

21 Robert Booth and Matthew Taylor, 'Jimmy Mubenga's Widow Shocked as Security Guards Cleared of Manslaughter', *Guardian*, 16 December 2014.

22 Ibid.

23 Yarl's Wood [online] (http://www.yarlswood.co.uk) (accessed 10 December 2015).

24 *Expecting Change: The Case for Ending the Detention of Pregnant Women* (London: Medical Justice, 2013).

25 Mark Townsend, 'Detainees at Yarl's Wood Immigration Centre "Facing Sexual Abuse"', *Observer*, 15 September 2013.

26 Ibid.

27 'Staff Fired over Sex with Detainee at Yarl's Wood Immigration Centre', BBC News [online], 29 October 2013 (http://www.bbc.co.uk/news/uk-england-beds-bucks-herts-24719300) (accessed 10 December 2015).

28 'UN Special Rapporteur Criticises Britain's "In-Your-Face" Sexist Culture', *Guardian*, 16 April 2014.

29 'Yarl's Wood', *File on 4*, BBC Radio 4, 24 June 2014.

30 Mark Townsend, 'Serco Whistleblower's Yarl's Wood Sex Claim', *Observer*, 25 May 2014.

31 'Yarl's Wood', *File on 4*.

32 Mark Townsend, 'Yarl's Wood: Labour Pledges to Investigate Claims of Sexual Abuse', *Observer*, 14 December 2014.

33 Amelia Gentleman, 'Female Detainees at Yarl's Wood Routinely Humiliated, Claims Report', *Guardian*, 14 January 2015.

34 *Channel 4 News*, 2 March 2015.

35 Rowena Mason, 'Theresa May "Allowed State-sanctioned Abuse of Women" at Yarl's Wood', *Guardian* [online], 3 March 2015 (http://www.theguardian.com/uk-news/2015/mar/03/yarls-wood-may-state-sanctioned-abuse-women) (accessed 10 December 2015).

36 Alan White, '"I Started to Go Mad in There": The Detention of Pregnant Asylum Seekers', *New Statesman*, 29 July 2013.

37 *Expecting Change*.

38 'Review Into the welfare in detention of vulnerable persons', Home Office, January 2016.

39 Radhika Sanghani, 'Inside Britain's "Worst" Immigration Removal Centre at Christmas', *Telegraph* [online], 24 December 2014 (http://www.telegraph.co.uk/women/womens-life/11308434/Yarls-Wood-Inside-Britains-worst-immigration-removal-centre-at-Christmas.html) (accessed 10 December 2015).

40 Cole Morton, 'Yarl's Wood: Undercover Tour of Detention Centre with Dreadful Reputation for Its Treatment of Asylum Seekers', *Independent*

[online], 16 November 2014 (http://www.independent.co.uk/news/uk/crime/yarl-s-wood-undercover-tour-of-detention-centre-with-dreadful-reputation-for-its-treatment-of-asylum-9863842.html) (accessed 10 December 2015).

41 *Report on an Unannounced Inspection of Yarl's Wood Immigration Removal Centre by HM Chief Inspector of Prisons, 17–28 June 2013, 30 Sept–1 Oct 2013*, HMIC, October 2013.

42 Maeve McClenaghan, 'Vulnerable Children Locked Up in Immigration Detention Centres for Adults due to Home Office Blunders, Bureau of Investigative Journalism [online], 22 June 2015 (https://www.thebureauinvestigates.com/2015/06/22/asylum-seeking-children-locked-up-adult-immigration-detention-centre-due-to-home-office-blunders/) (accessed 18 January 2016).

43 White, '"I Started to Go Mad in There"'.

44 Daniel Trilling, 'Why Does Britain Detain So Many Asylum Seekers?', *New Statesman*, 12 December 2013.

45 Jonathan Owen, 'Migrants Detained for up to Five Years in "UK Guantanamo Bay", Home Office Figures Show', *Independent* [online], 5 January 2015 (http://www.independent.co.uk/news/uk/politics/home-office-figures-show-migrants-detained-for-more-than-two-years-at-a-time-9959180.html) (accessed 10 December 2015).

46 'Immigration Enforcement Data: February 2015', Home Office, 26 February 2015.

47 Alan Travis, 'UK Border Agency Abolition is Another Sign of Politicians Spooked by UKIP', *Guardian* [online], 26 March 2013 (http://www.theguardian.com/uk/2013/mar/26/uk-border-agency-abolition-ukip) (accessed 10 December 2015).

48 Diane Taylor, 'Ministers Admit Trying to Forcibly Remove Tens of Thousands of People', *Guardian* [online], 22 March 2013 (http://www.theguardian.com/uk/2013/mar/22/ministers-forcibly-remove-people) (accessed 10 December 2015).

49 Alan White, 'The Trials of Roseline Akhalu', *New Statesman*, 15 January 2013.

50 Ibid.

51 Ibid.

52 Esme Madill, 'A Nation's Decency Put to the Test: Decision Due on

Transplant Patient's Perilous Removal to Nigeria', OpenDemocracy
UK [online], 19 September 2012 (https://www.opendemocracy.net/
ourkingdom/esme-madill/nation%E2%80%99s-decency-put-to-
test-decision-due-on-transplant-patient%E2%80%99s-perilous-re)
(accessed 10 December 2015).
53 Caitlin Green, 'Colin Firth Condemns "Cruelty" of Home Office
Decision to Deport Seriously Ill Woman to Nigeria', *Independent* [online],
4 October 2012 (http://www.independent.co.uk/news/uk/home-news/
colin-firth-condemns-cruelty-of-home-office-decision-to-deport-seri-
ously-ill-woman-to-nigeria-8198228.html) (accessed 10 December
2015).
54 White, 'The Trials of Roseline Akhalu'.
55 James Caven, 'Home Office Bar on Immigration Detention Centre Visit is
Appalling, Says MP', *Haringey Independent*, 27 August 2015.
56 'Yarl's Wood Removal Centre of "National Concern"', BBC News
[online], 12 August 2015 (http://www.bbc.co.uk/news/uk-33871283)
(accessed 10 December 2015).

Chapter 3: Disabilities and Employment

1 Explanatory Memorandum to the Employment and Support Allowance
(Transitional Provisions, Housing Benefit and Council Tax Benefit)
(Existing Awards) Regulations 2010, no. 875, Department for Work and
Pensions, 2010.
2 Hansard, HC Deb, 17 January 2013, vol. 556, col. 1071.
3 Patrick Butler, 'Ministers "Ignored Advice on Inhumane Fit-for-Work
Tests"', *Guardian*, 17 December 2013.
4 House of Commons work and pensions committee, *Employment and
Support Allowance and Work Capability Assessments*, 1st Report of Session
2014–15, HC 302, 16 July 2014.
5 Alan White, 'The Tragedy of Alice', *New Statesman*, 5 March, 2013.
6 Ibid.
7 Alan White, 'Why Did the Government's Fit-for-Work Test Turn into a
Disaster?' BuzzFeed [online], 23 July 2014 (http://www.buzzfeed.com/
alanwhite/why-did-the-governments-fit-for-work-test-turn-into-a-
disast#.vdEDr37OX) (accessed 11 December 2015).
8 Something I feel is counterproductive. Suicide is a complicated, tragic

phenomenon. Reducing its cause to mere financial stress contravenes the Samaritans' guidelines on reporting.

9 This and all previous quotes taken from 'Atos Work Capability Assessments', Hansard, HC Deb, 17 January 2013, vol. 556, cols. 1050–1101.

10 Kate Belgrave, 'Atos' [online] (http://www.katebelgrave.com/atos/) (accessed 18 January 2016).

11 'Atos Work Capability Assessments'.

12 Ibid.

13 Penman and Sommerlad Investigates, 'Atos Worker Sneers at "'Down and Outs'"', *Mirror* [online], 10 August 2011 (http://www.mirror.co.uk/opinion/money-opinion/p-s-investigates/atos-worker-sneers-at-down-and-outs-282744) (accessed 11 December 2015).

14 Amelia Gentleman, 'Greg Wood: Why I Blew the Whistle on Atos Fit-for-Work Test', *Guardian*, 31 July 2013.

15 'Dark Matter', *Judicial Information Bulletin*, April 2014.

16 'Atos seeks early exit from fit-to-work tests contract,' BBC News [online], 21 February 2014 (http://www.bbc.co.uk/news/uk-politics-26287199) (accessed 11 December 2015).

17 John Pring, 'Anger over "Libellous" Atos "Death Threat" Claims', Disability News Service [online], 28 February 2014 (http://www.disabilitynewsservice.com/anger-over-libellous-atos-death-threat-claims/) (accessed 11 December 2015).

18 John Pring, 'Atos Claims of Widespread "Assault" Were "Lies", Government Reveals', Disability News Service [online], 28 March 2014 (http://www.disabilitynewsservice.com/atos-claims-of-widespread-assault-were-lies-government-reveals/) (accessed 11 December 2015).

19 Matt Chorley, 'Sickness Benefit Tests Firm Pays the Government to Quit Its £500 Million Contract Early After Death Threats to Staff', *Mail* [Online], 27 March 2014 (http://www.dailymail.co.uk/news/article-2590590/Sickness-benefit-tests-firm-pays-government-quit-500million-contract-death-threats-staff.html) (accessed 11 December 2015).

20 'Dark Matter'.

21 Alejandro Lazo, 'Maximus Settles Fraud Case for $30.5 Million', *Washington Post*, 24 July 2007.

22 Linton Besser and Ali Russell, 'The Jobs Game', Four Corners [online], 12

March 2015 (http://www.abc.net.au/4corners/stories/2015/02/23/4183437. htm) (accessed 11 December 2015).

23 Ros Wynne Jones, 'US Firm Doing Tories' Dirty Work on Benefits Is Hit by Whistleblower's Shocking Allegations', *Mirror* [online], 14 January 2016 (http://www.mirror.co.uk/news/uk-news/firm-doing-tories-dirty-work-7182545) (accessed 18 January 2016).

24 Christine Murray, 'Flagship Work Programme a "Miserable Failure"', Reuters [online], 28 November 2012 (http://uk.reuters.com/article/uk-britain-work-idUKLNE8AQ00M20121128) (accessed 11 December 2015).

25 DWP press release, 26 September 2013.

26 'DWP Work Programme: How Is It Performing?', Centre for Social and Economic Inclusion [online], 20 March 2014 (http://cesi.org.uk/responses/dwp-work-programme-how-it-performing-1) (accessed 11 December 2015).

27 Centre for Social and Economic Inclusion blog, 22 July 2014.

28 'Work Programme – Improved Performance Not Delivered', Parliament [online], 2 July 2014 (http://www.parliament.uk/business/committees/committees-a-z/commons-select/public-accounts-committee/news/work-programme-chairs-statement/) (accessed 11 December 2015).

29 *Private Eye*, 19 April 2013.

30 *Private Eye*, 12 July 2013.

31 'Up to the Job?', *File on 4*, BBC Radio 4, 5 November 2013.

32 *Channel 4 News*, 12 March 2014.

33 'Welfare-to-Work Fraud Detection Inadequate, Say MPs', BBC News [online], 28 September 2012 (http://www.bbc.co.uk/news/uk-politics-19750551) (accessed 11 December 2015).

34 Alan White, 'Whistleblower Claims Work Programme Provider Attempted to Collect Fee for No Work', BuzzFeed [online], 4 December 2013 (http://www.buzzfeed.com/alanwhite/whistleblower-claims-work-programme-provider-attempted-to-co#.arA9YjqXr) (accessed 11 December 2015).

35 Rowena Mason and Louisa Peacock, '"Billion-Pound" Scandal in Welfare to Work', *Daily Telegraph*, 24 May 2012.

36 'Up to the Job?'

37 *Private Eye*, 24 January 2014.

38 Alan White, 'Why Eco-Actif Went Bust: A Brief History of UK plc', *New Statesman*, 1 November 2012.

39 Oliver Letwin, 'Payment by Results Will Transform Public Services for the Better', *Guardian* [online], 29 March 2012 (http://www.theguardian.com/commentisfree/2012/mar/29/no-drug-rehabilitation-no-fee) (accessed 11 December 2015).

40 '"Welfare to Out-of-Work": Colleen Baldwin on the Fall of Eco-Actif', Indus Delta [online], 9 August 2012 (http://indusdelta.co.uk/story/colleen_baldwin_blog_welfare_to_out_of_work/10751) (accessed 11 December 2015).

41 Dave Yip, 'Payment by Results Is Alluring but It's Still a Gamble', *Guardian* [online], 17 March 2011 (http://www.theguardian.com/public-leaders-network/2011/mar/17/payment-by-results-contracts-gamble) (accessed 11 December 2015).

42 Polly Toynbee, 'Anna's Charity Was Bid Candy. Now It's Bankrupt', *Guardian*, 20 July 2012.

43 '"Welfare to Out-of-Work"'.

44 *Outcome-Based Payment Schemes: Government's Use of Payment by Results*, National Audit Office, HC 86, 19 June 2015.

45 Patrick Worrall, 'FactCheck: Why Leaked A4e Data Suggests Work Programme Isn't Working', Channel 4 FactCheck blog, 24 October 2012 (http://blogs.channel4.com/factcheck/factcheck-why-leaked-a4e-data-suggests-work-programme-isnt-working/11729) (accessed 11 December 2015).

46 Bernard Ginns, '£20m Windfall for Emma Harrison as She Exits Welfare to Work Firm A4e', *Yorkshire Post*, 27 April 2015.

47 Ibid.

Chapter 4: Selling Off Lady Justice

1 Laura Smith, 'Nobody Can Hurt Him Now', *Guardian*, 4 July 2007.

2 '"Macho Culture" at Secure Training Centre Where Teenager Died, Inquest Hears', Community Care [online], 22 February 2007 (http://www.communitycare.co.uk/2007/02/22/macho-culture-at-secure-training-centre-where-teenager-died-inquest-hears/) (accessed 14 December 2015).

3 'Youth Custody: Myatt Inquiry Hears of Restraint Failures', Children and Young People Now [online], 21 February 2007 (http://www.cypnow.

co.uk/ypn/news/1069514/youth-custody-myatt-inquiry-hears-restraint-failures) (accessed 9 January 2016).

4 Alan White, 'The Brutality of the Shadow State: The Use of Force on Teenagers in Custody', *New Statesman*, 28 February 2013.

5 Alan Travis, 'Unlawful Restraint Widespread in Child Jails for a Decade, Says Judge', *Guardian* [online], 12 January 2012 (http://www.theguardian. com/society/2012/jan/12/unlawful-restraint-child-prisons) (accessed 14 December 2015).

6 White, 'The Brutality of the Shadow State'.

7 Eric Allison and Simon Hattenstone, 'G4S and Serco Pay Out in Youth Restraint Claims', *Guardian* [online], 24 October 2014 (http://www. theguardian.com/uk-news/2014/oct/24/g4s-serco-pay-out-100000-youth-restraint-claims-stc) (accessed 14 December 2015).

8 White, 'The Brutality of the Shadow State'.

9 *Twisted: The Use of Force on Children in Custody* (London: Howard League for Penal Reform, 2011).

10 Carolyne Willow, 'Gareth Myatt Died 10 Years Ago, But Prison Restraint on Children Continues', *Guardian* [online], 19 April 2014 (http://www. theguardian.com/commentisfree/2014/apr/19/gareth-myatt-died-prison-restraint-children-rainsbrook) (accessed 14 December 2015).

11 'Institute Staff Member Dragged Teen to Cell', Northampton *Chronicle* [online], 28 April 2010 (http://www.northamptonchron.co.uk/news/ local/institute-staff-member-dragged-teen-to-cell-1-898855) (accessed 9 January 2016).

12 Chris Green, 'Rainsbrook G4S Youth Prison Slammed by Ofsted Report as Children Suffer "Racist", "Degrading" Abuse from Guards High on Drugs', *Independent* [online], 20 May 2015 (http://www.independent. co.uk/news/uk/home-news/rainsbrook-g4s-youth-prison-slammed-by-ofsted-report-as-children-suffer-racist-degrading-abuse-from-10263121. html) (accessed 14 December 2015).

13 'Inspection of Rainsbrook Secure Training Centre: February 2015', Ofsted, CQC, HMIP.

14 Press Association, 'G4S Loses Contract to Run Rainsbrook Young Offender Facility', *Guardian* [online] 4 September 2015 (http://www. theguardian.com/uk-news/2015/sep/04/g4s-loses-contract-to-run-rainsbrook-young-offender-facility) (accessed 10 January 2016).

15 Alan White, 'A Firm That Ran a "Horror" Jail in America Is Taking Over a British Youth Prison', BuzzFeed [online], 11 January 2016 (http://www.buzzfeed.com/alanwhite/a-firm-that-ran-a-horror-jail-in-america-is-taking-over-a-br#.yo9M91NRD) (accessed 18 January 2016).

16 Mark Leftly, 'Coalition Is "Undermining" Prison Chiefs' Ability to Govern Effectively, G4S Warns', *Independent on Sunday*, 30 November 2014.

17 'G4S Medway Young Offenders Centre Staff Suspended over Abuse Claims', BBC News [online], 8 January 2016 (http://www.bbc.co.uk/news/uk-england-kent-35260927) (accessed 18 January 2016).

18 Alan White, 'Five Arrested over Private Youth Prison Abuse Allegations', BuzzFeed [online], 12 January 2016 (http://www.buzzfeed.com/alanwhite/lack-of-cctv-evidence-in-safeguarding-incidents-at-medway-si#.jyLBpOGeo) (accessed 18 January 2016).

19 Alan White, 'Staff At All G4S's Youth Prisons Will Now Wear Body Cameras', Buzzfeed [online], 25 Feb 2016 (http://www.buzzfeed.com/alanwhite/staff-at-all-of-g4ss-youth-prisons-will-now-wear-body-camera) (accessed 29 Feb 2016).

20 Alan White, 'G4S May Have Breached Contract Amid Abuse Allegations At Youth Prison', Buzzfeed [online], 22 Jan 2016, (http://www.buzzfeed.com/alanwhite/g4s-may-have-breached-contract-amid-abuse-allegations-at-you) (accessed 29 Feb 2016).

21 'Revealed: G4S youth jail faced abuse claims 12 years ago', *Guardian* [online], 26 Feb 2016, (http://www.theguardian.com/business/2016/feb/26/revealed-g4s-youth-jail-faced-abuse-claims-12-years-ago) (accessed 29 Feb 2016).

22 'How Are Privately-Run Prisons Performing?', BBC News [online], 8 October 2013 (http://www.bbc.co.uk/news/uk-england-birmingham-24442303) (accessed 14 December 2015).

23 'Oakwood Branded "Chaotic and out of Control" after Prisoners' Protest', Wolverhampton *Express and Star*, 12 October 2013.

24 'Report on an Unannounced Inspection of HMP Oakwood by HM Chief Inspector of Prisons, 10–21 June 2013', HM Inspectorate of Prisons, October 2013.

25 Steven Morris and Eric Allison, 'Tales from the Inside: Drugs and Disorder at G4S's Prison of the Future', *Guardian* [online], 29 April 2014 (http://

www.theguardian.com/society/2014/apr/29/tales-from-inside-oakwood-prison) (accessed 14 December 2015).

26 'HMP Oakwood on the Verge of Disaster', *Inside Time*, June 2014.

27 'Report on an Announced Inspection of HMP Oakwood by HM Chief Inspector of Prisons, 1–5 December 2014', HM Inspectorate of Prisons, February 2015.

28 Morris and Allison, 'Tales from the Inside'.

29 'How Are Privately-Run Prisons Performing?'

30 'Heavy Criticism for Doncaster Jail', *Daily Mail*, 13 August 2014.

31 'Transparency', Reform [online] (http://www.reform.uk/about/transparency) (accessed 18 January 2016).

32 Gabrielle Garton Grimwood, 'Prisons: The Role of the Private Sector', House of Commons Library, 30 January 2014.

33 'Female Prisoners Suffered "Intimidation and Abuse"', ITV News [online], 15 October 2013 (http://www.itv.com/news/update/2013-10-15/female-prisoners-suffered-intimidation-and-abuse/) (accessed 14 December 2015).

34 'Corporate Crime? A Dossier on the Failure of Privatisation in the Criminal Justice System', Howard League for Penal Reform, May 2014.

35 Ibid.

36 Rob Wilson, 'Ken Clarke: Austerity's Gone Far Enough', *Total Politics*, September 2013.

37 Emma Thomas, 'Prisons Are 99% Full as a Result of Closures', *Daily Mail*, 18 October 2013.

38 'The Ministry of Justice's Language Services Contract', National Audit Office, 10 September 2012.

39 Ibid.

40 Ibid.

41 Hansard, HC Deb, 20 June 2013, vol. 564, col. 307WH.

42 Aisha Maniar, 'Lost in Privatisation: Capita, Court Interpretation Services and Fair Trial Rights', Institute of Race Relations [online], 20 February 2014 (http://www.irr.org.uk/news/lost-in-privatisation-capita-court-interpreting-services-and-fair-trial-rights/) (accessed 14 December 2015).

43 'Ministry of Justice's Language Services Contract: Report Published', Parliament [online], 14 December 2012 (http://www.parliament.uk/

business/committees/committees-a-z/commons-select/public-accounts-committee/news/moj-language-services-report/) (accessed 14 December 2015).

44 Hansard, HC Deb, 20 June 2013, vol. 564, col. 307WH.

45 Aisha Maniar, 'Lost in Privatisation: Capita, Court Interpretation Services and Fair Trial Rights', *Institute of Race Relations* [online], 20 February 2014 (http://www.irr.org.uk/news/lost-in-privatisation-capita-court-inter-preting-services-and-fair-trial-rights/) (accessed 14 December 2015).

46 Wesley Johnson, '"Total Chaos" after Pet Dog Counted on Translators' Database', *Telegraph* [online], 14 December 2012 (http://www.telegraph.co.uk/news/politics/9742685/Total-chaos-after-pet-dog-counted-on-translators-database.html) (accessed 14 December 2015).

47 Hugh Muir, 'Look Who's Talking: Chris Grayling Gets a Wigging over Court Translators', *Guardian*, 27 May 2014.

48 Johnson, '"Total Chaos" after Pet Dog Counted on Translators' Database'.

49 Maniar, 'Lost in Privatisation'.

50 Marco Giannangeli and Ted Jeory, 'Interpreter's "Low Pay" Halts a Trial', *Express on Sunday*, 12 May 2013.

51 'Anxiang Du guilty of murder of Northampton family of four', BBC News [online], 27 November 2015 (http://www.bbc.co.uk/news/uk-england-25123910) (accessed 14 December 2015).

52 'Interpreting and Translation Services and Applied Language Solutions Contract', Parliament [online], 6 February 2013 (http://www.parliament.uk/business/committees/committees-a-z/commons-select/justice-committee/news/interpreters-and-als-report/) (accessed 14 December 2015).

53 Hansard, HC Deb, 20 June 2013, vol. 564, col. 300WH.

54 Maniar, 'Lost in Privatisation'

55 Ibid.

56 'Statistics on the Use of Language Services in Courts and Tribunals: Statistical Bulletin, 30 January 2012 to 31 January 2013', Ministry of Justice, 28 March 2013.

57 '£17 Million Lost in Translation', press release, Professional Interpreters for Justice, 13 December 2013 (http://www.iti.org.uk/attachments/article/544/%C2%A317%20million%20lost%20in%20court%20

}

interpreting%20fiasco%20(press%20release)%2013.12.13.pdf) (accessed 14 December 2015), using various statistical bulletins.

58 *Private Eye*, 29 November 2013.
59 'Court Interpreting Firm Capita Fined Thousands', BBC News [online], 22 January 2014 (http://www.bbc.co.uk/news/uk-25824907) (accessed 14 December 2015).
60 *Private Eye*, 9 January 2015.
61 Ibid.
62 Catherine Baksi, 'MPs Condemn "Shambolic" Court Interpreter Deal', *Law Society Gazette*, 4 February 2013.
63 Ibid.
64 Jack Doyle, 'Nearly 50,000 Criminals Spared Jail Offend Again within a Year: MPs Claim 'Shocking' Figures Show Failure by Probation Officers', *Mail* [Online], 19 December 2012 (http://www.dailymail.co.uk/news/article-2250255/Nearly-50-000-criminals-spared-jail-offend-year-MPs-claim-shocking-figures-failure-probation-officers.html) (accessed 14 December 2015).
65 Alan White, 'Probation Chiefs Voice Doubts about Outsourcing', *New Statesman*, 7 January 2013.
66 Ibid.
67 Ibid.
68 Ibid.
69 Ian Dunt, 'The Probation Service Is a Success Story – So Why Is Grayling Privatising It?', politics.co.uk, 9 May 2013 (http://www.politics.co.uk/comment-analysis/2013/05/09/comment-the-probation-service-is-a-success-story-) (accessed 18 January 2016).
70 Alan White, 'Three Reasons Chris Grayling's Outsourcing Plan for the Probation Service is a Terrible Idea', *New Statesman*, 27 May 2013.
71 Ibid.
72 Ibid.
73 Ian Dunt, 'Privatisation Lottery Admission Shows Grayling Misled the Commons', politics.co.uk, 25 July 2014 (http://www.politics.co.uk/news/2014/07/25/privatisation-lottery-admission-shows-grayling-misled-the-co) (accessed 14 December 2015).
74 White, 'Three Reasons Chris Grayling's Outsourcing Plan for the Probation Service is a Terrible Idea'.

75 *Private Eye*, 18 October 2013.

76 *Private Eye*, 2 May 2014.

77 'US: For-Profit Probation Tramples Rights of Poor', Human Rights Watch [online], 5 February 2014 (http://www.hrw.org/news/2014/02/05/us-profit-probation-tramples-rights-poor) (accessed 14 December 2015).

78 *Private Eye*, 2 May 2014.

79 Ibid.

80 Sadiq Khan, 'Chris Grayling's Probation Privatisation Is a Reckless Gamble', *Guardian*, 31 May 2014.

81 Alan Travis and Rajeev Syal, '"Poison Pill" Probation Contracts Could Cost £300m to £400m to Cancel', *Guardian*, 12 September 2014.

82 Khan, 'Chris Grayling's Probation Privatisation Is a Reckless Gamble'.

83 Maya Oppenheim, 'This Is Why You Should Care that Our Probation Service Has Just Been Privatized', Vice [online], 3 February 2015 (http://www.vice.com/en_uk/read/why-you-should-care-that-our-probation-service-has-just-been-privatised-119) (accessed 14 December 2015).

84 Alan Travis, 'Probation Officers Face Redundancy in Plan to Replace Them with Machines', *Guardian*, 1 April 2015.

85 Tom Harper, 'Probation Chiefs Cash In as 700 Staff Lose Jobs', *Sunday Times*, 19 April 2015.

86 Travis, 'Probation Officers Face Redundancy in Plan to Replace Them with Machines'.

87 'Community Rehabilitation Companies: Redundancy', Written Question 1762, Parliament.uk, 9 June 2015 (http://www.parliament.uk/business/publications/written-questions-answers-statements/written-question/Commons/2015-06-09/1762/) (accessed 18 January 2016).

88 Tamsin Rutter, 'Probation Service Split: "Staff Are Staring into the Abyss"', *Guardian* [online], 9 April 2015 (http://www.theguardian.com/public-leaders-network/2015/apr/09/probation-service-split-staff-demoralised-divided-private-services) (accessed 14 December 2015).

Chapter 5: NHS for Sale?

1 http://www.legislation.gov.uk/ukpga/2012/7/contents/enacted (accessed 14 December 2015).

2 'Health Reforms "Will Benefit Most Vulnerable in Society"', *Telegraph* [online], 10 May 2011 (http://www.telegraph.co.uk/news/health/news/8505422/Letter-Health-reforms-will-benefit-most-vulnerable-in-society.html) (accessed 14 December 2015).

3 Alan White, '"The Tail's Wagging the Dog": How Outsourcing Is Eroding NHS Services', *New Statesman*, 15 April 2013.

4 Ibid.

5 Ibid.

6 'Health Group Warns It Will Take the NHS to Court', *Suffolk Free Press*, 16 December 2012.

7 White, '"The Tail's Wagging the Dog"'.

8 Nigel Bennett, 'NHS Response to WATCH's Concerns on Serco's Proposals' [online], 13 December 2012 (http://nigelbennett.mycouncillor.org.uk/2012/12/13/nhs-suffolk-response-to-watch-concerns-to-sercos-proposals/) (accessed 14 December 2015).

9 White, '"The Tail's Wagging the Dog"'.

10 Ibid.

11 Matt Stott, 'Suffolk's Privatized Community Healthcare Run by Serco Set for NHS Return as Hospitals Name Preferred Bidders', *East Anglian Daily Times*, 19 May 2015.

12 *Private Eye*, 21 February 2014.

13 Felicity Lawrence, 'Serco Investigated over Claims of "Unsafe" Out-of-Hours GP Service', *Guardian* [online], 25 May 2012 (http://www.theguardian.com/society/2012/may/25/serco-investigated-claims-unsafe-hours-gp) (accessed 15 December 2015).

14 See 'Memorandum on the Provision of the Out-of-Hours GP Service in Cornwall', National Audit Office [online] (http://www.nao.org.uk/report/health-memorandum-on-the-provision-of-the-out-of-hours-gp-service-in-cornwall/) (accessed 15 December 2015).

15 Ibid.

16 Sean Farrell, 'Serco to Lose Out-of-Hours GP Services and Hospital Management Contracts', *Guardian* [online], 13 December 2013 (http://www.theguardian.com/business/2013/dec/13/serco-lose-contract-gp-services-nhs-outsourcing) (accessed 15 December 2015).

17 Melanie Newman, '"Appalling Service" Provided by Healthcare at Home Leaves Patients without Drugs', Bureau of Investigative Journalism

[online], 2 June 2014 (https://www.thebureauinvestigates.com/2014/06/02/appalling-service-provided-by-healthcare-at-home-leaves-patients-without-drugs/) (accessed 15 December 2015).

18 'Major Shareholders', Circle Holdings [online], April 2015 (http://www.circleholdingsplc.com/investor-relations/shareholder-information) (accessed 18 January 2016).

19 James Lyons, 'Fury as Tory Party Donors Are Handed NHS Contracts Worth £1.5 Billion under Health Reforms', *Mirror* [online], 8 February 2014 (http://www.mirror.co.uk/news/uk-news/fury-tory-party-donors-handed-3123469) (accessed 15 December 2015).

20 *Private Eye*, 7 February 2014.

21 Isabel Hardman, 'Who Privatised Hinchingbrooke Hospital? And Does It Matter?', *Spectator* [online], 10 December 2014 (http://blogs.spectator.co.uk/spectator-surgery/2014/12/who-privatised-hinchingbrooke-hospital-and-does-it-matter/) (accessed 15 December 2015).

22 Andrew Levy, 'Private Firm Turned Failing NHS Hospital into Award-Winner: From "Basket Case" to Best in Country for Patient Care', *Mail* [Online], 19 May 2014 (http://www.dailymail.co.uk/news/article-2632191/Private-firm-turned-failing-NHS-hospital-award-winner-From-basket-case-best-country-patient-care.html) (accessed 15 December 2015).

23 *Private Eye*, 24 January 2014.

24 *Private Eye*, 7 February 2014.

25 *Private Eye*, 22 March 2014.

26 *Private Eye*, 29 May 2014.

27 Richard Murphy, 'NHS Privatisation: The Loss Leader Model', Tax Research UK [online], 10 August 2014 (http://www.taxresearch.org.uk/Blog/2014/08/10/nhs-privatisation-the-loss-leader-model/#sthash.ufBlmRnF.dpuf) (accessed 15 December 2015).

28 *Private Eye*, 30 May 2014.

29 Circle Holdings plc, 'Statement Regarding Hinchingbrooke', 9 January 2015, available at FE Investigate [online] (http://www.investegate.co.uk/circle-holdings-plc--circ-/rns/statement-regarding-hinchingbrooke/201501090700107435B/) (accessed 15 December 2015).

30 Tom Levitt, 'Circle Was Not the Problem at Hinchingbrooke Hospital', *Guardian* [online], 20 January 2015 (http://www.theguardian.com/

society/2015/jan/20/circle-failure-hinchingbrooke-hospital-poor-nhs-contract) (accessed 15 December 2015).

31 Ben Glaze, 'Hinchingbrooke Hospital: Fury as Private Firm's £1 Billion 10-Year NHS Contract Fails', *Mirror* [online], 18 March 2015 (http://www.mirror.co.uk/news/uk-news/hinchingbrooke-hospital-fury-private-firms-5352895) (accessed 15 December 2015).

32 Andy Lines, 'Controversial American Health Firm That Donates to Tories Handed Huge NHS Contract', *Mirror* [online], 3 September 2013 (http://www.mirror.co.uk/news/uk-news/nhs-hospital-corporation-america-donates-2246513) (accessed 15 December 2015).

33 Michelle Roberts, 'A Third of NHS Contracts Awarded to Private Firms', BBC News [online], 10 December 2014 (http://www.bbc.co.uk/news/health-30397329) (accessed 15 December 2015).

34 Charlie Cooper, 'NHS Services Cut in Nottingham after Doctors Quit Rather Than Work for Private Firm', *Independent* [online], 17 December 2014 (http://www.independent.co.uk/news/uk/politics/nhs-services-cut-in-nottingham-after-doctors-quit-rather-than-work-for-private-firm-9931763.html) (accessed 15 December 2015).

35 *Private Eye*, 21 February 2014.

Chapter 6: The Trouble with Social Care

1 'The Shadow State', Social Enterprise UK, December 2012

2 Alan White, 'What the Forgotten Victims of Operation Bullfinch Can Teach Us about Stopping Child Abuse', *New Statesman*, 5 November 2013.

3 'Grooming: Who Cares?', *The Report*, BBC Radio 4, 31 May 2012.

4 'The Shadow State'.

5 Ibid.

6 Jonathan Stanley, 'Yes, Private Homes Do Care for Their Children' *Guardian* [online], 29 November 2012 (http://www.theguardian.com/commentisfree/2012/nov/29/children-welfare-priority-private-homes) (accessed 15 December 2015).

7 Alan White, 'The Rise of the Shadow State: The Truth about Outsourcing', *New Statesman*, 3 December 2012.

8 Polly Toynbee, 'Now Troubled Children Are an Investment Opportunity', *Guardian*, 13 May 2014.

9 Patrick Butler, 'Government U-Turn over Privatising Child Protection Services', *Guardian*, 21 June 2014.

10 'Behind Closed Doors: Elderly Care Exposed', *Panorama*, BBC One, 30 April 2014.

11 Alan White, 'This Is the Shocking Face of Abuse in Britain's Elderly Care System', BuzzFeed [online], 30 April 2014 (http://www.buzzfeed.com/alanwhite/this-is-the-shocking-face-of-abuse-in-britains-elderly-care#. eqmB70Gny) (accessed 15 December 2015).

12 Ibid.

13 Ibid.

14 Ibid.

15 Will Lodge, 'Improvements Made at Old Deanery Care Home in Bocking, Inspectors Find,' *East Anglian Daily Times*, 4 March 2015.

16 Emma Innes, 'Dementia Sufferer, 78, Died in Agony because Care Home Didn't Keep the Pain Relief She Needed on Site for "Cost" Reasons', *Mail* [Online], 24 September 2013 (http://www.dailymail.co.uk/health/article-2429901/Dementia-sufferer-78-died-agony-care-home-didnt-pain-relief-needed-site-cost-reasons.html) (accessed 15 December 2015).

17 White, 'This Is the Shocking Face of Abuse in Britain's Elderly Care System'.

18 *Private Eye*, 1 November 2013.

19 Ibid.

20 Euan McLelland, 'Man Fed Dog Biscuit at BUPA's Kirknowe Nursing Home in Wishaw', *Daily Record* [online], 2 May 2012 (http://www.dailyrecord.co.uk/news/local-news/man-fed-dog-biscuit-bupas-2551924) (accessed 15 December 2015).

21 Ibid.

22 See 'Financial Results', BUPA [online] (https://www.bupa.com/Corporate/our-performance/financial-results) (accessed 18 January 2016).

23 Jo Macfarlane, 'Scandal of Neglect in Britain's Care Homes: NHS Survey of 63,000 Elderly Residents Reveals One in Three Are Living in Fear of Abuse', *Mail* [online], 5 January 2013 (http://www.dailymail.co.uk/news/article-2257703/Scandal-neglect-Britains-care-homes-NHS-survey-63-000-elderly-residents-reveals-living-fear-abuse.html) (accessed 15 December 2015).

24 'Cuts in Social Care', UNISON Local government Report, February 2011.

25 White, 'This Is the Shocking Face of Abuse in Britain's Elderly Care System'.

26 *Private Eye*, 16 November 2012.

27 Ibid.

28 Leigh Day, 'Settlements Agreed in Winterbourne View Abuse Case' [online], 28 November 2013 (https://www.leighday.co.uk/News/2013/ November-2013/Settlements-agreed-in-Winterbourne-View-abuse-case) (accessed 15 December 2015).

29 White. 'This Is the Shocking Face of Abuse in Britain's Elderly Care System'.

30 Ibid.

31 *Private Eye*, 5 April 2013.

32 Vidhya Alakeson, 'Social Care Commissioners Should Ditch Zero-Hours Contracts', *Guardian*, 26 March 2014.

33 *Domiciliary Care UK Market Report 2011* (London: LaingBuisson, 2011).

34 *Private Eye*, 5 April 2013.

35 Ibid.

36 *Private Eye*, 10 January 2014.

37 Daniel Boffey, 'Doncaster Care Workers Set to Intensify Strike in Fight for Living Wage', *Guardian* [online], 9 August 2014 (http://www.theguardian.com/society/2014/aug/09/former-nhs-carers-intensify-strike-over-pay) (accessed 15 December 2015).

38 'Social Care Funding Outlook "Bleak"', *Croydon Guardian* [online], 8 May 2013 (http://www.croydonguardian.co.uk/news/10404574.Social_care_funding_outlook__bleak_/) (accessed 15 December 2015).

39 Mithran Samuel, 'Social Care Professionals Oppose Outsourcing, Finds Survey', Community Care [online], 3 May 2011 (http://www.communitycare.co.uk/2011/05/03/social-care-professionals-oppose-outsourcing-finds-survey/) (accessed 15 December 2015).

40 Robert Booth, 'High Court Rejects Legal Challenge to Barnet's "easy-Council" Plans', *Guardian* [online], 29 April 2013 (http://www.theguardian.com/society/2013/apr/29/high-court-challenge-barnet-easycouncil) (accessed 15 December 2015).

41 Aditya Chakrabortty, 'Outsourced and Unaccountable: This Is the Future of Local Government', *Guardian*, 16 December 2014.

42 'The Shadow Cuts Part One', *New Statesman*, 28 May 2013.

43 Ibid.

44 Ibid.

45 'The Barnet Group Ltd Local Authority Trading Company: Privatising Adults and Housing Services', Barnet Unison, January 2012.

46 'Branch Guide to Council Finances and Privatisation', Unison, June 2013.

47 Ibid.

48 Ibid.

Chapter 7: Accountability

1 'Scrap Immigration Texts Say Men Targeted in Error', Channel 4 News [online], 17 October 2013 (http://www.channel4.com/news/scrap-immigration-texts-say-men-targeted-in-error) (accessed 17 December 2015).

2 Rajeev Syal, 'DWP to Blame for Fitness-to-Work Tests Fiasco, MPs Say', *Guardian* [online], 8 February 2013 (http://www.theguardian.com/society/2013/feb/08/dwp-fitness-to-work-fiasco) (accessed 17 December 2015)

3 'Department for Work and Pensions: Contract Management of Medical Services', Parliament.uk, 8 February 2013 (http://www.parliament.uk/business/committees/committees-a-z/commons-select/public-accounts-committee/news/contract-management-of-medical-services/) (accessed 17 December 2015).

4 'Work Fitness Tests "Shocking" Says Islington Council', BBC News [online], 21 October 2013 (http://www.bbc.co.uk/news/uk-england-london-24609466) (accessed 17 December 2015).

5 'Hugh Muir's Diary', *Guardian*, 19 December 2012.

6 Shiv Malik, 'DWP Draws Up Plans to Ditch Ridiculed Jobs Website', *Guardian*, 17 March 2014.

7 Hugh Muir, 'Seek and Ye Shall Find – But Don't Expect Iain Duncan Smith to Help', *Guardian* [online], 19 December 2013 (http://www.theguardian.com/politics/2013/dec/19/hugh-muir-diary-iain-duncan-smith) (accessed 17 December 2015).

8 Malik, 'DWP Draws Up Plans to Ditch Ridiculed Jobs Website'.

9 'Government Website Plagued with Bogus and Duplicated Job Ads', Channel 4 News [online], 7 August 2014 (http://www.channel4.com/news/universal-jobmatch-bogus-misleading-ads-nao) (accessed 18 January 2016).

10 Ibid.

11 'Iain Duncan Smith's Universal Job Match Fiasco', Another Angry Voice [online], 17 March 2014 (http://anotherangryvoice.blogspot.co.uk/2014/03/universal-job-match-fiasco-ids.html) (accessed 17 December 2015).

12 'Major Projects Authority Annual Report 2014–15', Cabinet Office, June 2015.

13 Richard Vize, 'Is This the Proof that Outsourcing Wastes Money?', Public Procurement Insider, 3 June 2014 (http://www.publicprocurementinsider.com/2014/06/03/is-this-the-proof-that-outsourcing-wastes-money-guest-post/) (accessed 17 December 2015).

14 Solomon Hughes, 'Meet the Most Powerful Court You've Never Heard Of', BuzzFeed News [online], 16 May 2015 (http://www.buzzfeed.com/solomonhughes/what-is-the-lcia#.urWa3BOLN) (accessed 17 December 2015).

15 Dominic Casciani, 'Home Office Ordered to Pay £224m to E-Borders Firm', BBC News [online], 18 August 2014 (http://www.bbc.co.uk/news/uk-28840966) (accessed 17 December 2015).

16 'Employment and Support Allowance Needs Fundamental Redesign, Say MPs', Parliament.uk, 23 July 2014 (http://www.parliament.uk/business/committees/committees-a-z/commons-select/work-and-pensions-committee/news/esa-wca-report-substantive/) (accessed 17 December 2015).

17 John Bingham, 'Success of "Mega-Charities" Hides Struggle for Survival for Tens of Thousands of Others', Telegraph [online], 18 June 2013 (http://www.telegraph.co.uk/news/uknews/10125812/Success-of-mega-charities-hides-struggle-for-survival-for-tens-of-thousands-of-others.html) (accessed 17 December 2015).

Chapter 8: Transparency

1 Sadiq Khan, 'Bringing Transparency to Public Contracts', Politics Home [online], 28 October 2013 (https://www.politicshome.com/economy-and-work/articles/opinion/sadiq-khan-mp-bringing-transparency-public-contracts) (accessed 18 December 2015).

2 Mark Townsend, 'Yarl's Wood: UN Special Rapporteur to Censure UK Government', Observer, 4 January 2015.

3 Mark Townsend, 'Yarl's Wood: Labour Pledges to Investigate Claims of Sexual Abuse', *Observer*, 14 December 2014.

4 Ian Dunt, 'How the Home Office, Serco and G4S Catastrophically Mishandled Asylum Contracts', politics.co.uk, 24 April 2014 (http://www.politics.co.uk/blogs/2014/04/24/how-the-home-office-serco-and-g4s-catastrophically-mishandle) (accessed 18 December 2015).

5 Alan White, 'Outsourcing and Housing for Asylum Seekers', *New Statesman* [online], 3 June 2013 (http://www.newstatesman.com/politics/2013/06/rape-cannot-be-monetized-outsourcing-and-housing-asylum-seekers) (accessed 18 December 2015).

6 House of Commons public accounts committee, *COMPASS: Provision of Asylum Accommodation*, 54th Report of Session 2013–14, HC 1000, 24 April 2014.

7 Dunt, 'How the Home Office, Serco and G4S Catastrophically Mishandled Asylum Contracts'.

8 'The Poverty Barrier: The Right to Rehabilitation for Survivors of Torture in the UK', Freedom from Torture, July 2013.

9 Richard Garside, 'The Great Criminal Justice Contracts Monopoly', Centre for Crime and Justice Studies [online], 17 March 2014 (http://www.crimeandjustice.org.uk/resources/great-criminal-justice-contracts-monopoly) (accessed 18 December 2015).

10 Jamie Ross, 'Scottish Government Demands Inquiry Into "Concerning" Treatment Of Glasgow Refugees', Buzzfeed [online], 18 Feb 2016 (http://www.buzzfeed.com/jamieross/scottish-government-demands-investigation-into-treatment-of#.dxr2xNdaj) (accessed 29 Feb 2016).

11 Nicholas Watt, 'Chris Grayling Accused of Trying to Manipulate Parliamentary Answers', *Guardian* [online], 18 February 2014 (http://www.theguardian.com/politics/2014/feb/18/chris-grayling-accused-manipulate-parliamentary-answers) (accessed 18 December 2015).

12 Ibid.

13 Hansard, HC Deb, 16 December 2013, vol. 572, cols. 499W–500W.

14 Hansard, HC Deb, 3 February 2014, vol. 575, col. 117W.

15 Larisa Brown, 'Burglars in Prison Paid £20 a Week to Quiz You about Your Valuables', *Mail* [Online], 21 August 2013 (http://www.dailymail.co.uk/news/article-2398602/Prisoners-paid-ask-families-want-save-money-house-insurance.html) (accessed 18 December 2015).

16 Letter from Roger Davis, MoJ, to 'Farah D', 2 June 2014, available at https://www.whatdotheyknow.com/request/209212/response/524331/ attach/3/FOI%2090554%20reply%20to%20Farah%20D%20request.pdf (accessed 18 December 2015).

17 Alan White, 'Female Prisoners Are Making Designer Items in a Private Prison', BuzzFeed [online], 17 January 2016 (http://www.buzzfeed.com/ alanwhite/female-prisoners-are-making-designer-items-in-a-private-pris#.jxvmJyVxR) (accessed 18 January 2016).

18 Ian Dunt, 'MoJ Pulls the Wool over Its Own Eyes in G4S and Serco Contracts', politics.co.uk, 6 January 2015 (http://www.politics.co.uk/ blogs/2015/01/06/moj-pulls-the-wool-over-its-own-eyes-over-g4s-and-serco-cont) (accessed 18 December 2015).

19 Caroline Molloy, 'What Is G4S Doing in England's NHS?', Our NHS [online], 16 July 2013 (https://www.opendemocracy.net/ournhs/caro-line-molloy/what-is-g4s-doing-in-englands-nhs) (accessed 18 December 2015).

20 Ibid.

21 Ibid.

22 Paul Milligan, 'Retired Newsagent Died after His Wheelchair Tipped Over in the Back of a G4S Ambulance', *Mail* [Online], 9 March 2013 (http:// www.dailymail.co.uk/news/article-2290607/Retired-newsagent-died-wheelchair-tipped-G4S-ambulance.html) (accessed 18 December 2015).

23 'Latest with Atos', Carer Watch's Blog, 26 August 2011 (https://carerwatch. wordpress.com/2011/08/26/latest-with-atos-2/) (accessed 18 December 2015).

24 Emily Butselaar, 'Benefits Test Company Threatens Critics with Libel Action', Index on Censorship [online], 23 August 2011 (https://www. indexoncensorship.org/2011/08/benefits-test-company-threatens-crit-ics-with-libel-action/) (accessed 18 December 2015).

25 'A Fine Problem for the DWP's Contractor', *Evening Standard*, 11 June 2014.

26 Patrick Butler, 'Funding Cuts Leave Charities Scared to Speak Up, Says Study', *Guardian*, 22 January 2013.

27 *Private Eye*, 14 June 2013.

28 Working Links is described as a 'platinum' corporate partner on a now deleted CSJ web page. It is thanked on page 10 of a report from the CSJ

called *It Happens Here: Equipping the United Kingdom to Fight Modern Slavery*, published in March 2013.

29 Eric Allison and Simon Hattenstone, 'G4S Paid Author of "Independent" Youth Prison Report as Consultant', *Guardian*, 6 August 2015.

30 'Open Data: Unleashing The Potential', gov.uk, 28 June 2012 (https://www.gov.uk/government/publications/open-data-white-paper-unleashing-the-potential) (accessed 18 December 2015).

Chapter 9: Lobbying and Conflicts of Interest

1 *Private Eye*, 18 October 2013.

2 Ibid.

3 Ibid.

4 Alan Travis, 'Probation Officers Face Social Media Gag as Outsourcing Row Rumbles On', *Guardian* [online], 21 March 2013 (http://www.theguardian.com/society/2013/mar/21/probation-officers-social-media-gag-outsourcing) (accessed 18 December 2015).

5 *Private Eye*, 14 June 2013.

6 *Newsnight*, BBC Two, 21 November 2013.

7 Rowena Mason, 'Doctors Using NHS in "Abhorrent" Way to Push Private Practice, Whitehall Boss Admits', *Telegraph* [online], 1 April 2013 (http://www.telegraph.co.uk/news/9965124/Doctors-using-NHS-in-abhorrent-way-to-push-private-practice-Whitehall-boss-admits.html) (accessed 18 December 2015).

8 Available at http://web.archive.org/web/20130308102036/http://conference.nhsconfed.org/sponsors-and-exhibitors/sponsorship/networking-sessions/ (accessed 18 January 2016).

9 James Lyons, 'Fury as Tory Party Donors Are Handed NHS Contracts Worth £1.5 Billion under Health Reforms', *Mirror* [online], 8 February 2014 (http://www.mirror.co.uk/news/uk-news/fury-tory-party-donors-handed-3123469) (accessed 15 December 2015).

10 Solomon Hughes, 'NHS Contract Awarded to Private Firm Despite Rival Bid Being "£7m Cheaper"', BuzzFeed News, 27 January 2015 (http://www.buzzfeed.com/solomonhughes/nhs-contract-stoke#.naP0qaXDk) (accessed 18 December 2015).

11 'Sir Stuart Rose to Advise on NHS Leadership', press release, Department of Health, 14 February 2014, available at https://www.gov.uk/government/

news/sir-stuart-rose-to-advise-on-nhs-leadership (accessed 18 December 2015).

12 *Private Eye*, 9 January 2009.

13 Toby Helm and Rajeev Syal, 'Storm over Blunkett Role with Private Jobs Firm', *Observer*, 1 February 2009.

14 Amardeep Bassey, 'Failing Birmingham Care Home Moundsley Hall Made £11,000 Donation to Bromsgrove Conservatives', *Birmingham Mail* [online], 15 June 2014 (http://www.birminghammail.co.uk/news/midlands-news/failing-birmingham-care-home-moundsley-7270726) (accessed 18 December 2015).

15 'Moundsley Hall Nursing and Residential Home', Care Quality Commission [online], 13 June 2014 (http://www.cqc.org.uk/location/1-143441646) (accessed 18 December 2015).

16 Melanie Newman and Oliver Wright, 'Tory Donor's Nursing Home Shame', *Independent*, 17 July 2014.

17 'Yvette Cooper's Speech to Labour Party Annual Conference 2012', Labour Party [online], 3 October 2012 (http://archive.labour.org.uk/yvette-cooper-speech-to-labour-party-annual-conference-2012) (accessed 18 December 2015).

18 *Private Eye*, 16 November 2012.

19 Solomon Hughes, 'A Labour Deputy-Leader Candidate Is Being Funded by Corporate Lobbyists for Austerity', Vice [online], 14 July 2015 (http://www.vice.com/en_uk/read/solomon-hughes-caroline-flint-labour-deputy-leadership-campaign-901) (accessed 18 December 2015).

20 *Newsnight*, BBC Two, 23 May 2013.

21 Clare Sambrook, 'Woolwich: Lord Reid, the Security Industry's Salesman', OpenDemocracy UK [online], 23 May 2013 (https://www.opendemocracy.net/ourkingdom/clare-sambrook/woolwich-lord-reid-security-industrys-salesman) (accessed 18 December 2015).

22 *Private Eye*, 23 August 2013.

23 Michael Buchanan, 'Work Programme Chief Alan Cave Joins Contractor Serco', BBC News [online] 12 October 2012 (http://www.bbc.co.uk/news/uk-19931604) (accessed 18 December 2015).

24 *Private Eye*, 11 December 2015.

25 'MoD Halts Helicopter Deal as Police Probe "Irregularities"', *Telegraph* [online], 8 February 2011 (http://www.telegraph.co.uk/news/uknews/

defence/8310344/MoD-halts-helicopter-deal-as-police-probe-irregularities.html) (accessed 18 December 2015).

26 John Grayson and Ed Lewis, 'G4S and the Corporate State', New Left Project [online], 2 August 2012 (http://www.newleftproject.org/index.php/site/article_comments/g4s_and_the_corporate_state) (accessed 10 December 2015).

27 *The Role of Major Contractors in the Delivery of Public Services*, National Audit Office, HC 810, 12 November 2013.

28 *Today*, BBC Radio 4, 14 March 2014.

29 *Private Eye*, 30 May 2014.

30 Ibid.

31 Nigel Morris, 'Extend Freedom of Information Rules to Include Private Companies on Government Contracts, 'uggests Minister', *Independent* [online], 18 March 2014 (http://www.independent.co.uk/news/uk/politics/extend-freedom-of-information-rules-to-include-private-companies-on-government-contracts-suggests-9200425.html) (accessed 18 December 2015).

32 Edward Curwen, 'Serco Profits Fall as Contracts Decline', *The Times*, 7 December 2015.

33 Julia Kollewe, 'Serco Reports Sharp Drop in Profits after Crisis-Hit Year', *Guardian*, 5 March 2014.

34 *The Role of Major Contractors in the Delivery of Public Services*.

Chapter 10: Market Failure

1 Solomon Hughes, 'Meet the Most Powerful Court You've Never Heard Of', BuzzFeed News [online], 16 May 2015 (http://www.buzzfeed.com/solomonhughes/what-is-the-lcia#.urWa3BOLN) (accessed 17 December 2015).

2 *Private Eye*, 16 May 2014.

3 Ian Quinn, 'NHS London Drops Clinicenta a Year after Enquiry', Pulse [online], 28 January 2011 (http://www.pulsetoday.co.uk/nhs-london-drops-clinicenta-a-year-after-inquiry/11051590.article) (accessed 18 January 2016).

4 'The Scandal of Dirty Wards in Nottingham's Hospitals', *Nottingham Post* [online], 11 August 2015 (http://www.nottinghampost.com/life-death-says-horrified-MP/story-27581081-detail/story.html) (accessed 17 January 2016).

5 *Private Eye*, 10 August 2014.

6 'EAT Win for Carillion Swindon Workers', GMB [online], 5 September 2014 (http://www.gmb.org.uk/newsroom/eat-win-for-carillion-swindon-workers) (accessed 20 December 2015).

7 *Private Eye*, 19 December 2015.

8 Alan White, 'US Outsourcing Company Abandons Plans to Sue Michael Gove's Department', BuzzFeed [online], 4 January 2016 (http://www.buzzfeed.com/alanwhite/us-outsourcing-company-abandons-plans-to-sue-michael-goves-d) (accessed 18 January 2016).

9 A few days after the tagging story broke, Nick Buckles, whom we last heard about in Chapter 1, quit as chief executive of G4S. He received a pay-off of £1.2 million. It included his basic annual salary of £830,000 and a £332,000 pension allowance.

10 'Probe of G4S and Serco Tagging Contracts Begins', BBC News [online], 4 November 2013 (http://www.bbc.co.uk/news/uk-24805255) (accessed 20 December 2015).

11 Shane Croucher, 'Electronic Tagging Scandal: How G4S Mishandled Its Ministry of Justice Contract', *International Business Times* [online], 18 March 2014 (http://www.ibtimes.co.uk/electronic-tagging-scandal-how-g4s-mishandled-its-ministry-justice-contract-1440160) (accessed 20 December 2015).

12 Ibid.

13 Ibid.

14 Gill Plimmer, 'Capita Benefits as Rivals Fail to Deliver', *Financial Times*, 20 December 2015.

15 *Private Eye*, 31 May 2013.

16 Rajeev Syal, 'Hodge Accuses Government of "Shocking Complacency" over G4S and Serco', *Guardian*, 9 September 2014.

17 Gill Plimmer, 'G4S Back in Favour at Whitehall', *Financial Times*, 28 April 2014.

18 G4S Twitter account, 18 June 2015 (https://twitter.com/G4S/status/611482201365082112) (accessed 10 January 2016).

19 *Private Eye*, 16 May 2014.

20 House of Commons public affairs committee, *Transforming Contract Management*, 23rd Report of Session 2014–15, HC 585, 26 November 2014.

21 Alan Travis and Rajeev Syal, '"Poison Pill" Probation Contracts

Could Cost £300m to £400m to Cancel', *Guardian*, 12 September 2014.

22 Gill Plimmer and Sarah Neville, 'G4S and Serco Won Whitehall Work Despite Being "on Probation"', *Financial Times*, 10 December 2014.

23 'Electronic Tagging: Written Question – 218417', parliament.uk, 21 January 2015 (http://www.parliament.uk/business/publications/written-questions-answers-statements/written-question/Commons/2014-12-11/218417/) (accessed 20 December 2015).

24 'Don't Demonise G4S and Serco, CBI Says', Centre for Crime and Justice Studies [online], 19 November 2013 (http://www.crimeandjustice.org.uk/news/dont-demonise-g4s-and-serco-cbi-says) (accessed 20 December 2015).

25 Gill Plimmer and Jim Packard, 'Ministers Move to Limit Fallout from Serco/G4S Debacle', *Financial Times*, 20 November 2013.

26 Colin Cram, 'Is the Ministry of Justice to Blame for the G4S Overcharging Scandal?' *Guardian* [online], 19 July 2013 (http://www.theguardian.com/public-leaders-network/2013/jul/19/ministry-of-justice-g4s-overcharging) (accessed 20 December 2015).

27 Hansard, HC Deb, 19 December 2013, vol. 572, col. 122WS.

28 Nigel Morris and Rachel Pells, 'Serco Given Yarl's Wood Immigration Contract despite "Vast Failings"', *Independent* [online], 24 November 2014 (http://www.independent.co.uk/news/uk/politics/serco-given-yarl-s-wood-immigration-contract-despite-vast-failings-9880772.html) (accessed 20 December 2015).

29 'Yarl's Wood: Undercover in the Secretive Immigration Centre', Channel 4 News [online], 2 March 2015 (http://www.channel4.com/news/yarls-wood-immigration-removal-detention-centre-investigation) (accessed 20 December 2015).

30 Oliver Wright, 'Atos "Misled Ministers" to Win Lucrative Contract Assessing Disabled for Benefits', *Independent*, 21 March 2014.

31 Ibid.

32 John Pring, '"Liars!" MPs Use DNS Investigation to Accuse Atos over PIP Contract', Disability News Service [online], 21 March 2014 (http://www.disabilitynewsservice.com/liars-mps-use-dns-investigation-to-accuse-atos-over-pip-contract/) (accessed 20 December 2015).

33 John Pring, 'New Questions over Seetec Work Choice "Scam" Allegations',

Disability News Service [online], 1 November 2013 (http://www.disabilitynewsservice.com/new-questions-over-seetec-work-choice-scam-allegations/) (accessed 20 December 2015).

34 House of Commons public accounts committee, *Contracting Out Public Services to the Private Sector*, 47th Report of Session 2013–14, HC 777, 14 March 2014.

35 Ibid.

36 Ibid.

37 *Today*, BBC Radio 4, 18 March 2014.

38 Chris Green and Oliver Wright, 'Capita Accused of Using Major Government Contract to Short-Change Companies, Driving Some out of Business', *Independent* [online], 10 February 2015 http://www.independent.co.uk/news/uk/politics/capita-accused-of-using-major-government-contract-to-short-change-small-companies-driving-some-out-10037349.html) (accessed 20 December 2015).

39 Mark Wallace, 'Serco and G4S Ripped Us Off – the Public Sector Must Learn to Play Hardball', *Guardian* [online], 13 March 2014 (http://www.theguardian.com/commentisfree/2014/mar/13/serco-g4s-public-sector-hardball-government-taxpayers) (accessed 20 December 2015).

40 Charlotte Jee, 'HMRC's Aspire Costs Set to More than Double to £10.4bn', ComputerWorld UK [online], 22 July 2014 (http://www.computerworlduk.com/news/it-management/hmrcs-aspire-costs-set-more-than-double-104bn-3531977/) (accessed 20 December 2015).

41 Tom Gash, 'G4S and Competition Regulation in Public Services', Institute for Government [online], 10 April 2014 (http://www.instituteforgovernment.org.uk/blog/7676/g4s-and-competition-regulation-in-public-services/) (accessed 20 December 2015).

Chapter 11: Conclusion

1 'The Serco Insider: What It's Really Like to Work for the Outsourcing Giant', *Guardian* [online], 10 April 2014 (http://www.theguardian.com/public-leaders-network/2014/apr/10/serco-employees-targets-treated-children-contracts) (accessed 21 December 2015).

2 Sam Knight, 'Can Winston Churchill's Grandson Save Serco? And Is It Worth Saving?', *Guardian*, 2 July 2015.

3 *Private Eye*, 15 May 2015.

4 *Investors Chronicle*, November 2015.

5 Gill Plimmer and Sarah O'Connor, 'UK Government Outsourcing Raises Questions over Pay', *Financial Times*, 23 March 2015.

6 Ibid.

7 Gerry Holt, 'G4S Staff Hit Out over Olympics Security "Shambles"', BBC News [online], 18 July 2012 (http://www.bbc.co.uk/news/uk-18877744) (accessed 21 December 2015).

8 House of Commons home affairs committee, *Olympics Security*, 7th Report of Session 2012–13, HC 531, 18 September 2012.

9 Alan White, 'The Rise of the Shadow State: What Can We Do about It?', *New Statesman*, 4 December 2012.

10 Ibid.

11 Ibid.

12 'The Shadow State', Social Enterprise UK, December 2012.

13 Ibid.

14 White, 'The Rise of the Shadow State'.

15 Knight, 'Can Winston Churchill's Grandson Save Serco?'

16 'The Shadow State'.

17 Steve Denning, 'What Went Wrong at Boeing?', *Forbes* [online], 21 Jan 2013 (http://www.forbes.com/sites/stevedenning/2013/01/21/what-went-wrong-at-boeing/) (accessed 21 December 2015).

18 Chris Wajzer, 'Outsourcing: Green Light for Contract Transparency', *Public Finance* [online], 30 March 2015 (http://www.publicfinance.co.uk/opinion/2015/03/outsourcing-green-light-contract-transparency) (accessed 21 December 2015).

19 Speech on open data delivered 10 December 2015 in Berlin (https://www.gov.uk/government/speeches/open-data-matt-hancock-speech) (accessed 17 January 2016).

20 *Investors Chronicle*, November 2015.

21 John Grayson and Ed Lewis, 'G4S and the Corporate State', New Left Project [online], 2 August 2012 (http://www.newleftproject.org/index.php/site/article_comments/g4s_and_the_corporate_state) (accessed 10 December 2015).

22 Sadiq Khan, 'Bringing Transparency to Public Contracts', Politics Home [online], 28 October 2013 (https://www.politicshome.com/

economy-and-work/articles/opinion/sadiq-khan-mp-bringing-transparency-public-contracts) (accessed 18 December 2015).

23 Oliver Wright, 'Labour Would Strip G4S and Serco of Contracts', *Independent*, 27 December 2013.

24 Ibid.

25 Clare Sambrook, 'Gove's Own Operation Trojan Horse: The Privatisation of Our Schools', OpenDemocracy UK [online], 16 July 2014 (https://www.opendemocracy.net/ourkingdom/clare-sambrook/goves-own-operation-trojan-horse-privatisation-of-our-schools) (accessed 21 December 2015).

26 As I reported in 2012: 'Only one in five people polled by Social Enterprise UK knew that the majority of children's homes are now owned by private companies. The majority of people polled for the report had never heard of Atos or Serco, yet these firms and others like them, are receiving and are responsible for many billions of pounds of taxpayers' money.'

Index